start
influencing stop talking,

stop talking, start influencing

12 insights from brain science to
make your message stick

JARED COONEY HORVATH | PhD, MEd

First published 2019

Exisle Publishing Pty Ltd
PO Box 864, Chatswood, NSW 2057, Australia
226 High Street, Dunedin, 9016, New Zealand
www.exislepublishing.com

A CiP record for this book is available from the National Library of Australia.

ISBN 978-1-925335-90-3

Designed by Sarah Johnston
Typeset in Adobe Caslon 11pt / Headings in Poppins Bold
Printed in China

This book uses paper sourced under ISO 14001 guidelines from well-managed forests and other controlled sources.

10 9 8 7 6 5 4

Disclaimer
While this book is intended as a general information resource and all care has been taken in compiling the contents, neither the author nor the publisher and their distributors can be held responsible for any loss, claim or action that may arise from reliance on the information contained in this book.

To Bub for your love and
support throughout this process

This book is so engaging it is hard to put down, and it's absolutely full of fascinating and useful ideas. I recommend it to everyone who has ever tried to teach anyone anything!

Helen Street, PhD — Founder and Chair, The Positive Schools Initiative;
Honorary Research Fellow, University of Western Australia

This is a great explanation of not only the *how*, but also the *why* behind great presentations. These exceptional insights from neuroscience will make your message pop like never before.

Barbara Oakley, PhD — Author of *Learning How to Learn* and *A Mind for Numbers*

This is an awesome book — fascinating, helpful, and a blast to read. I highly recommend it to teachers, coaches, trainers, speakers, parents ... anyone who has ever attempted to pass information or skills along to another person.

Dr Todd Rose, EdD — Director, Mind, Brain, and Education,
Harvard Graduate School of Education

If you want a book about the brain and learning that is fun, engaging, and seriously based on evidence — then this it. Watch a neuroscientist at work and realize how much we can learn from brain science. Horvath knows how to excite the brain, to feed it, to make it fun — and he does it all while invoking stimulating emotions on every page.

John Hattie, PhD — Professor Emeritus, Melbourne Graduate School of Education;
Author of *Visible Learning* and *Visible Learning for Teachers*

I have been waiting years (decades) for a book like this to be written! Finally, brain research that's rigorous, understandable, and actually applicable to work and life. Important for marketing, branding, sales, training, culture, change management — just about any aspect of business you can think of. This is science in action and I love it.

Sergio Brodsky — Head of Strategy, Initiative Global Media Agency

To everyone in creative, marketing, branding, sales, content — I can't recommend this book enough.

Gemma Hunter — Global Executive Creative Director, MediaCom

I've been in this business for almost 20 years, and this is the first time I've come across some of these ideas. Not only is this book new, fresh, and important — it's also incredibly fun to read.

Brandon Exline — Vice President, CCMC Management

In our rapidly changing world, life-long learning is proving to be of paramount importance for healthy and meaningful adaptation — and I can think of no better person to be your guide through this topic than Dr Horvath.

Dr Patrycja Slawuta, PhD — Founder & Director, SelfHackathon

Stop Talking, Start Influencing combines brain research and captivating storytelling with practical real-world application. A must-read for anyone interested in making an impact on the world.

Dr Sarah M. McKay, DPhil (Oxon)— Founder, Neuroscience Academy;
Author of *The Women's Brain Book*

A ground-breaking book. Dr Horvath expertly illuminates the neuroscience behind learning and provides powerful yet simple applications to improve learning in the classroom, the boardroom or the playing field. Essential reading.

Cathy Brandon, MAPsych — Director, Genazzano Institute of Learning & Brain Sciences;
Co-author of *Thinking Skills for Peak Performance*

At last! By showing us *WHY* instructional strategies succeed or fail, Jared truly is enabling us to become Picassos of teaching. Read. Learn. Teach!

Elisabeth Lenders, MEd, MACE — Principal, Kingswood College

Dr Horvath has done what is sorely needed in this world of quick fixes and short cuts: he's put together the truth of the science of learning. If you're serious about teaching and learning, you need to read this book.

Vin Walsh, PhD — Professor of Human Brain Research, University College London

Contents

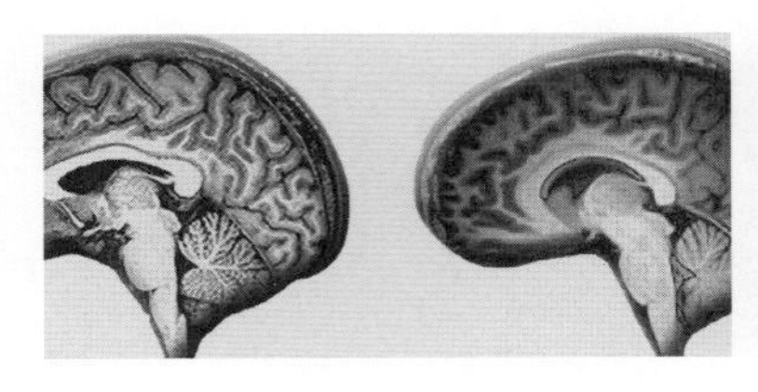

ILLUSTRATION 1. TWO SIMPLE HORSES

Introduction

We are all teachers.

If you've ever walked a colleague or client through a new program or procedure, you're a teacher.

If you've ever coached a novice how to swing a golf club, hit a baseball or kick a football, you're a teacher.

If you've ever stood in front of an audience and presented a new idea or concept, you're a teacher.

If you've ever been a parent … enough said.

Here's the problem: despite the fact that many of us spend time each and every day disseminating knowledge to others, very few of us have ever been schooled in how best to pass along this knowledge so that others can understand, remember and apply it. Simply put, we've never been taught how to teach. To get around this, many of us turn to books (much like this one) that offer a plethora of tips and techniques we can use to make our teaching more effective. Surely, if we simply follow these 'how to' guides we should be able to inspire and influence those around us just like the greats.

Unfortunately, these guides almost never work. To understand why, take a look at the illustration opposite.

One of those horses was drawn by the great Spanish artist Pablo Picasso. The other was drawn by my six-year-old niece. Despite the fact that both are incredibly simple in appearance, I don't imagine you're having much difficulty differentiating the two. Why?

Although Picasso is most often recognized for his blocky, childlike figures, many people don't know that he was a master of technique. In fact, over the course of his life, Picasso was able to learn, perfect and adapt almost every major art style.

Figure Sketch
Age 12

Portrait
Age 15

Expressionism
Age 22

Cubism
Age 33

Neo-Classicism
Age 42

Surrealism
Age 64

ILLUSTRATION 2. THE MANY STYLES OF PICASSO

When my niece drew the horse on the bottom, she did so from a relatively shallow level of understanding: every line can be taken at face value and it's easy to recognize the *pure* simplicity in her technique. However, when Picasso drew the horse on the top, he did so from a deep and nuanced understanding of his craft: each curve represents choice, comprehension and purpose that belies the *apparent* simplicity of the figure.

This is why 'how to' guides rarely work. Although the tips and techniques may be useful under certain circumstances, without a deeper understanding of how people learn and remember, we must blindly follow these instructions with no clear sense of *why* they work or fail. As such, our efforts often come across more like my niece's horse: we are stuck imitating surface simplicity with no real ability to modify, adapt or personalize the techniques to evolving, changing situations.

I often liken this to cooking. If I give you a detailed, step-by-step recipe to bake a cake, I imagine you'd be able to follow the instructions quite easily. Mix three eggs with some butter, add whole milk, whisk in some flour ... fairly simple. But what would happen if you had no eggs? Or were allergic to milk? Without a deeper understanding of the purpose for and interaction between each ingredient, you can easily become derailed and have no clue how to press forward and tweak the recipe to suit your unique kitchen, your unique tastes or your unique requirements.

If we want our teaching to be effective, we must move beyond simple recipes and dig deeper into the mechanisms behind *why* each recipe works. In other words, we must become Picassos of teaching.

This is my goal with this book. Through exploring brain research, diving into psychological phenomena and undertaking a number of fun experiments, I will present to you twelve core concepts of how people think, learn and remember. My aim is not to simply help you apply these concepts, but to deeply understand each so as to ensure any knowledge you hope to impart to others is understood, sticks with and influences them — regardless of the situation or environment.

Before we dive in, however, there are two things you should probably know.

First, the concepts we will explore are *foundations* of learning: as such, they are supported by a wealth of brain and behavioural research. In this instance, when I say 'research', I don't mean a single obscure study from 1970 conducted with rats in the Siberian wilderness — I mean well-characterized, well-replicated research spanning decades of scientific toil. For this reason, I don't want you to simply take my word for anything. Rather, at the end of the book you will find a link to a generous online reference section that will allow you to dive into any topic you wish to probe further.

Second, whenever I teach a class, group or team I adhere to a single philosophy: if I cannot get my learners to *experience* a concept I am discussing, then I do not yet truly understand that concept myself. I have tried my best to apply the same philosophy to this book. For this reason, you will notice that, at times, I have made seemingly random formatting and stylistic choices. Although things may occasionally feel odd and confusing, I assure you every decision has been made for a very specific learning purpose. Although my use of an image, phrase or game may not always be immediately apparent, I promise everything will make perfect sense by the time you reach the end of this book.

Now, if you're sick of repeating yourself ad nauseam to your colleagues and clients; if you're tired of endlessly drilling your athletes and students without seeing meaningful improvement; if you've had enough of pouring your heart into presentations only to see no lasting impact among your audience, then settle in.

It's time to stop talking and start influencing.

1.

Text + Speech

What is reading, but silent conversation.

— *Charles Lamb*

Imagine it's Friday night. You and a friend are parked in the middle of a crowded pub nursing a couple over-priced craft beers, while all around you people rowdily reminisce about the events of the week. It's auditory chaos — yet despite the noise echoing throughout the room, you find you're able to maintain a coherent conversation. True, you may have to shout in order to be heard over the dozens of competing voices, but you have no real difficulty homing in on and following your friend's ideas.

Now imagine it's Wednesday afternoon. You and your colleagues are settled around a large conference table, subtly rocking in your ergonomic wheelie chairs, while at the front of the room a presenter is speaking in front of a PowerPoint slide riddled with titles, bullet points and references. There is no question the presenter is knowledgeable

ILLUSTRATION 3. PUB VS POWERPOINT

and engaging — but despite your best efforts you simply can't seem to focus on or follow any of the ideas being presented.

On the surface, these two scenarios couldn't appear more different. But what if I told you that the reason you're able to coherently converse while in a busy pub is the *same* reason you're unable to remember much from the majority of PowerPoint presentations? To understand how these two scenarios are related, all you've got to do is shift your attention to the activity you are undertaking at this very moment: *reading*.

The secret history of reading

We tend to think of reading as a largely silent activity. Barring the occasional muffled cough or embarrassed giggle, libraries aren't traditionally known for being boisterous hubs of activity.

For this reason, it might come as a surprise to learn that silent reading wasn't always in fashion. In fact, until the late seventh century, reading *out loud* was the most common practice. Far from being havens of peace and quiet, ancient libraries were likely places of clamorous chatter as even solitary readers could be heard mumbling words aloud to themselves. The act of silent reading was so rare in the past that Saint Augustine felt it worthy of mention in his seminal *Confessions*: 'When Ambrose read, his eyes ran over the columns of writing and his heart searched out the meaning, but his voice and tongue were at rest. Often … I have seen him reading silently, never in fact otherwise. I ask myself why he read this way?'

---

readingaloudwasfacilitatedbythewayancienttextswerewrittenmore
specificallyancienttextscontainednospacesbetweenwordsnopunctuation
marksandnocapitallettersinfactifyougotoyourlocallibraryormuseumyou
willlikelyfindmanyexamplesofancientgreekandlatinmanuscripts
scrawledinthisstyle

This form of writing is called *scriptura continua* and it demonstrates that reading was largely an oral activity. Of what need are spaces, punctuation or capitalization when text is read aloud? To see what I mean, simply go back and read that last passage out loud: you'll likely notice that many important aspects of language — things like pacing, inflection and intention — naturally emerge out of your vocalization with little-to-no deliberate effort on your part.

If the concept of reading as a vocal activity seems a bit odd or ancient, simply look around: the legacy of this practice is everywhere in modern civilization. University lectures are predicated upon the act of one individual reading aloud important information to a group of listeners (in fact, the French word 'lecture' translates to 'reading'). Church services commonly involve someone reading aloud to the gathered congregation. Scientific conferences, political addresses, even weekly progress meetings are all structured around the ancient practice of individuals reading aloud in public settings.

At the turn of the eighth century, Irish monks began adding spaces between words and as this trend spread throughout Europe, so too did the practice of *silent reading*. So, thanks to a group of ancient monks, you can enjoy the remainder of this book safe in the knowledge that it never need be turned into oral speech …

… or does it?

It only takes a moment of consideration to realize that the concept of 'silent' reading can't be entirely accurate. If you pull your attention back and focus on what is occurring in your head as you read this sentence, likely the first thing you'll notice is that you hear something — or, more accurately, *someone*.

Embedded deep within your head there is a voice reading aloud each word as your eyes pass over it. Nine times out of ten you can identify that voice as your own, but this isn't always the case:

'I ate his liver with a side of fava beans and a nice Chianti.'

'I did not have sexual relations with that woman.'

'That's one small step for man, one giant leap for mankind.'

If you're familiar with these phrases, then as you read them there's a strong chance you heard Hopkins' chilling precision, Clinton's confident drawl and Armstrong through a scratchy receiver. It turns out, when we read words strongly associated with a specific person, we hear his or her voice (of course, this only happens when we are reasonably familiar with the person whose words we are reading. I don't imagine anyone out there, except perhaps my mother, would be hearing my voice right now — hi Mom!).

Clearly, silent reading is far from silent; but of what possible importance could this be to the theme of this chapter? To understand why I took you on this whirlwind tour of reading history, we need to briefly shift gears and explore a seemingly unrelated topic.

ILLUSTRATION 4. HIS SILKY BARITONE LIVES IN YOUR HEAD

Twice the work, half the impact

Experiment 1

For this, you will need two sources of audio that contain spoken language (I find the easiest set-up is to use a television and a radio).

1. Pop on the television and find a 'talking head' show. The content doesn't matter — could be the news, could be sports, could be the weather — just find a channel with someone speaking.
2. Flip on the radio and tune it to an AM 'talk' station. Again, don't worry about the content — just find a station with someone speaking.
3. Your goal is to try to *simultaneously understand* both the words coming from the television and the words coming from the radio. Give it a shot ...

You probably found that experiment impossible (and quite annoying). Maybe you noticed you were able to understand the words coming from the television, but in order to do so you had to ignore the words coming from the radio. Maybe you also noticed you were able to feel the moment when your attention would 'flip' between the two voices — almost like a physical switch in your head.

Scientists call this *dichotic listening* and it demonstrates that, although we can *listen to* multiple people speaking at the same time, we can only truly *understand* one person speaking at a time. Here's the important bit: when we try to understand two different streams of oral speech simultaneously (as above), we typically fail to understand anything at all! It's a bit like trying to watch two different episodes of your favourite television show at the same time: although the episodes would doubtless be related (same characters, same music, same storylines), you would be forced to quickly shift your attention back and forth. As you do this, you would necessarily begin to miss key information from each. After enough time, everything would simply become disjointed and meaningless, leaving you uncertain and confused (Who is that guy again? Why is she angry all of a sudden? Wait, where's Eddard Stark?).

To understand why dichotic listening doesn't work, we need to take a quick trip through the brain.

There are three major areas of the brain that allow us to understand oral speech. The first is the *auditory cortex*. This is the part of the brain that processes the pure characteristics of incoming sounds, things like pitch and volume. Of importance is that both sides of your brain contain this region. This is why, during our experiment, you were able to *hear* both the television and the radio: your brain has plenty of neural real estate to process sound coming into both ears without much fuss. But, of course, the goal of the experiment wasn't simply to hear both auditory streams; it was to *understand* both auditory streams.

The next area of the brain that allows us to understand oral speech is the *Broca/Wernicke network*. This part of the brain processes and makes sense of the spoken word. Importantly, this network exists in only *one* side of your brain (for most people, it's the left). This means that, even though the basic sounds of language are initially processed in both sides of the brain, oral speech must eventually be funnelled into this singular brain network. As you can likely guess, this quickly leads to a bottleneck.

This bottleneck is controlled by the third area of the brain that allows us to understand oral speech: the *left inferior frontal gyrus*. When trying to understand two people speaking at the same time, it's believed that this region effectively blocks one voice while the other is allowed to pass through the Broca/Wernicke bottleneck. This was that physical 'switch' you might have felt during our experiment. Essentially, as you jumped back and forth between paying attention to the television and the radio, the left inferior frontal gyrus was jumping back and forth between which stream of information it was blocking out.

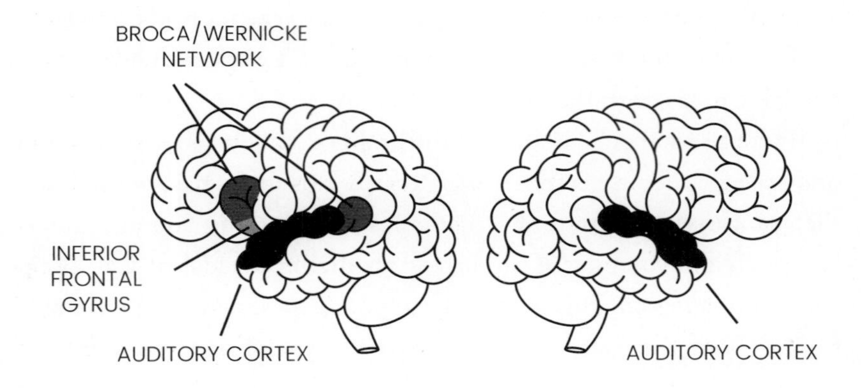

ILLUSTRATION 5. YOUR BRAIN LISTENING TO ORAL SPEECH

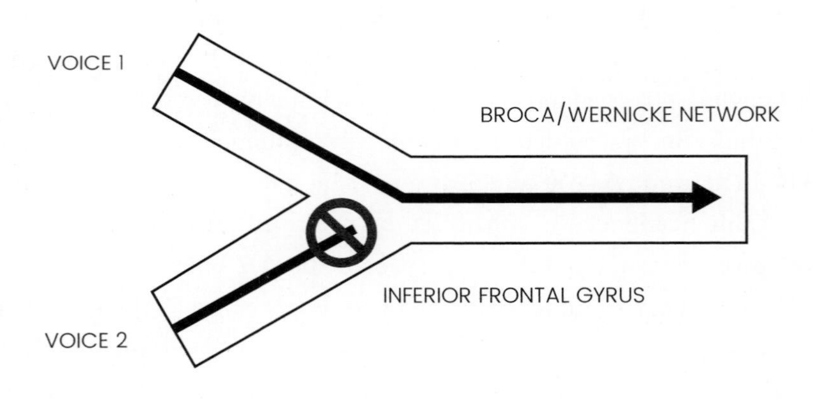

ILLUSTRATION 6. THE BROCA/WERNICKE BOTTLENECK

I often envision this bottleneck as dozens of busy travellers all trying to cram through a single-file security line at the airport. Where this metaphor falls apart is in the fact that, given enough time, all travellers will eventually make it through the line and to their waiting planes. With the Broca/Wernicke network, however, any information that does not immediately make it through the bottleneck *disappears completely* — there is no backlog or waitlist. All oral speech blocked by the left inferior frontal gyrus is, for all intents and purposes, gone for good: you can no longer access or process any of that information.

Now, let's bring all the pieces together.

Dichotic reading?

Experiment 2

For this, you will need one source of audio that contains spoken language (a television will suffice) and one source of reading material (hint: you're holding one right now!).

1. Pop on the television and find a 'talking head' show. As before, the content doesn't matter — just find a channel with someone speaking.
2. Open your reading material to a passage you are not intimately familiar with (you can just flip forward in this book to any paragraph you've not yet read).
3. Your goal is to try to listen to the television while silently reading this book — and *simultaneously understand* both streams of information. Give it a shot …

Considering our busy modern lifestyles, many of us squeeze reading into whatever free time we may have: on the train to work, in a busy cafe, in line at the bank. As such, we're used to reading in noisy environments and rarely have difficulty understanding what we read. Perhaps this is why it comes as a shock to many that we are *unable* to understand something we are *reading* while simultaneously trying to understand something someone else is *saying*.

To see why this is, let's go back to the brain:

Take a look at the image opposite. See anything familiar?

When reading, the first neural region to demonstrate activation is the *visual cortex*. This is the part of the brain that processes the pure visual characteristics of incoming sights: things like colours, edges and motion. The fact that this activates early during the reading process makes perfect sense, as you must first be able to 'see' words before you can read them.

Here's where things get interesting. Almost immediately after the visual cortex activates, the *auditory cortex* and the Broca/Wernicke network fire up. But why would the speech areas of the brain activate when silently reading? Simple: the historic switch from oral to silent reading was no real switch at all — it was merely a shifting of verbalization from the vocal chords into the brain. In other words, your brain processes your silent reading voice in a manner *almost identical* to the way in which it processes an actual, out-loud speaking voice. For this reason, attempting to read while listening to someone speak is the same as trying to understand two people speaking at the same time — it can't be done!

Let me say that again: it is impossible to understand something you are reading while simultaneously trying to understand a voice you are listening to.

This is the reason for the imagination exercise at the beginning of this chapter. When maintaining a conversation in a busy pub, your auditory cortex is madly processing the myriad of voices coming into your ears from all directions. However, your left inferior frontal gyrus acts to single out and funnel your partner's unique voice through the Broca/Wernicke bottleneck, thereby allowing you to understand it.

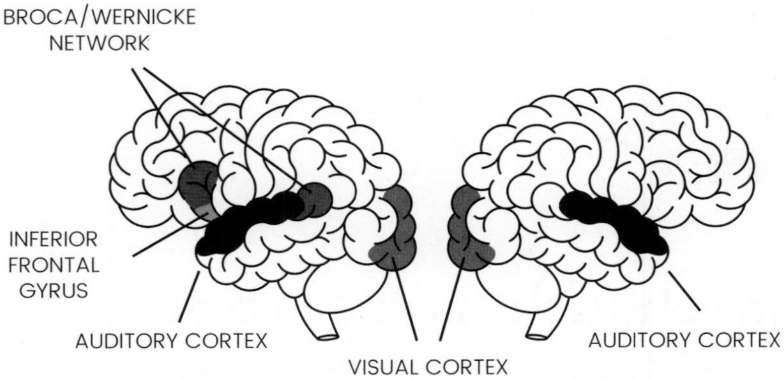

BROCA/WERNICKE NETWORK

INFERIOR FRONTAL GYRUS

AUDITORY CORTEX

VISUAL CORTEX

AUDITORY CORTEX

ILLUSTRATION 7. YOUR BRAIN SILENTLY READING ... SEE ANYTHING FAMILIAR?

As such, even though you can *hear* dozens of clashing voices at the same time, they all become meaningless noise as you zero in on and *understand* only one.

Similarly, in the staff meeting, as the presenter speaks in front of a text-heavy PowerPoint slide, your auditory cortex is madly processing both the sound of the speaker's voice *and the sound of your own silent reading voice.* The issue arises at the bottleneck: at this point, you must decide which stream of information you are going to let pass through to the Broca/Wernicke network.

As noted above, if you were to select a single stream (say, your silent reading voice), you'd be able to understand that just fine while the speaker's voice is blocked out and becomes meaningless noise. More commonly, however, we attempt to take in all the information we can — continuously jumping back and forth between the slides and the speaker. Same as trying to simultaneously watch two different episodes of a television show, whenever we do this our understanding of *both* streams of information suffers significantly.

This is why, quite often, people leave PowerPoint presentations more confused than when they went in.

Implications for leaders, teachers and coaches

1. No (or minimal) text on slides

Like it or hate it, slideware programs are now a mainstay of boardrooms, classrooms and locker rooms. Unfortunately, many people use these tools as a cheap substitute for note cards, filling each slide with copious amounts of text ('If I forget to speak about an important topic, the audience can simply read it from the slide behind me').

You likely now understand why this practice doesn't work. Just as you were unable to read this book while listening to the television, neither can your audience read your slides while listening to you speak: something must be blocked and eliminated at the Broca/Wernicke bottleneck. So what happens? The audience typically attempts to jump back and forth between you and your slides, causing them to lose important information from each. In fact, a number of studies have demonstrated that individuals who receive information in a single manner (oral *or* text) consistently comprehend and remember more than individuals who receive the same information simultaneously in both manners (oral *and* text).

Accordingly, the next time you're asked to give a presentation, do not put text on your PowerPoint slides (and if you're worried you won't be able to remember all the key points you wish to discuss during your presentation, construct a set of note cards you can hold onto and read from).

But wait — if including text on our slides hinders learning, what can we include on our slides to assist learning? We'll explore this in the next chapter.

BURNING QUESTION 1:

KEYWORDS

'What if a slide contains some words, but not many? For instance, can I include keywords on my slides?'

Interestingly, the need to internally translate visual text into auditory speech *only occurs when many words are being read in succession*, as in the case of a complete sentence, paragraph or slide of text. When we read a small number of highly familiar words, then we can bypass vocalization and, instead, directly access their meaning.

For this reason, including a very small number of keywords on each slide (generally, less than seven) might not interfere with anyone's ability to listen to your speech. However, as noted above, in the next chapter we will explore additional material that can be added to slides to improve overall audience understanding.

ILLUSTRATION 8. DON'T DO THIS!

BURNING QUESTION 2:
IDENTICAL WORDS

'What if the words on my slide are the same words I am saying out loud during my talk? Will this still create interference?'

The simple answer: yes.

The reason for this concerns pacing. The average person speaks at a rate of about 130 words per minute, while the average person reads at a rate of about 220 words per minute – with highly skilled readers maxing out around 1000 words per minute (meaning some of you will finish this chapter faster than the time it takes to brew a cup of tea).

Accordingly, when an audience is presented with identical written and spoken words, the tendency will be to read ahead of or out of sequence from the presenter. Once this occurs, we are back in the same boat as before, with the words generated by the silent reading conflicting with the words generated by the oral voice, thereby leading to a bottleneck.

Beyond interference, the practice of simply reading aloud words contained on a PowerPoint slide has long been shown to frustrate and bore audiences. In fact, when individuals attend talks that consist of a presenter speaking words identical to those on slides, they actually learn *less* than if they were to simply take the slides home and read them quietly on the couch. Clearly, this is a habit to avoid at all costs.

2. No (or minimal) text on handouts

Oftentimes during a talk, lesson or coaching session, presenters will supply their audience with handouts meant to supplement their oral speech. Unfortunately, if these handouts contain text, then we can expect the same issues as above. In order to read a handout during a presentation, people must stop listening to the speaker. Conversely, when listening to the speaker, there's no chance they will be able to read the handouts. Therefore, try to distribute any text-based handouts *after* your talk is complete. If you must include handouts during an oral presentation, remember the keyword limit (see p. 17) and see the next chapter for additional ideas.

3. Follow the speaker

We know not to use text-based slides or handouts when we give a presentation … but what about when we attend a presentation by someone who has not yet learnt this concept? As you're now aware, in order to get the most from this presentation you'll need to select one stream of information to focus on and stick with it. But which to choose?

My advice (though, admittedly, it's anecdotal) is to *always pay attention to the speaker*. Whereas the slides are static and unchanging from one minute to the next, presenters will often respond to the mood of the audience, peppering their talk with stories, asides and off-the-cuff remarks that didn't make it onto the slides. For this reason, you can expect to get more relevant, more coherent and simply *more* information from speakers than from their notes.

If you're really worried you're missing key ideas, you can always ask for a copy of the slides once the presentation is complete. This way, you can devote your full attention to reading and comprehending them in the comfort of your own home.

BURNING QUESTION 3:

NOTE-TAKING

'What about taking notes? Does writing down words during an oral presentation trigger the Broca/Wernicke bottleneck?'

Interestingly, the answer to this question depends upon the type of notes being taken.

Note-taking can be divided into two distinct categories: *shallow* and *deep*. When taking shallow notes, the goal is simply to take as many notes as possible during an oral presentation — essentially, jotting down a complete transcript of what is being said. Luckily, this type of note-taking does *not* appear to bottleneck; all sounds that hit your ears can make it onto the page.

Here's the rub: whenever you take shallow notes, you can expect to *learn* next to nothing. As an example, think of court stenographers — these incredible note-takers can type upwards of 300 words per minute and can copy down nearly every word said during even the most chaotic of trials. However, if you quiz stenographers about the details of a particular court case, they typically have only a fleeting memory of the proceedings with no real sense of the larger story or its ultimate meaning.

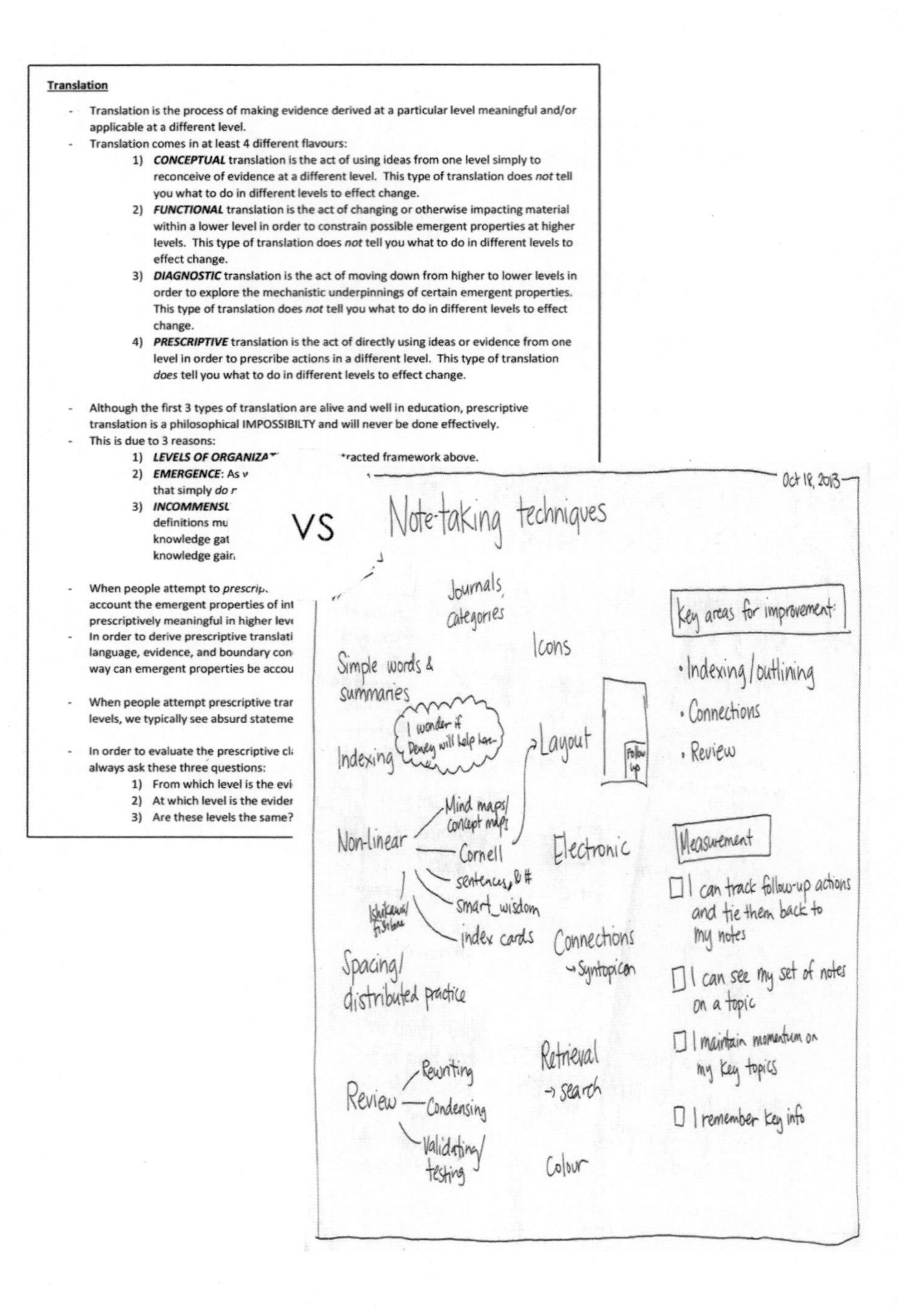

Translation

- Translation is the process of making evidence derived at a particular level meaningful and/or applicable at a different level.
- Translation comes in at least 4 different flavours:
    1) ***CONCEPTUAL*** translation is the act of using ideas from one level simply to reconceive of evidence at a different level. This type of translation does *not* tell you what to do in different levels to effect change.
    2) ***FUNCTIONAL*** translation is the act of changing or otherwise impacting material within a lower level in order to constrain possible emergent properties at higher levels. This type of translation does *not* tell you what to do in different levels to effect change.
    3) ***DIAGNOSTIC*** translation is the act of moving down from higher to lower levels in order to explore the mechanistic underpinnings of certain emergent properties. This type of translation does *not* tell you what to do in different levels to effect change.
    4) ***PRESCRIPTIVE*** translation is the act of directly using ideas or evidence from one level in order to prescribe actions in a different level. This type of translation *does* tell you what to do in different levels to effect change.
- Although the first 3 types of translation are alive and well in education, prescriptive translation is a philosophical IMPOSSIBILTY and will never be done effectively.
- This is due to 3 reasons:
    1) ***LEVELS OF ORGANIZA*** ... racted framework above.
    2) ***EMERGENCE***: As v ... that simply *do r*
    3) ***INCOMMENSU*** ... definitions mu ... knowledge gat ... knowledge gair
- When people attempt to *prescrip* ... account the emergent properties of int ... prescriptively meaningful in higher leve
- In order to derive prescriptive translati ... language, evidence, and boundary con ... way can emergent properties be accou
- When people attempt prescriptive trar ... levels, we typically see absurd stateme
- In order to evaluate the prescriptive cl ... always ask these three questions:
    1) From which level is the evi
    2) At which level is the evider
    3) Are these levels the same?

ILLUSTRATION 9. SHALLOW VS DEEP NOTE-TAKING

This is because when we take shallow notes, the only things of importance are the *sound* and *order* of the words being spoken, not the meaning of or story behind those words.

Conversely, when taking *deep notes*, the goal is to make sense of and organize the words being spoken in order to derive a deeper meaning. These notes often appear somewhat chaotic with many scribbles, links and doodles. Unfortunately, when note-taking like this, the bottleneck comes back into play: as you focus on organizing the words you are jotting down, the voice of the speaker becomes background noise.

Study after study has revealed that even though deep note-taking might trigger the bottleneck and lessen the overall amount of information taken in during a presentation, it serves to strengthen the understanding of and memory for those ideas noted down. In other words, though you may learn *less*, you can expect to learn *better*. For this reason, when taking deep notes, be sure to only take down those ideas you deem important enough to commit to memory.

This leads to a second important issue. Many people argue that taking notes using a computer is worse than taking notes using traditional pen and paper. The truth is, it's not the tool *per se* that matters — it's the *type of notes* each tool best caters to that matters. Many people can type words on a keyboard much faster than they can write them out by hand. For this reason, computers tend to cater to shallow notes: people vigorously typing out each word as they hear it simply because they can. Conversely, hand-writing tends to cater to deep notes: people processing and organizing information within their minds because they know they won't be able to jot down every word spoken.

As such, there is nothing inherently wrong with taking notes on a computer — except that these notes are typically constructed in a shallow manner, thereby leading to weaker learning. And there is nothing inherently better about taking notes by hand — except that this type of note-taking almost always requires deep processing, thereby leading to stronger learning.

4. Computerized text and speech is no different

When designing digital programs or tutorials, it is common to include both text and speech elements. So long as the user has control over these features and can turn them on and off at will, this might be an excellent design choice. The problem arises when these features are blindly combined, so that words and text appear together regardless of user preference.

As you can now guess, including simultaneous text and speech elements within a single program — even when the text and speech are identical — serves only to impair comprehension and retention of the presented material. For this reason, consider ways to allow for users to manage, control or otherwise access written and spoken elements.

In addition, many websites now embed audio and video elements alongside more common text-based material. Again, as this forces users to divide their attention between the text and audio/video, try to ensure audio options are available and clearly demarcated. Conversely, consider embedding audio or video clips in a pop-out screen or new tab, as this will allow users to focus completely on the audiovisual material without interference from text elements.

AT A GLANCE

It is impossible to simultaneously read words while listening to someone speak.

- » Silent reading ain't so silent.
- » Due to the Broca/Wernicke bottleneck, only one stream of verbal information can be understood at any one time.
- » Trying to jump quickly between reading words and listening to oral speech impairs memory for both streams of information.

APPLICATIONS

1. No (or minimal) text on PowerPoint slides.
   - » Keywords are fine (generally, less than seven).
   - » If written and spoken text match ... we still run into the same problem.
2. No (or minimal) text on handouts.
3. Follow the speaker.
   - » Shallow note-taking can impair learning.
   - » Deep note-taking can improve learning.
   - » Computers cater to shallow note-taking.
   - » Pen and paper caters to deep note-taking.
4. Computerized text and speech is no different.

2. Images + Speech

We hear and apprehend only what we already half know.

— *Henry David Thoreau*

ABBA.

Dancing Queen.

I take little pride in admitting it, but for a short period during my formative teenage years, this was easily my favourite song. In fact, I'd say I listened to it upwards of 300 times throughout the mid-90s — and during all that time I was absolutely certain that the opening lyrics were: 'You can dance, you can *die*, having the time of your life'. To be honest, this did always strike me as slightly macabre, but come on … it's ABBA … what else could I expect?

Jump to earlier this year. I'm at work surfing YouTube when I randomly stumble upon the original *Dancing Queen* music video.

Despite my long history with this song, I had only ever *heard* ABBA sing it — now, I would actually be able to *watch* ABBA sing it.

Fully expecting to be transported to my glorious youth, I hit play ... that's when I saw it. During the opening verse, both singers clearly rounded their pursed lips into an unmistakable 'J' form. For the first time in my life, I heard the correct lyrics: 'You can dance, you can *jive*'. The song was never about someone passing away; it's always been about someone getting down (which, in hindsight, makes a whole lot more sense).

So what happened? How is it possible that watching someone sing a song could overwrite twenty years of memory forged by listening to that song?

Hear with your eyes, see with your ears

My *Dancing Queen* debacle was a real-world example of the McGurk Effect, a psychological phenomenon that illustrates how what we *see* can drive what we *hear*.

If you were to take part in a typical McGurk experiment, it would go something like this. You're sitting in front of a computer screen, watching a man exaggeratedly mouth the word 'baba' while over a set of speakers you hear him saying that same word. Every second or so you hear it: 'baba ... baba ... baba'.

Suddenly, while the voice continues unchanged over the speakers, the man on the screen starts mouthing a different word. Rather than pressing his lips together to form 'ba', he deliberately puts his front teeth against his lower lip and exaggeratedly makes a 'fa' form.

That's when it happens.

Rather than the clear 'b' syllable you've been hearing all along, you start to hear a much softer 'f'. Even though you know the audio

ILLUSTRATION 10. THE MCGURK EFFECT

hasn't changed in any way, you start to hear a totally different word: 'fafa … fafa … fafa'.

Convinced the researchers must be playing some sort of trick on you, you close your eyes. With the face gone, the audio clearly reverts to what it's been all along: 'baba'. But as soon as you open your eyes and focus back on the man's face, the voice shifts again to 'fafa'.

Many people seem willing to accept that vision can drive hearing (perhaps this has to do with the tangible nature of visual objects as opposed to the largely 'invisible' nature of sound waves). However, it might come as a bit of a shock to learn that this relationship isn't a one-way street. For as many instances as we can find of vision driving hearing, there are an equal number of *hearing* driving *vision*.

Perhaps the best-known example is something known as the Shams Illusion. If you were to take part in a typical Shams experiment, it would start similarly to the McGurk experiment above. You're sitting in front of a blank computer screen. Suddenly, at random intervals, a loud beep plays over the pair of speakers while, simultaneously, a small circle quickly appears and disappears on the screen.

Occasionally, two loud beeps play in rapid succession over the speakers while two circles quickly appear and disappear on the screen. It's all fairly simple — when you hear one beep, you see one circle; when you hear two beeps, you see two circles. Nothing to get too excited about.

Of course, it's all an illusion. Regardless of how many beeps are played over the speakers, only *one* circle is ever flashed on the computer screen. At no time do two circles ever appear on the screen — yet you'd swear you see two circles every time you hear two beeps. This is essentially the flipside of the McGurk Effect. Whereas before what you saw changed what you heard, in this illusion what you hear changes what you see.

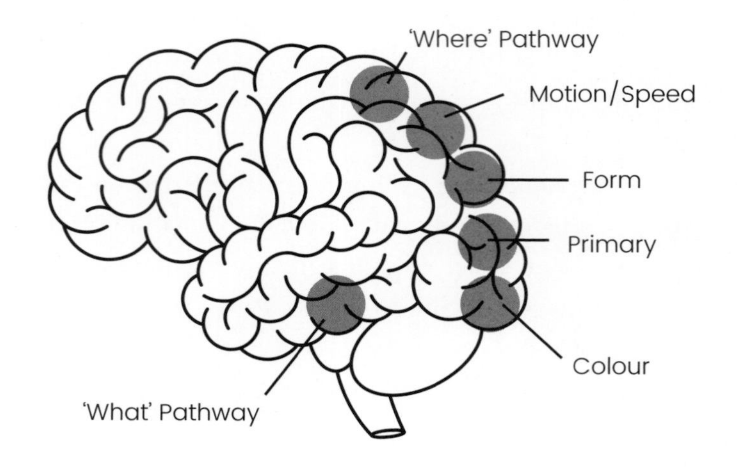

ILLUSTRATION 11. YOUR VISUAL BRAIN

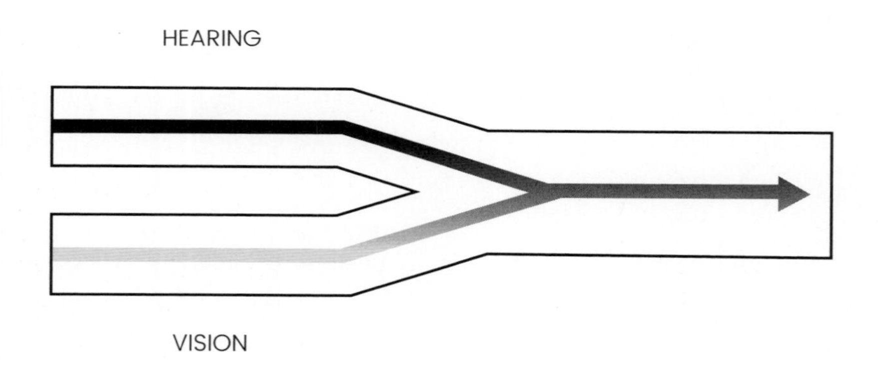

ILLUSTRATION 12. SIGHT AND SOUND MIX FREELY — NO BOTTLENECK!

The ecological shift

There's clearly a strong and integrated relationship between what we see and what we hear. But how does all of this work?

In the last chapter we learnt that when we hear something, this information is first processed along the sides of the brain within the auditory cortex.

Conversely, when we see something, this information is first processed along the *back* of the brain within the visual cortex. This very large neural area is divided into several distinct regions, each of which serves to process a different aspect of whatever it is we are looking at. For instance, when watching a bird fly, different regions of the visual cortex process the edges of the bird, the colour of the bird, the motion of the bird, etc.

Earlier, we saw that trying to funnel two different streams of information down a single processing channel causes a bottleneck which leads to a loss of information. Luckily, hearing and vision utilize different processing channels. This not only eliminates any bottleneck, but also allows us to combine hearing and vision into a single, consolidated signal. This process is what is meant by *sensory integration*.

Importantly, sensory integration is not an additive process (A + B = A and B) — it is an ecological process (A + B = C). As an example, imagine if you dropped a dozen non-native beetles into an otherwise balanced garden. The results wouldn't simply be the same garden plus beetles. Rather, this one addition would change everything: the food chain, the nutrients in the soil, the survival conditions. The same is true for hearing and vision. In a very real sense, when what we hear joins with what we see, a completely new entity emerges. Perhaps no process has better epitomized the phrase 'The whole is greater than the sum of its parts'.

Let's see what this all means in the real world.

Every Saturday night, three good friends get together. When Jerry and Casey arrive at Karen's house, Karen is sitting in her room writing some notes. She quickly gathers the cards and stands up to greet her friends at the door. They follow her into the living room but, as usual, they can't agree on exactly what to play. Casey eventually takes a stand and they begin. Early in the evening, Casey notices Karen's hand and the many diamonds. As the night progresses, the tempo of play increases. Finally, Karen says 'Let's hear the score.' They listen carefully and comment on their performance. When all is done, Karen's friends go home, exhausted but happy.

ILLUSTRATION 13. INTERPRETATION — PART I
(INSPIRED BY ANDERSON ET AL. 1977)

Interpretation

Let me quickly acknowledge the elephant in the room: over the next couple of sections I am going to attempt to demonstrate how hearing and vision combine to generate meaning. To that end, I'm not 100 per cent sure a book is the best medium with which to accomplish this task. However, as we learnt in the previous chapter, reading written text is similar to listening to oral speech. As such, although the examples we'll use aren't ideal, they should be effective enough to get the basic points across.

To begin, I'd like you to take a look at the picture opposite, then read the passage following it.

Again, allowing for the fact that *reading* is standing in for *listening*, I imagine you found this passage relatively simple and straightforward. It's an innocuous tale of a group of friends gathering for a weekend card game. Fair enough.

Now I'd like you to take a look at the image on the next page and read the passage following it.

Same story, same words, same sounds entering your ears — yet the accompanying image changes how you interpret this auditory information. When the image changes, words like *notes*, *score* and *performance* suddenly take on a totally different meaning. Similarly, phrases like 'She quickly gathers the cards and stands up' and 'the tempo of play increases' resonate in completely novel ways. Importantly, this interaction works both ways: the sounds you are hearing (or, in this case, reading) impact the way you interpret each visual image. In the first sequence, you likely attached the name Casey to one of the male characters and took special interest in Karen's flush draw. Conversely, in the second sequence, you likely attached the same name to one of the female characters and took special interest in the rings adorning Karen's bow hand.

This is what I meant earlier by an *ecological* process. As information enters your eyes, it changes the way you process and interpret

Every Saturday night, three good friends get together. When Jerry and Casey arrive at Karen's house, Karen is sitting in her room writing some notes. She quickly gathers the cards and stands up to greet her friends at the door. They follow her into the living room but, as usual, they can't agree on exactly what to play. Casey eventually takes a stand and they begin. Early in the evening, Casey notices Karen's hand and the many diamonds. As the night progresses, the tempo of play increases. Finally, Karen says 'Let's hear the score.' They listen carefully and comment on their performance. When all is done, Karen's friends go home, exhausted but happy.

ILLUSTRATION 14. INTERPRETATION – PART II
(INSPIRED BY ANDERSON ET AL. 1977)

information entering your ears. Similarly, as information enters your ears, it changes the way you process and interpret information entering your eyes. The whole is greater than the sum of its parts.

Comprehension

Again, allowing for the fact that we are confined to using reading as a substitute for hearing, read the passage below.

> If the balloons popped, the sound wouldn't be able to carry since everything would be too far away from the correct floor. A closed window would also prevent the sound from carrying, since most buildings tend to be well insulated. Since the whole operation depends on a steady flow of electricity, a break in the middle of the wire would also cause problems. Of course, the fellow could shout, but the human voice is not loud enough to carry that far. An additional problem is that a string could break on the instrument. Then there could be no accompaniment to the message. Clearly, the best situation would involve less distance. Then there would be fewer potential problems. With face-to-face contact, the least number of things could go wrong.

If you're like most people, you probably found this a bit odd. At a base level, the words in this passage are simple and easy to follow — but what do they mean? Although these words make sense, there is simply nothing tying them all together into a coherent concept. In fact, if I were to test your memory for what you'd just read, you might be able to recall a fleeting detail here or there, but overall you'd likely perform quite poorly.

Now, take a look at the image on the next page.

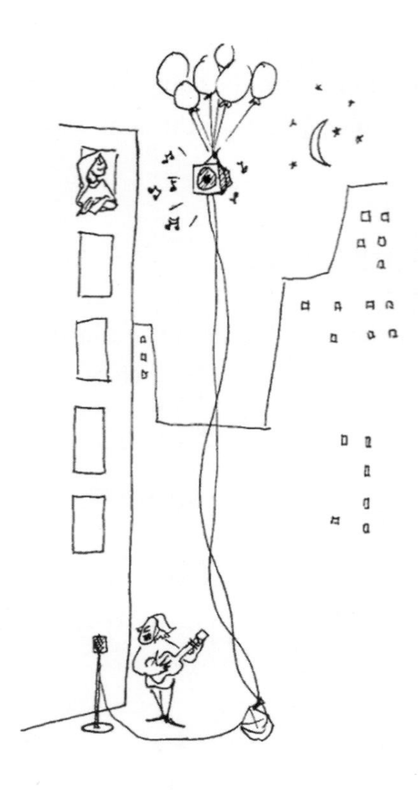

ILLUSTRATION 15. SENSORY INTEGRATION DRIVES COMPREHENSION (FROM BRADMAN & JOHNSON, 1972)

Suddenly, the earlier passage makes sense. With the inclusion of the visual information, what you hear comes to life: specific details are spotlighted, patterns are formed and coherence is reached. Whereas before you could *read* the words, now you *comprehend* them.

But, as before, this isn't a one-way street: if I were to have first shown you the picture in isolation — with no accompanying sounds/ words — you likely would have found it cute but ultimately lacking in specificity. With the accompanying passage, certain details take on special importance (the wires tying the speaker to the ground console, the number of floors between the singer and the woman) while other details fade to the background (the moon in the sky, the city buildings) and meaningful comprehension is achieved.

Is all of this really necessary?

You may have noticed that, in each of the examples above, I could have simply added additional words in order to clarify details. For instance, I could have said, 'Imagine a man is playing a guitar, and that this guitar is plugged into an amplifier, and that the amplifier is being hoisted six storeys off the ground by a dozen balloons …'. This would have gotten the point across, no picture needed.

So, what's the point of including images with spoken words?

EXPEDIENCE AND SPECIFICITY

It boils down to expedience and specificity. To demonstrate, below is the original written description of a famous literary character. Read it and see how long it takes for you to determine which character this is describing.

> *His limbs were in proportion, and I had selected his features as beautiful. His yellow skin scarcely covered the work of muscles and arteries beneath; his hair was of a lustrous black, and flowing; his teeth of a pearly whiteness; but these luxuriances only formed a more horrid contrast with his watery eyes, that seemed almost of the same colour as the dun white sockets in which they were set, his shrivelled complexion and straight black lips.*

ILLUSTRATION 16. THIS IS MUCH EASIER

Expedience: images allow us to process an incredible amount of information in an amazingly short time. Whereas it probably took you about 30 seconds to read the original written description, it likely took you about 0.2 seconds to recognize the image opposite.

'But wait,' you might be saying. 'You could have simply said the words "Frankenstein's monster" and I'd have gotten it just as quickly'. This is absolutely true — which brings us to the second topic.

Specificity: over the last century, there have been dozens of variations of Frankenstein's monster. Beyond Mary Shelley's original description and Boris Karloff's definitive portrayal, there is Peter Boyle's comical spin in *Young Frankenstein*, Robert De Niro's emotional deconstruction in the 1994 film version, Rory Kinnear's pale gothic take in the television program *Penny Dreadful*. If I had simply said the words 'Frankenstein's monster' then continued with a lengthy oral discussion of this character, there is simply no guarantee everyone would be conjuring up the same mental images of the monster. Seeing as the images we conjure up will change how we interpret and comprehend the words we hear, using a picture ensures everyone is on the same page and building the same understanding.

In summary: audio alone works fine. Visuals alone work fine. But audio and visuals together can be transcendent.

Implications for leaders, teachers and coaches

1. Use (predominantly) images on slides

In the previous chapter, we learnt that filling a PowerPoint slide with text will force the audience to choose between listening to the words you speak or reading the words you wrote; they cannot do both simultaneously. So what should we be putting on our slides? You've probably guessed the answer: images.

As outlined above, not only can visual images and oral speech be processed simultaneously, but this combination will also assist the audience in interpreting, comprehending and learning the presented material. In fact, memory can increase up to 20 per cent when images and speech are combined (as opposed to presenting them in isolation). Furthermore, the inclusion of images with speech has been shown to enhance audience engagement, receptivity and judgments of likability. In all seriousness, scientific research has demonstrated that when you replace text with images on your PowerPoint slides, your audience will view you as better prepared and more professional, and they will *like* you more — no joke!

BURNING QUESTION 1:

QUANTITY

'How many images should I include on each slide?'

When people first learn of the power of images, they can sometimes go a little overboard. The thought process is clear enough: if adding one picture can improve memory, then adding *ten* pictures should blow memory right out of the water. Unfortunately, more is not always better.

Earlier, we learnt that people can analyze and recognize images incredibly quickly (around 0.2 seconds). Unfortunately, this speed is confined to *one complex image at a time*. In order to comprehend multiple complex images appearing simultaneously, people must process each in turn. This not only increases the time it takes to interpret multiple images, but also drains attentional resources and impairs memory for the different images being analyzed. In fact, if I were to show you multiple visual scenes simultaneously, your memory would be up to 50 per cent worse than if I were to show you those same scenes one at a time.

For this reason, when designing PowerPoint slides, try to imagine you are flipping through personal photos with a friend. You'd never reminisce by throwing a dozen photos haphazardly on a table and attempting to discern them all simultaneously. Rather, the natural (and effective) practice is to go through them one photo at a time, allowing each to be analyzed and discussed in turn.

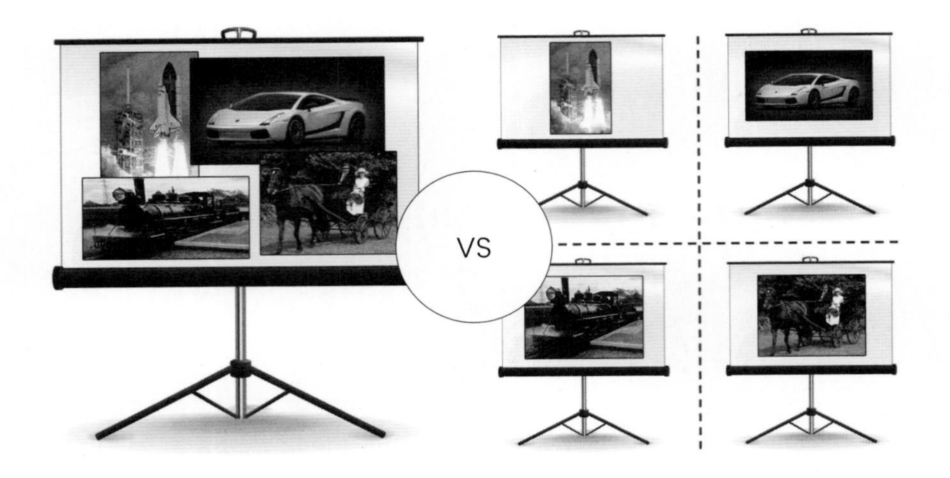

ILLUSTRATION 17. ONE IMAGE PER SLIDE IS PLENTY

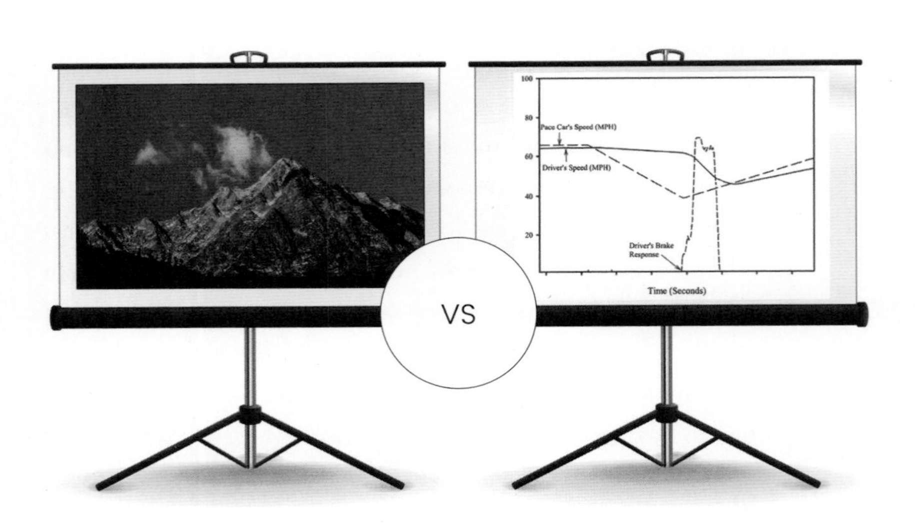

ILLUSTRATION 18. GRAPHS ARE NOT PROCESSED LIKE TYPICAL IMAGES

BURNING QUESTION 2:

GRAPHS AND TABLES

'What about graphs? Does it only take 0.2 seconds for people to interpret them?'

If you remember nothing else from this chapter, please let it be this: graphs and tables *are not* like other images. The reason we are able to analyze complex scenes in the blink of an eye is largely due to the fact that most scenes have an underlying pattern or 'gist'. For instance, if I show you a picture with 1000 evergreen trees, you don't need to analyze each individual tree in order to get the gist and recognize the image as one of a forest.

Unfortunately, graphs and tables rarely have a gist. Rather, they are meaningful only in their *specific details* — every number, letter and shape carries information necessary to comprehend the whole. For this reason, deciphering graphs and tables is far from fast and almost never easy. In fact, each time we pop a graph or table onto a PowerPoint slide, it's akin to projecting a Where's Waldo image: although *we* might know exactly where to look to locate the information relevant to our talk, the audience must weed through a complex maze in order to decipher the meaning of what they're seeing. As you can probably guess, when the audience is forced to expend attention and mental energy analyzing a graph or table, this almost always comes at the cost of them listening to and understanding your speech.

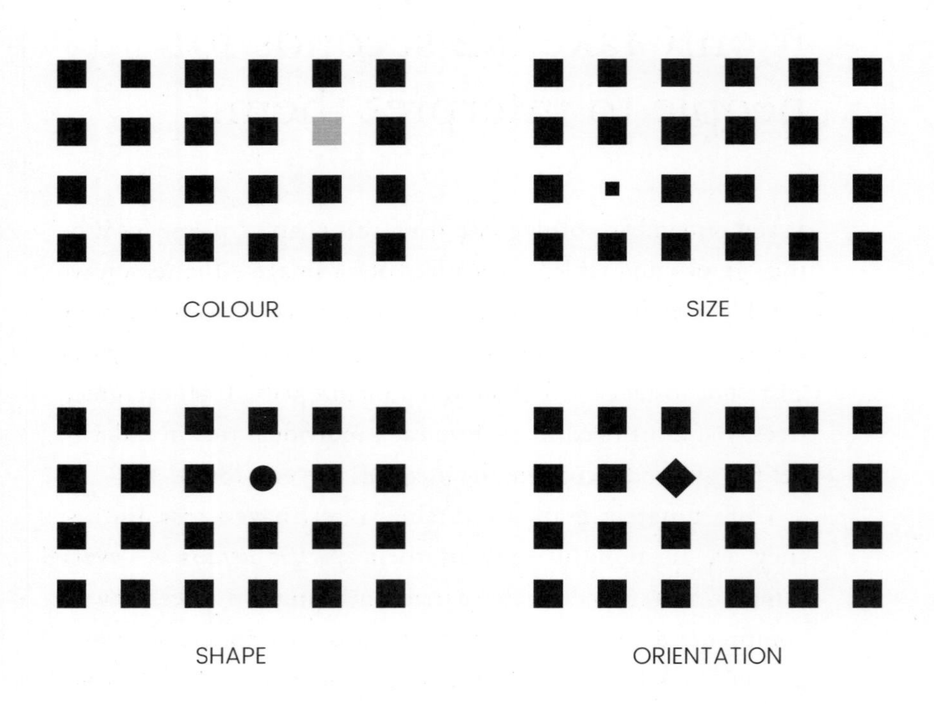

ILLUSTRATION 19. THE POP-OUT EFFECT

When including a graph or table during a presentation, one option is to present it piecemeal. For example, you might start by displaying and explaining only the axes, then layer on data one line at a time, explaining each new section as it appears. This process allows you to quickly walk the audience through the figure to ensure they are focused on the correct information at the correct moment and are not wasting precious cognitive resources trying to decrypt a complicated figure.

The next best option is to explicitly highlight or delineate relevant aspect/s of the figure to guide the audience's attention only to those areas worth analyzing. Luckily, human beings will almost automatically home in on any aspect of an image that breaks an otherwise uniform pattern. Psychologists call this the Pop-Out effect. Grey in a sea of black; **bold** in a sea of standard; CAPITAL in a sea of lowercase. When the audience can easily discern where to look, they will more easily comprehend the point you are making.

BURNING QUESTION 3:

RELEVANCE

'Do images need to be relevant to the topic I am discussing?'

Unfortunately, the terms *engagement* and *learning* are not synonymous. When an audience is engaged, this means they are primed and ready to learn ... but this does not ensure they will actually do any learning.

I bring this up to highlight the fact that including cute, silly or otherwise irrelevant images during an oral presentation has been shown to boost *engagement* but potentially impair *learning*. Conversely, including relevant images that support verbal content has been shown to help audiences build deeper connections and ultimately increase *learning*, but to potentially decrease *engagement*.

As such, the issue of image relevance is predicated upon the purpose you are trying to achieve. During the early stages of a presentation, when your goal might be to ensure the audience is on board and excited to hear what you have to say, then irrelevant images might prove your greatest ally. However, during the later stages of a presentation, when your goal might be to ensure the audience understands and will remember the issues being discussed, then irrelevant images might be your greatest enemy. Simply being clear on your ultimate intention for an included image will help you determine how relevant that image needs to be to the words you're speaking.

2. Use (predominantly) images on handouts

Any handouts given to an audience during a presentation should follow the same general rules as those that apply to PowerPoint slides. Last chapter, we saw that handouts with textual information will force the audience to choose between reading or listening. Luckily, handouts with visual images will not drive this same selection: people will be able to analyze images on handouts *while* continuing to comprehend the speaker. As such, try to ensure any hard-copy information handed out during a presentation is largely visual rather than textual. Keep in mind, however, the issues outlined above concerning quantity, relevance and the unique nature of graphs and tables.

3. Use images to support digital narration/text

This may be beating a dead horse, but the issues inherent with oral speech, written text and visual images do not change when a presentation or artefact goes digital. Accordingly, when developing a novel program or website that includes oral or textual elements, try to support these with images. As before, if the goal is simply to hook people's attention and get them engaged and excited, then the relevance of these images is largely unimportant. However, if the goal is to meaningfully convey information in order to drive learning, then ensure images are relevant to and support the textual information.

4. Beware of the Attenborough Effect

People seem to love sleek, sexy, flashy products. All you have to do is look at the rapid evolution of movie visual effects to realize that the more 'wow factor', the more audiences will clamour for it. The same appears to be true in learning situations. When people watch high-gloss, well-produced videos or presentations, most feel as though they have understood better and learnt more than those who watched the same material presented in a drier, less fancy manner.

Here's the issue: it's all an illusion. Regardless of how sexy or well put together a video or presentation appears, the actual learning that occurs does not appear to change. We call this the Attenborough Effect. If you've ever watched one of those sleek David Attenborough nature specials, you were likely hooked and swore you'd always remember every moment. Truth is, though, that if I were to test your memory one week after watching the show, you're likely to have forgotten exactly as much as someone who watched the same material presented in a more straightforward manner with simple speech and static images.

This is all to say, don't sweat the small stuff when trying to develop specific teaching materials. If you have two hours to prepare a presentation, and the ultimate goal of that presentation is to ensure others will understand and learn from the presented material, then your time will be much better spent refining your story, content, and ideas than trying to create sleek and sexy material meant to wow your audience.

AT A GLANCE

Listening to speech while looking at images can improve learning and memory.

- » Hearing and vision are processed separately and undergo an ecological combination: the whole is more than the sum of the parts.
- » Hearing and vision combine to guide interpretation and comprehension.
- » Visual images allow for an expedience and specificity not easily matched by oral speech.

APPLICATIONS

1. Use (predominantly) images on PowerPoint slides.
   - » One image at a time is plenty.
   - » Relevant images can support learning; irrelevant images can support engagement.
   - » Graphs and tables *are not* like regular images!
2. Use (predominantly) images on handouts.
3. Use images to support digital narration/text.
4. Beware of the Attenborough Effect.
   - » Engagement is not the same as learning.

1952

GET A-HEAD!

FOR ADULTS
AT
NO CHARGE

ADULT EDUCATION
CLASSES

MANY COURSES · · MANY PLACES

Intermission 1

Please take around 15 seconds to study and enjoy this old adult education poster.

3.

Space

A place for everything, everything in its place.

— *Charles A. Goodrich*

A warning: this chapter might feel a bit confusing. But, rest assured, there is method behind the madness. I promise everything will make sense by the end.

Now, let's tuck in!

» In 2016, American student Alex Mullen correctly memorized a shuffled deck of 52 playing cards in 19.41 seconds.
» In 2013, Swedish author Johannes Mallow correctly memorized a string of 1080 binary digits in five minutes.
» In 2015, Indian vegetable vendor Suresh Kumar Sharma correctly memorized the first 70,030 digits of π.

These are, without a doubt, awe inspiring feats of memory. But perhaps what's more incredible is that the people who accomplished them are, for all intents and purposes, completely normal; they aren't savants, they don't have photographic memories and they weren't genetically endowed with super-human brains. They are working with the same neural hardware as you and I. So how'd they do it?

Each of them utilized a 2000-year-old memory technique called the *method of loci*. This technique employs a relatively simple two-step process. The first step is *elaboration*. In general, human beings are horrible at memorizing common or unremarkable material (ever sat through an endless board meeting?) but incredible at memorizing surprising or shocking material (ever seen or been in a car accident?). Exploiting this, elaboration is a process whereby mundane material is mentally replaced with extraordinary images. For instance, if you were trying to memorize a deck of cards, you might mentally replace the three of clubs with an image of Elvis wearing a bikini and shaking his hips in a kiddie pool filled with pudding. With elaboration, the weirder the better.

The second step is *placement*. After converting each card into an elaborate image, you select a specific location you are intimately familiar with (say, a childhood home) and 'place' each image within progressive landmarks throughout that location (say, at the front door, in the entry hallway, by the kitchen, etc.). Placement allows you to easily memorize elaborated items in a specific order. This means, when it comes time to recall the playing cards, all you have to do is take a mental stroll through your location and call out each image as you see it ('at the front door I see Elvis in a pool of pudding — three of clubs; as I step through the door into the entry hallway I see Madonna riding a Burmese tiger — six of diamonds').

The fact that nearly every mental athlete utilizes variations of this same technique suggests there is a very strong relationship between spatial locations and memory — but how exactly does it work?

"The news belongs to the people."

The Daily News

WEATHER
TODAY: Mostly sunny, High 75, Low 61

VOL. 1 . . . No. 001 CONNECTICUT, TUESDAY, SPETEMBER 1, 1953 10 cents

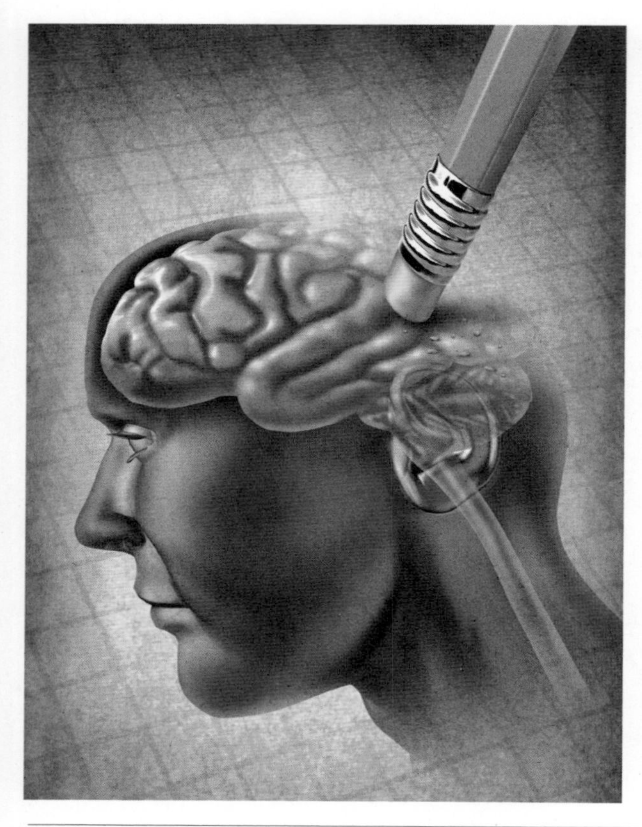

MAN'S MEMORY GOES MISSING

MANCHESTER – Memory comes in several different forms. For instance, ***working memory*** is our ability to briefly maintain recently experienced information. This is why you can remember the beginning of this sentence and form coherent meaning out of the words you are reading now. Additionally, ***procedural memory*** is our largely unconscious ability to activate physical movements and skills. This is why you can brush your teeth, throw a ball, and

Continued Below

cook an egg with little-to-no deep thought.

Typically when we speak about memory, however, we are referring to ***declarative memory.*** This is our ability to remember specific facts or events – for instance, what you ate for breakfast this morning, the capital of France, or your favourite childhood teacher.

Although we have been researching this form of memory for centuries, there is still a lot to learn. For instance, we don't know where in the brain these memories are stored or what in the heck these memories actually are (are they elecomagnetic patterns? Maybey they're a series of linked molecules?).

Despite this, it is safe to say a large chunk of what what we *do* understand about this form of memory comes from a single individual: Henry Molaison.

Continued on P. 2

NORMAL BRAIN

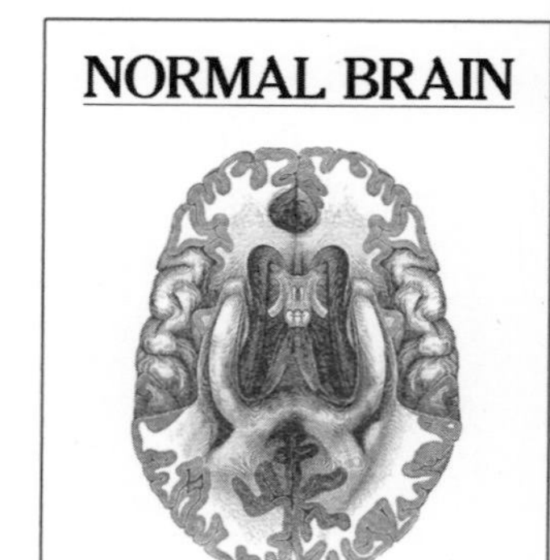

Continued from P. 1

At the age of seven, Henry began suffering from recurrent seizures. Although they started out relatively minor, they became increasingly more severe as he aged. By the time Henry turned 27, he was suffering from over a dozen black-outs a week making it impossible for him to maintain a job or live a normal life. After drugs proved ineffective at treating these seizures, Henry decided to undergo a radical and experimental surgery. Seeing as Henry's seizures always started within a specific region of the brain called the ***Hippocampus***, doctors decided to open his skull and remove this part of his brain.

Incredibly, the surgery was a success: Henry lived an additional 55 years suffering only one or two seizures per year. Unfortunately, after having his Hippocampus removed, Henry lived an additional 55 years without ever forming a new declarative memory.

Put simply, the hippocampus is the gateway to memory

Though he could remember much of his life prior to the surgery, he couldn't hold on to any new information for longer than a couple minutes. He would re-read the same magazines time and time again, couldn't remember the fact that his father had passed away, and would introduce himself anew to doctors he had met hundreds of times previously. In fact, until the day he died in 2008, Henry likely thought he was still a 27-year-old living in 1953.

HENRY'S BRAIN

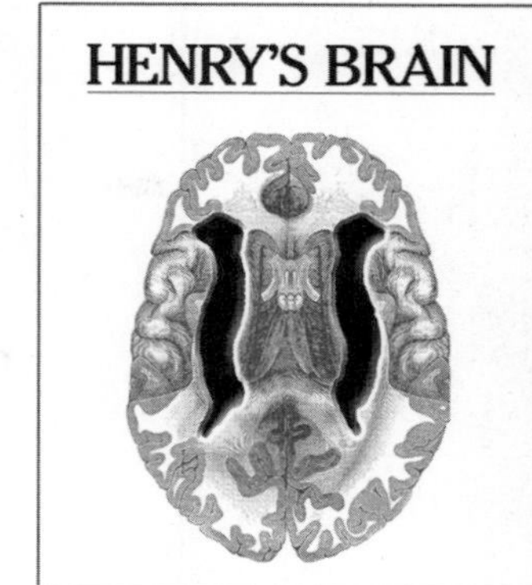

The fact that Henry could remember events that occurred *prior* to the surgery suggests that memories are not stored in the Hippocampus. But, the fact that he could no longer form any *new* memories suggests novel information/experiences must pass through the Hippocampus in order to become memories. Put simply, *the Hippocampus is the gateway to memory.*

Let's take a closer look at this important and interesting brain structure.

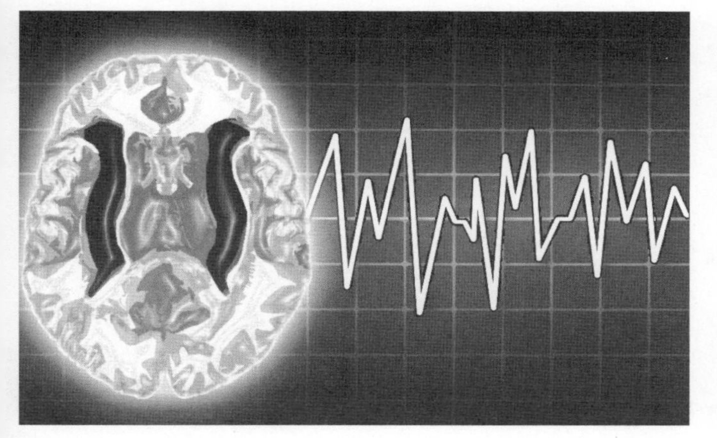

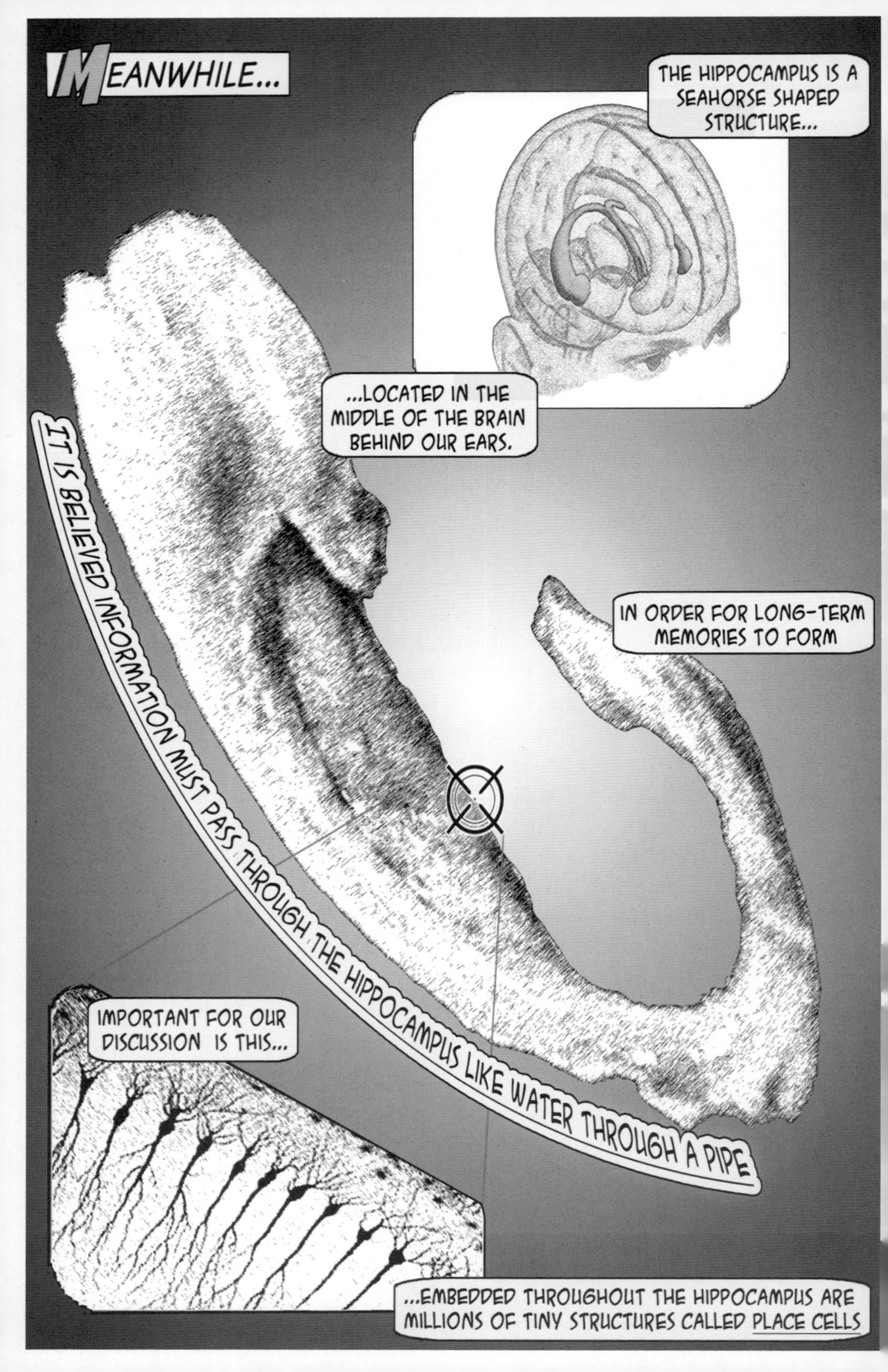
MEANWHILE...
THE HIPPOCAMPUS IS A SEAHORSE SHAPED STRUCTURE...
...LOCATED IN THE MIDDLE OF THE BRAIN BEHIND OUR EARS.
IN ORDER FOR LONG-TERM MEMORIES TO FORM
IT IS BELIEVED INFORMATION MUST PASS THROUGH THE HIPPOCAMPUS LIKE WATER THROUGH A PIPE
IMPORTANT FOR OUR DISCUSSION IS THIS...
...EMBEDDED THROUGHOUT THE HIPPOCAMPUS ARE MILLIONS OF TINY STRUCTURES CALLED PLACE CELLS

LIKE A GPS DEVICE, PLACE CELLS ENCODE THE SPATIAL LAYOUT OF LOCATIONS, OBJECTS, AND OUR PHYSICAL RELATIONSHIP TO THEM.
THIS ALLOWS US TO CONSTRUCT A MENTAL MAP OF THE WORLD AROUND US.
IF YOU WERE IN A MAZE, YOUR PLACE CELLS WOULD REFLECT BOTH THE LAYOUT OF THAT MAZE AND YOUR SPECIFIC LOCATION AS YOU WALK THROUGH IT.
ALZHEIMER'S DISEASE GREATLY DAMAGES THESE PLACE CELLS.
THIS IS WHY MANY SUFFERERS OFTEN BECOME DISORIENTED AND CAN GET LOST EVEN WITHIN FAMILIAR LOCATIONS.

Look Inside!

WHY WE'VE GOT PLACE CELL FEVER!

MEMORY & SPACE

JULY 1988 $1.75 £1.65

SPACE is INTEGRAL

The fact that the Hippocampus, our gateway to memory, is riddled with place cells suggests space is an *essential* component of memories. In fact, if I were to show you a screen with several images scattered around (a bicycle on the top left, a snake on the bottom right, etc.), then I removed the images and asked you a question about one (what colour was the snake?), your eyes would move to the portion of the screen where the relevant image used to be — even though there's no longer anything there!

LOOKING @ NOTHING

Researchers call this phenomenon *Looking at Nothing*. Importantly, this occurs even when we do not explicitly focus on the spatial layout of the original images. Like it or hate it, our place cells *subconsciously* create mental maps which are automatically encoded within each newly formed memory.

9 771234 567003 01

CORY SEZ:

"Think about the last time someone cleaned up your desk without your knowing. Even though you likely never explicitly memorized where your stapler, mug, and notebooks were placed, odds are it was immediately apparent when these objects were moved. This is because your place cells were automatically encoding this information for you."

PLUS...
Two reasons why space is an integral aspect of declarative memories

Mental maps are incredibly strong guiding cues. For instance, if I ask my brother to recall what we did during a trip to Albuquerque when we were children, he'd probably stare blankly back at me. But, if I remind him that we stayed in a two-storey motel across the street from an ancient-looking Dairy Queen and next-door to an abandoned strip mall, he'd likely be able to use these spatial details to reconstruct the complete memory of our escapades (a dare involving a skateboard, several trashcans, and a very angry mom).

This is why the Method of Loci discussed at the start of this chapter works so well. Although it's incredibly difficult to remember hundreds of mental images in the correct order (regardless of how elaborate they are), it is incredibly easy to remember the spatial layout of the house we grew up in, the high school we attended, or the route we take to work. As such, expert memorizers organize their elaborated images within these mental maps and use each as a guiding cue to complete the pattern and call up the proper image order.

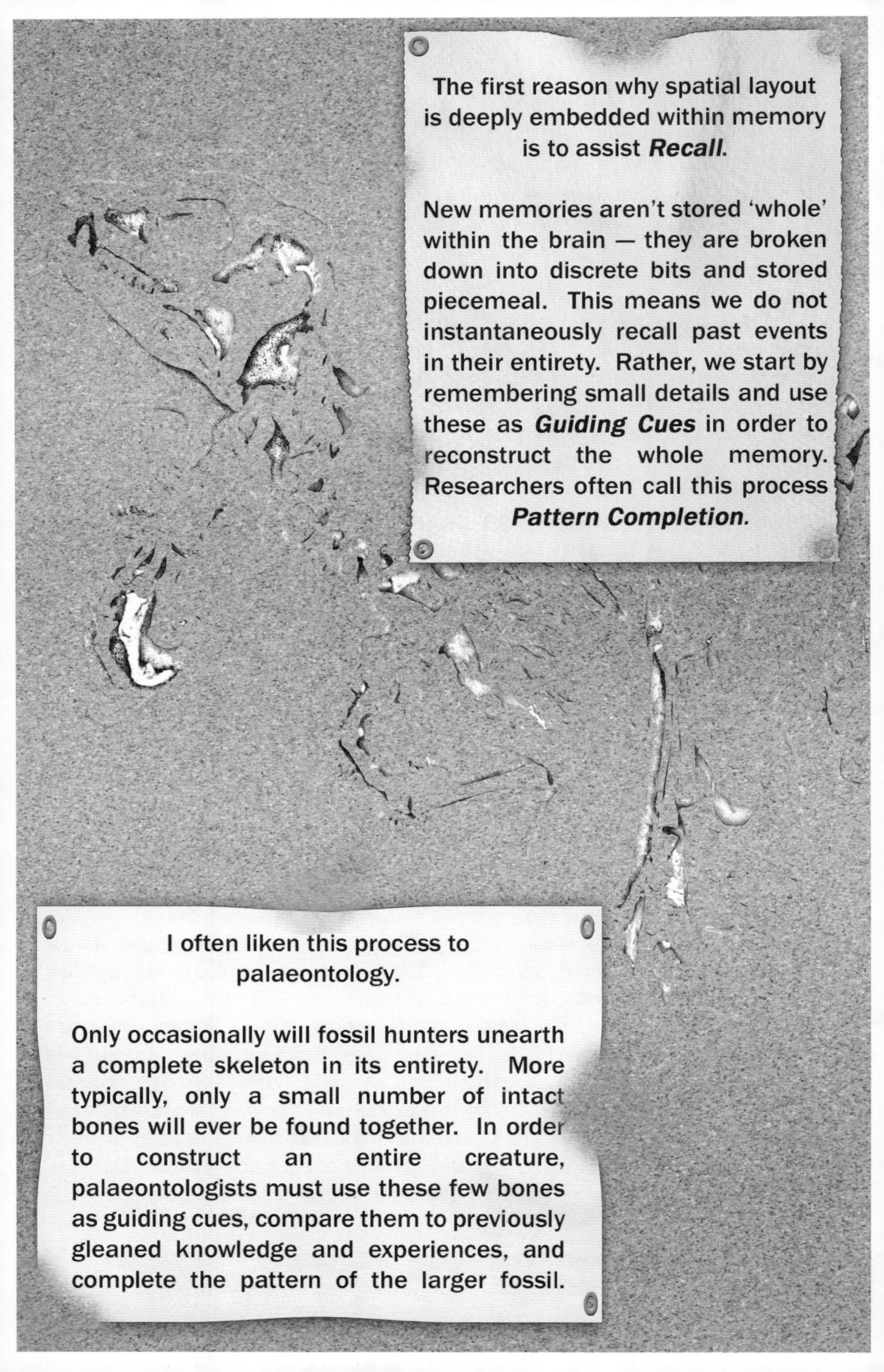
The first reason why spatial layout is deeply embedded within memory is to assist ***Recall.***

New memories aren't stored 'whole' within the brain — they are broken down into discrete bits and stored piecemeal. This means we do not instantaneously recall past events in their entirety. Rather, we start by remembering small details and use these as ***Guiding Cues*** in order to reconstruct the whole memory. Researchers often call this process ***Pattern Completion.***

I often liken this process to palaeontology.

Only occasionally will fossil hunters unearth a complete skeleton in its entirety. More typically, only a small number of intact bones will ever be found together. In order to construct an entire creature, palaeontologists must use these few bones as guiding cues, compare them to previously gleaned knowledge and experiences, and complete the pattern of the larger fossil.

PRED

The second reason why spatial layout is deeply embedded within memory is to assist *prediction.* For a long time, researchers thought the brain was a passive receiver: information would enter the body through the senses, speed along into the brain, and trigger off whatever response was required. We now know that, far from sitting back and observing the world, the brain is constantly and actively trying to forecast what is about to occur. When you see '*the grass is always___*', your brain is able to anticipate and complete the sentence long before your eyes reach the blank space.

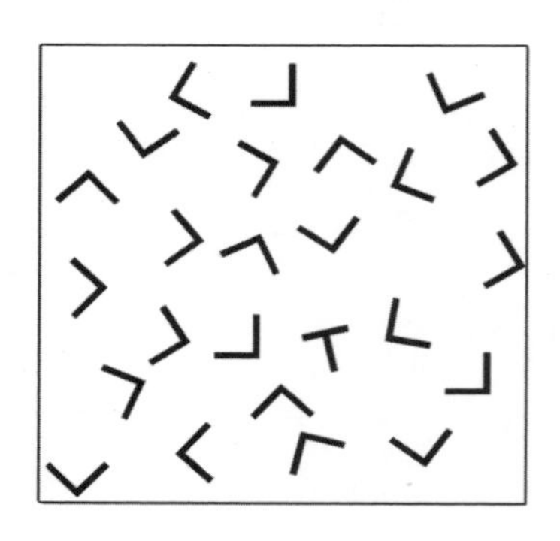

In a simple experiment, individuals are shown hundreds of grid-like images and asked to find the single 'T' shape hidden amidst a forest of 'L' shapes. Although each grid appears to be different from the others, researchers coyly insert one identical grid several dozen times. Typically, individuals never consciously recognize this repeating grid — but this doesn't stop their predictive brains from recognizing it! After only a couple repetitions, people are able to locate the 'T' in the repeated grid much quicker, though they can not explain why.

CTION

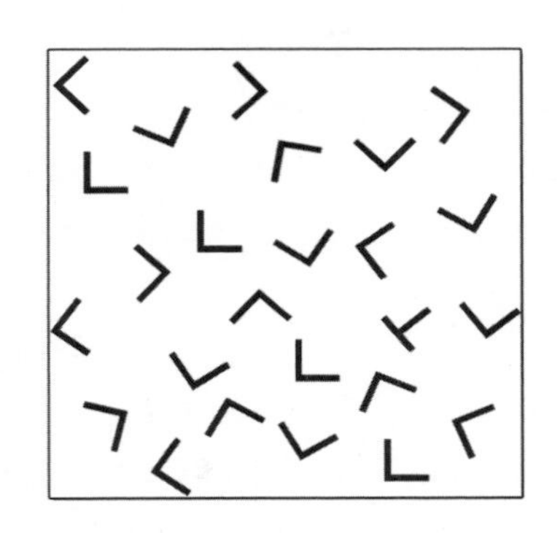
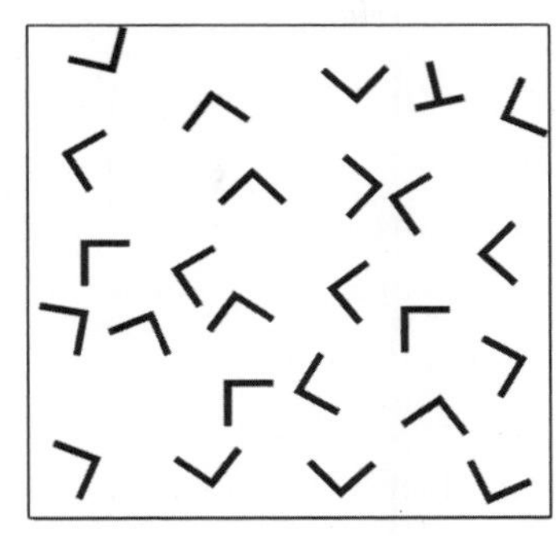

This is why many scientists now refer to the brain as an *Advanced Prediction Machine.* The fact that our brain fights to stay one step ahead of reality allows us to rapidly select thoughts and behaviours most relevant to each circumstance. Importantly, the predictions made by our brains are predicated almost exclusively on our previous experiences — in other words, our *memories.* Seeing as spatial organization is an integral feature of memories, this means mental maps serve not only as a guiding cue to recall previous events, but also as a guiding cue to predict future ones.

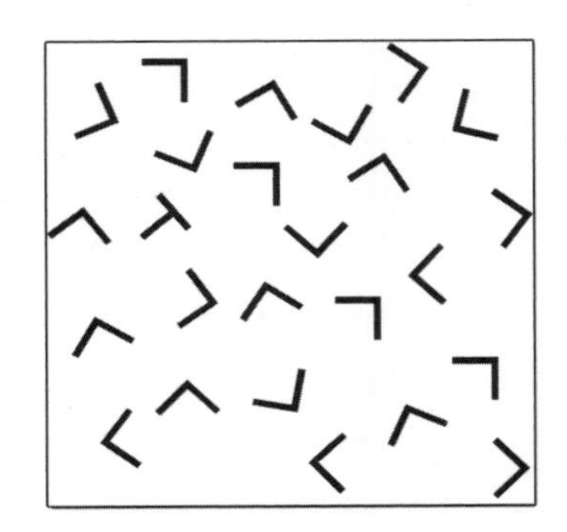

Researchers call this *Contextual Cuing* and, in a nut-shell, it demonstrates that human beings will implicitly and largely subconsciously memorize physical layouts, create mental maps, and use these to form predictions in order to drive future behaviours. So long as the world matches these predictions, individuals will respond faster and more efficiently to relevant situations.

Bringing it home

Think about how you read the first two chapters of this book. As you turned each page, you simply knew the page number would be in the bottom corner, the book and chapter names would be next to those, and the words would flow in paragraphs from left to right, top to bottom. I am fairly certain you never took the time to explicitly memorize this layout — rather, after reading a few pages that utilized this format, you subconsciously formed a prediction of how each future page would look. In fact, if we were to measure your brain activity while reading the first few chapters, we'd likely see a significant *decrease* in activity within the hippocampus: a sign that your place cells were quietening down as they'd already constructed an effective mental map. As long as each new page matched this prediction, you were able to progress through the book relatively quickly and effortlessly.

Now, think about how you read this chapter. As you turned each page, the spatial layout failed to match your prediction, meaning you had to expend time and effort analyzing each new format. In fact, if we were to measure your brain activity when reading this chapter, we'd likely see a significant *increase* in activity within the hippocampus: a sign that your place cells were vigorously trying to construct a new mental map to predict future pages.

Unfortunately, the inability to predict the layout of each page likely killed the 'flow' you typically achieve while reading. This, in turn, may have made this chapter feel disjointed and ultimately impaired your ability to connect with the material. Hopefully, though, this experience has helped demonstrate the benefits of spatial predictability and the negative impact of spatial discontinuity.

We'll finish with this: now that you're aware of the integrated nature of spatial layouts and predictability, chances are you'll start to see this relationship everywhere. Have you ever noticed that the majority of traffic lights are placed at the same height? How about that newsreaders always have the video screen over their same shoulder every broadcast? Or that sports networks always include stats in the same location on the screen during games, regardless of who is playing? This is *contextual cueing* in action. When you can accurately predict where in space relevant information is likely to occur, you expend less time and energy interpreting that information.

Imagine how much trickier driving would be if you had to search high and low for each road sign because they weren't all attached to posts of the same height?

Implications for leaders, teachers and coaches

1. Ensure slides are consistently formatted

In the last couple chapters, you learnt that omitting text from PowerPoint slides and adding relevant images can improve learning. After this chapter, it should be clear that haphazardly slapping images about will force the audience to expend mental resources trying to decipher and create a mental map for each successive slide.

On the basis of *contextual cueing*, ensure all slides are spatially organized in a consistent manner; more specifically, ensure images and keywords appear in the same location from one slide to the next and are approximately the same size across slides. In this way, the audience can quickly and implicitly learn this layout, form a prediction and free up mental resources, allowing them to focus more deeply on the content at hand. In fact, individuals presented with material in a spatially consistent format demonstrate up to 35 per cent better memory than those presented with identical material in a random, spatially inconsistent format.

So, choose a layout and stick with it!

BURNING QUESTION 1:

PREDICTION BREAKING

'What happens if I change up an otherwise consistent format?'

Any time a spatial layout fails to match a prediction, a small signal called the *mismatch negativity* is triggered within the brain. This signal automatically forces attention to focus on the area where the prediction was incorrect.

For instance, right now I imagine you have a pretty good prediction of how your bedroom is organized. As such, if someone were to sneak in and secretly rotate your bed 90 degrees, the next time you walked into your bedroom your attention would reflexively be drawn to this shift.

Importantly, we can exploit this automatic response to drive learning. If, during a presentation, there is a key idea or concept you wish to emphasize, one way to ensure the audience is paying attention is to *intentionally* break their spatial prediction. The idea is simple: after displaying several slides using the same layout, you can assume the audience will have implicitly learnt this format and formed a prediction for how proceeding slides will appear. As such, any time you project a slide that *fails* to match this predicted format, this will trigger a mismatch negativity and the audience will have no choice but to pay attention to whatever is on the screen.

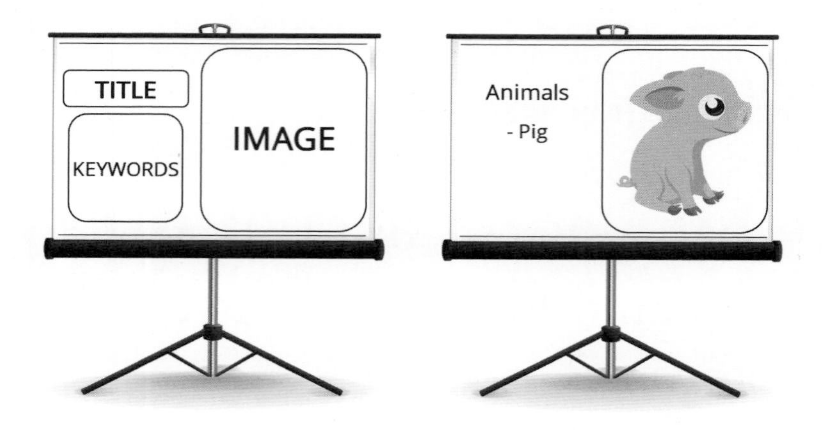

ILLUSTRATION 20. CONSISTENCY FREES UP MENTAL RESOURCES

ILLUSTRATION 21. BREAK CONSISTENCY TO FORCE ATTENTION

Remember: this strategy only works once a layout has been learnt and a prediction formed. If the format of every slide is different, no mental map will ever be constructed and your ability to break the audience's prediction will be lost. Therefore, use this technique sparingly.

BURNING QUESTION 2:

SIGNALLING

'How else can I guide people's attention to relevant information?'

Signalling is an incredibly simple (if under-utilized) technique whereby a specific region of space is highlighted in order to guide attention. For instance, imagine you hired one of those smoke-trailing airplanes to write a love letter in the sky. One way to ensure your partner sees this message would be to point to the sky and say, 'Look up there.' That's how easy it is — and, unlike contextual cueing (which is implicit and requires several repetitions), signalling is explicit and immediately shifts others' attention to an area of importance.

During a meeting or presentation, signalling is as easy as circling, pointing to or otherwise delineating relevant material. Though this strategy might seem painfully simple, keep an eye out: you'll quickly notice how rarely people apply this incredibly obvious technique. In fact, the next time you are wasting mental energy trying to decipher a busy chart or wondering what page of the handout a presenter is referencing, just think back to this moment.

2. Ensure handouts and documents are consistently formatted

Contextual cueing can (and should) be applied to handouts and/or other documents. If you develop a consistent and predictable artefact format, others will implicitly learn where to look to quickly and easily find whatever information they need. This will, ultimately, reduce the effort required to decipher material and free up cognitive resources for learning and memory (however, see Implication 5 below for an important caveat).

BURNING QUESTION 3:

PRINT VS DIGITAL

'Do people learn more by reading hard-copy books or digital e-books?'

I am often surprised how controversial this topic can be. But at the risk of angering some readers, I do think it is important to discuss.

When material is short and simple (around two pages or less), there doesn't appear to be much difference between print and digital. However, when material is longer than a couple of pages, *then* print almost always outperforms digital.

The reason for this is because hard-copy reading materials have a very clear and static spatial layout. This means information presented in print exists in an unambiguous, unchanging, three-dimensional region of space. For instance, if you're reading a print version of this book, this sentence will always be *right here*. Until these pages decay into dust, you will always be able to triangulate these words near the top of the page, on the right-hand side, about a quarter of the way through the book. This location is part of the memory you are forming right now and can be used in the future as a guiding cue to recall this information.

Digital reading materials, on the other hand, have neither a clear nor a static spatial layout. For instance, if you are scrolling through a PDF version of this book, this sentence will have started at the bottom of your screen, is now somewhere near the middle, and will soon disappear out the top. Without a physical location for this information, you lose the ability to use spatial layout as a guiding cue for later recall.

To address this, many e-readers have eliminated the scroll bar and, instead, allow users to 'flip' between digital pages. Although this is slightly better (as information in this format does have a two-dimensional location), it still omits the important third-dimension of *depth* only extant in print.

With that said, PDFs and e-readers have a number of advantages over print (the ability to change font size, the ability to search for keywords, backlighting for night reading, etc.). Thus, digital copies suit different purposes better than print. However, when it comes to *learning and memory*, print should be your medium of choice.

3. Use a consistent format on webpages and applications

There's a growing trend in web design whereby content is stacked vertically on one seemingly never-ending page (requiring extensive use of the scroll bar). As you just learnt, when information does not have a clear and

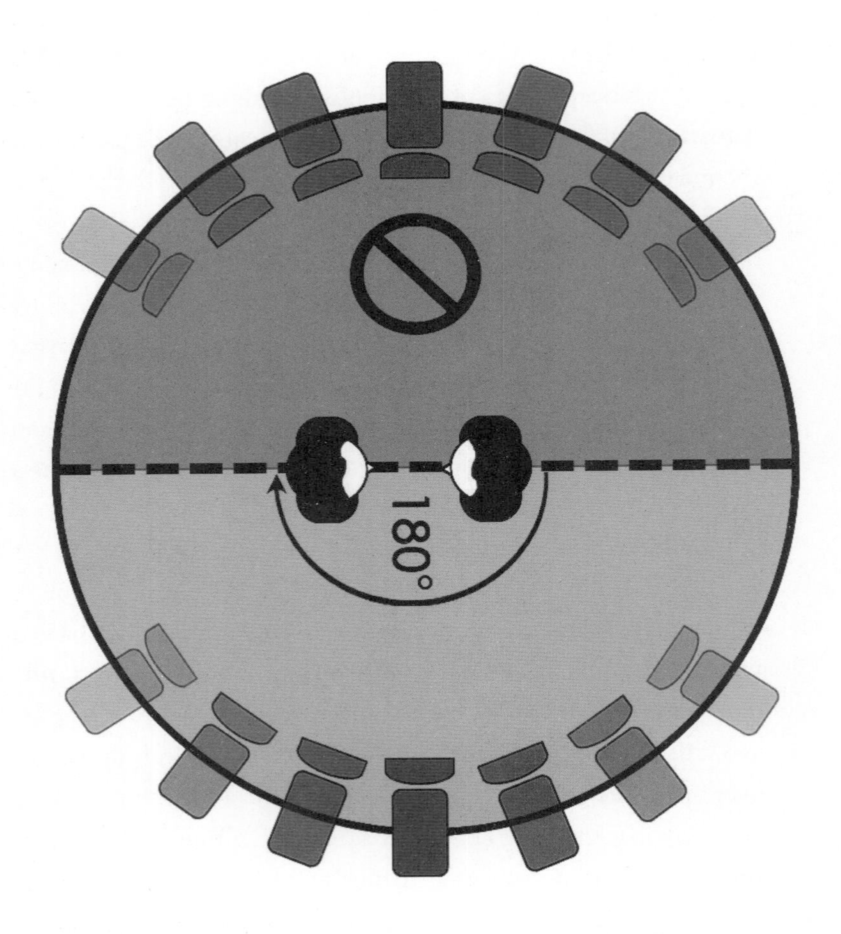

ILLUSTRATION 22. CROSSING THE LINE — A FILM FAUX PAS

unambiguous location, comprehension and memory will suffer. As such, if your purpose for a website is to help users easily access, learn from and remember material, then employing a static and consistent design across multiple web pages will help your audience implicitly learn the spatial layout and know where to look to find required information.

When using a stacked, scroll-based design, there are two strategies to consider employing to support learning. The first involves *static images*. If each block of information is anchored to a unique picture, it's possible users will be able to use these images to both locate and recall relevant information at a later date. The second strategy involves *static buttons or peripheral elements*. Some websites include menu bars, links and ads that move with the page as the user scrolls up and down. Unfortunately, as you may have guessed, when elements move with the screen it is impossible to anchor any ideas or information to them. As such, if you lock these items in place on each webpage, users will have the opportunity to tie ideas to them and use each to locate and recall relevant information later.

The same issues apply to app and program interfaces. There is a reason most smartphones use identically sized buttons arranged in an identical grid across identical screens: this way, users know exactly where to look to find any program they desire (even after upgrading to a new phone). This consistency frees up mental resources, allowing users to interact with programs rather than simply trying to locate them.

4. Hold perspective during video lessons

In film and television, there is a blunder called *crossing the line*. In short, whenever a scene contains two or more people, an invisible 180-degree line is formed that dictates how the action flows. Filmmakers know to never let the camera cross this line unless they want their audience to suddenly become confused and lose the plot.

Perhaps the best example of this concept in action involves sports on TV. During a game, all cameras are typically set up on one side of the field; this way, each team moves in a consistent direction until quarter-break or half-time (e.g. the red team is always running right-to-left). Imagine if, in the middle of a play, the camera suddenly crossed the line and the red team inexplicably started running left-to-right. As a viewer you'd become wildly confused and devote all your attention and energy to figuring out what just happened. Forget the game — did you miss something? Is it half-time? Is this a replay?

To ensure viewers are learning from video material, maintain a consistent perspective. The more times the camera crosses the line, the less predictable the video will become and the more energy will be spent trying to update mental maps.

5. Avoid spatial predictability when complacency is a worry

Though spatial predictability is a solid technique to boost learning and memory, there are times when learning and memory aren't our primary purpose.

For instance, imagine if you worked at a construction site and prior to each shift you were required to fill out a safety checklist. In this scenario, if you saw the same checklist in the same format each day, you'd soon stop devoting explicit attention to it and start checking each box in the same order. Unfortunately, mindlessly ticking boxes because a spatial layout has become highly predictable is probably the last thing we want in this scenario.

Accordingly, be very clear on your desired outcome when employing spatial predictability. If complacency is a worry, consider ways to frequently adjust formats. In this way, you can ensure individuals must devote explicit attention and cognitive resources to the task of discerning each layout. Though this may impair memory, it can serve other 'non-learning' purposes.

AT A GLANCE

Predictable spatial layouts free up mental resources and can boost learning and memory.

- » The hippocampus, our gateway to memory, is lined with place cells.
- » Place cells embed spatial layout into each newly formed memory.
- » Spatial layout can be used as a guiding cue to help recall previously learnt or experienced information.
- » Spatial layout can also be used to form predictions for the future (which is why predictability can free up attention and reduce mental effort).

APPLICATIONS

1. Ensure slides are consistently formatted.
   - » Break consistency to force attentional focus.
   - » Signal relevant information or features to help guide people's attention.
   - » Signalling is especially important for graphs and tables.
2. Ensure handouts and documents are consistently formatted.
   - » Print is better than digital when it comes to longer texts.
3. Use a consistent format on webpages and applications.
4. Hold perspective during video review.
5. Avoid spatial predictability when complacency is a worry.

4. Context/State

> It's not where you take things from — it's where you take things to.
>
> —*Jean-Luc Godard*

When I was ten years old I watched my great-uncle Mooney perform one of the most incredible feats of golfing skill I have ever seen.

Mooney spent his entire life in the same white weatherboard home with one of those expansive backyards common in parts of the east coast of the United States. In the far corner of the lawn, away from the house, was a concrete incinerator about the same size and shape as an oil drum.

On this particular day, I was sitting on the porch watching my uncle use an old shovel to dig out a dead tree stump by the side of his house.

When the trunk was out, he walked over to the incinerator, reached in, pulled out half a dozen golf balls and tossed them haphazardly around his lawn. I assumed he was simply clearing the balls out to make room for the tree trunk … but I was wrong.

Mooney walked up to the nearest golf ball, took aim and, using his shovel like a golf club, chipped the ball high into the air and dropped it perfectly into the incinerator! He then proceeded to do the same for each remaining ball. It didn't matter how far away it was or how it was sitting in the grass — one smooth swing with the shovel was all it took to pop the ball up and sink it back into the open concrete tub. Six shovel swings, six perfect shots.

I was floored. When I asked how he'd learnt to do that, he explained that during the Great Depression he needed to come up with a creative way to make money. His idea: teach himself how to chip golf balls into the incinerator using the only 'club' readily available to him — his father's work shovel. After he had honed his skills, he started inviting still-wealthy golfers over from the local course for a little wager: they could pick any spot on the lawn and Mooney would bet 5 cents he could pitch the ball closer to the incinerator using his shovel than they could using their golf clubs. Over time, this little wager became so popular that golfers would bypass the course and head directly to Mooney's house to spend the entire afternoon chipping around his backyard for cash.

Here's where things get interesting. One day, a group of golfers invited Mooney to the local course to participate in an 'official' chipping competition. They even let him bring his shovel. Everyone was supremely confident my uncle would win — so imagine their collective shock when Mooney lined up his first shot … and completely missed. He didn't simply miss the hole, he missed the entire green. Chalking it up to nerves, he lined up his second shot … and missed again. Out of ten shots, he was only able to land the ball on the green twice.

So what happened? Why is it Mooney could hit a target the size of a manhole cover when in his backyard, but he couldn't hit a target the size of a swimming pool when at the local course?

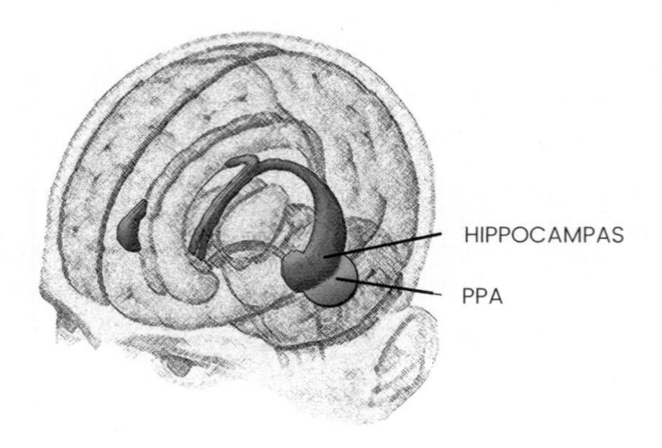

ILLUSTRATION 23. THE PARAHIPPOCAMPAL PLACE AREA (PPA)

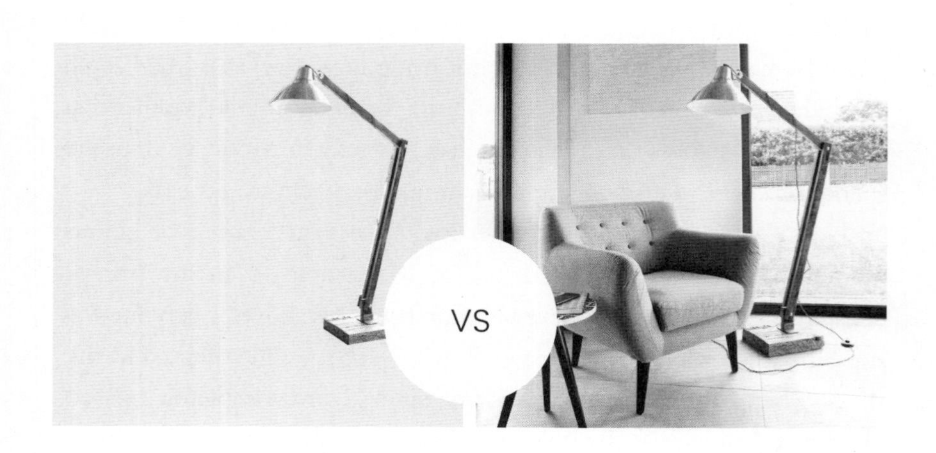

ILLUSTRATION 24. THE PPA PROCESSES ENVIRONMENTS

Context-dependent

In the last chapter we explored the hippocampus, our gateway to memory. In this chapter I want to focus on a small area of the brain at the base of the hippocampus called the *parahippocampal place area* (to make it easier we'll just call it the PPA). This small structure constantly and continuously feeds information through the hippocampus, suggesting that whatever information is being processed there must form an integral aspect of nearly every memory we create. So what is the PPA processing?

To find out, researchers popped individuals into a brain scanner, showed them dozens of images of everyday objects and simply asked them to remember as many as they could. Here's the twist: some objects were displayed against a blank white background while others were displayed within a realistic setting. It turns out the PPA showed strong activation *only* when objects were placed within realistic settings — even though people weren't explicitly paying attention to or trying to memorize those settings.

Just as in the last chapter, where we learnt that place cells automatically encode and embed spatial layouts within new memories, it appears the PPA automatically encodes and embeds the physical characteristics of the surrounding environment within new memories. Furthermore, just as with spatial layouts, we can use these physical characteristics as guiding cues in order to reconstruct memories and guide future predictions.

Perhaps the best demonstration of this concept comes from an experiment conducted in the 1970s. A team of deep-sea divers were asked to memorize a list of words while they were 6-metres (20 feet) underwater. The following day, half the divers returned to their 6-metre depth while the other half remained on dry land, and all were asked to recall as many words as they could from the previous day. What do you think happened?

Even though nobody was explicitly focusing on the blue water, colourful reefs and tropical fish surrounding them as they learnt the

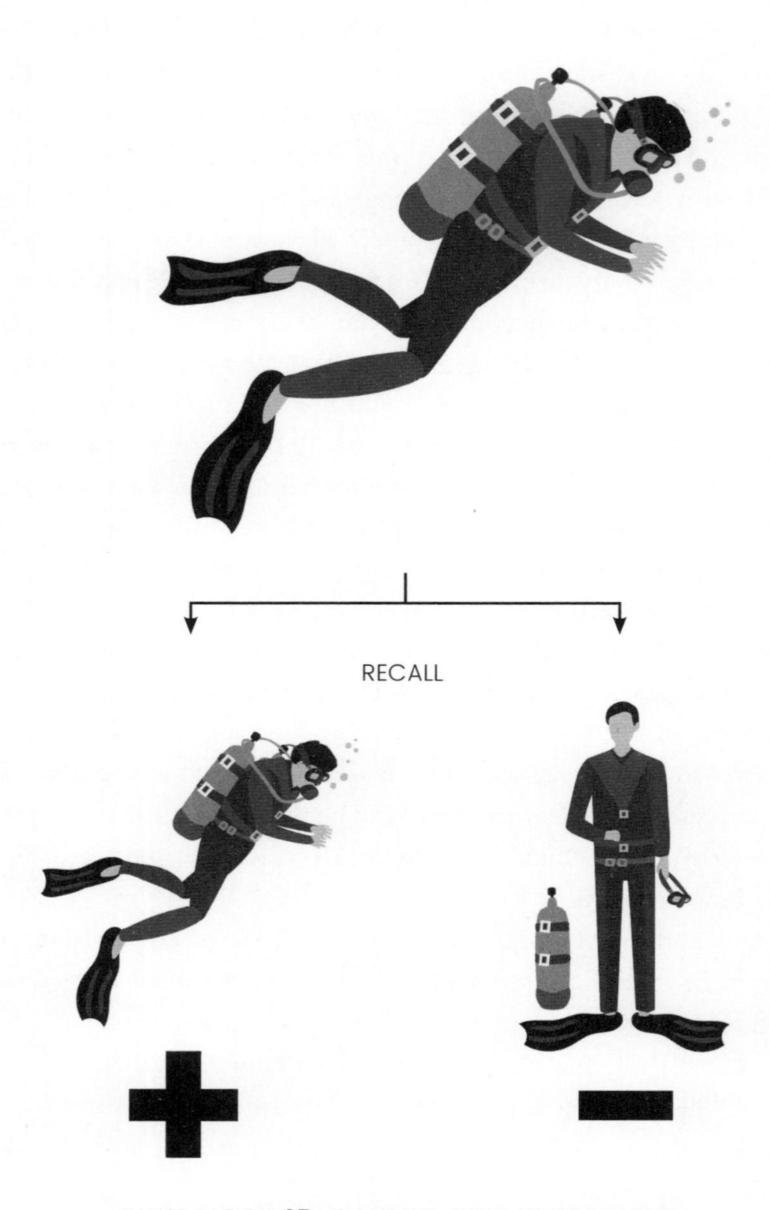

ILLUSTRATION 25. CONTEXT-DEPENDENT MEMORY

words, this information was nonetheless encoded and embedded within everyone's memories. As such, those divers who recalled their words underwater were able to recall 35 per cent more than those who recalled their words on dry land.

Environments contain more than physical features: they also contain smells, sounds, textures, etc. These 'sensory' aspects of the environment are also encoded within each memory we create. Right now, whatever odours are entering your nose, noises entering your ears and textures pressing against your skin will form part of your memory for this sentence — whether you're explicitly paying attention to these sensations or not.

In short, *where* we do our learning forms an integral aspect of *what* we ultimately learn. Researchers call this *context-dependent learning* and it's the reason why we don't always recognize co-workers when we bump into them outside the workplace, why certain smells can trigger vivid memories, and why returning to places from our childhood can bring back long-forgotten episodes.

State-dependent

Beyond the external environment, there is another dimension that appears to be embedded within each new memory we form: our internal environment.

To understand what I mean, imagine the following scenario.

> It's Friday night and you've just arrived at a bar for a networking event. Like almost everyone else, you're not a huge fan of randomly chatting with strangers — so to make the proceedings a bit easier you quickly toss back a few cocktails ... just enough to grease the wheels.
>
> Overall, the event goes well. As you crawl into bed that night, you take one last look through the dozen business cards

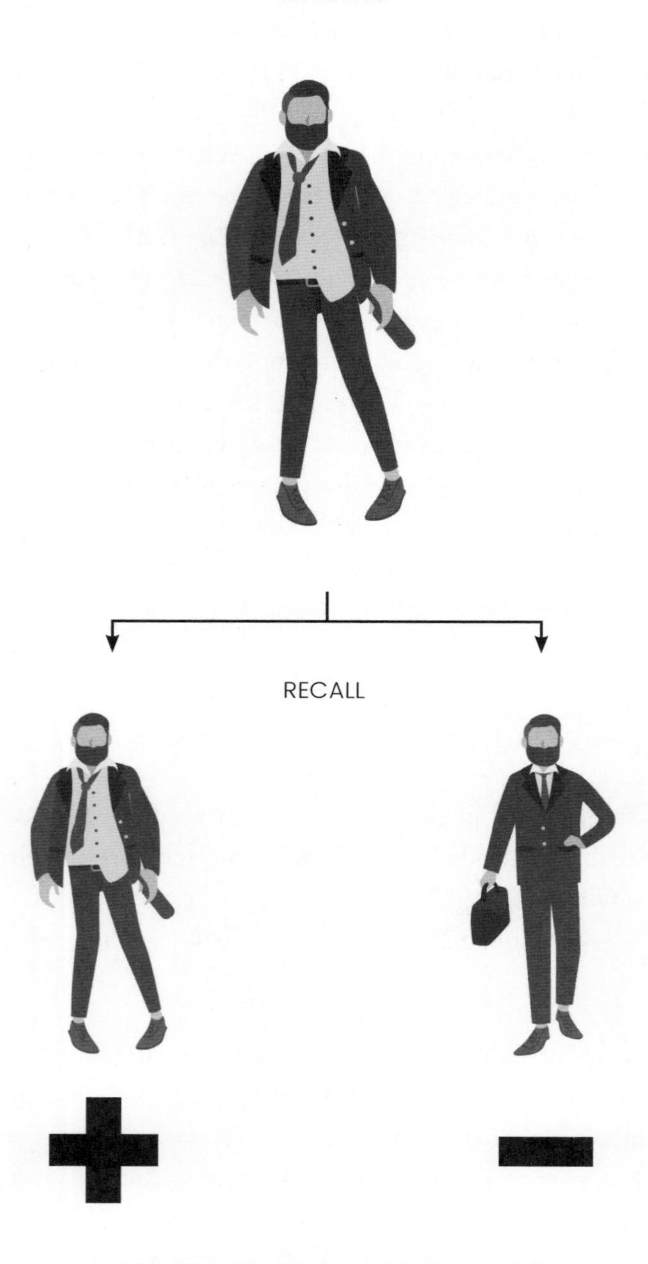

ILLUSTRATION 26. STATE-DEPENDENT MEMORY

you managed to collect. Some are job opportunities, a few are possible project collaborations, and one is a potential romantic connection. You doze off, excited about your future prospects.

In the morning, as you open your eyes, you make a startling realization … you can no longer remember which card was collected for which purpose! You can vaguely recognize a few names, but the specifics are gone. Was Alex a potential job contact or a love interest? Was Jerome a collaborator or someone you promised to hook up with a job?

What a disaster.

Here's the question I want you to consider: what is one of the most effective actions you could undertake in order to jog your memory and remember which cards go with which purpose?

The answer: have a drink! Seeing as you were drunk when collecting each card, you can use drunkenness as a guiding cue to reconstruct the relevant memories. In fact, a story like this appears in a physiology textbook from the 1800s. In that account, an Irish delivery man decided to indulge in a liquid lunch and, during this drunken episode, accidentally misplaced an expensive package. Sober the following morning, he couldn't remember where he had lost the parcel — however, after getting drunk again that afternoon, he was able to walk straight to the house where he'd mistakenly left it. Similar effects have been found with individuals under the influence of caffeine, nicotine, marijuana, psychedelics, and uppers and downers of all sorts.

Beyond pharmaceuticals, this same concept applies to emotions. Any new memory we form while happy, sad, angry, scared or disgusted will be infused with this emotion and easier to access in the future when in that same emotional state.

This is why the military conducts training drills under extreme pressure. It's unlikely soldiers will ever need to draw upon combat skills while sipping margaritas by the pool on a lazy Sunday. Instead, they will most likely need to apply these skills during moments of high stress and volatility. As such, the military ensures the internal state of soldiers as they train matches the internal state they will likely be in when they need to perform.

In short, *how we feel* during learning forms an integral aspect of *what* we ultimately learn. Researchers call this *state-dependent learning*, and it is the reason why sometimes we can't click into work until after the third latte, why some days we can't engage with a long-term project, and why we sometimes screw up the simplest of tasks under high-pressure circumstances.

Seeking independence

Right now, you might be a bit sceptical.

Sure, you may not have recognized Barb from accounting when you bumped into her in the frozen food aisle, but you had no problem recognizing Dennis from sales when you caught him at the movie theatre. And you might not have been able to recall details of your relaxing holiday while sitting through a stressful board meeting, but you had no problem discussing details of that frightening, turbulence-filled plane ride while sitting through a peaceful dinner party.

Clearly, if everything we learnt was forever tied to the specific circumstances in which we learnt it, nothing would ever get done; we'd have to constantly re-learn the same concepts each time we left the house. This means there must be a process by which information can *decouple* from a specific context and become accessible at any time across any scenario.

Indeed, there is. The secret is variety.

EPISODIC AND SEMANTIC MEMORY

To understand what I mean, we need to dig a bit deeper into memory.

In the 'newspaper column' image from the last chapter, we learnt that declarative memory is our ability to remember specific facts or events. It turns out, declarative memories come in two distinct flavours: episodic and semantic.

Episodic memories are facts or events *tied to a specific time and place*. For instance, I can recall dropping my niece's ice-cream cake on the kitchen floor on the afternoon of her fifth birthday. Semantic memories, on the other hand, are facts or events *independent of any particular time and place*. For instance, I know that the term 'birthday' signifies the anniversary of an individual's birth.

Are the following episodic or semantic memories?

---

1. Last year, a dog bit my ankle when I walked past his yard.
2. Dogs typically have four legs.
3. Back in 2000, I knocked over and shattered a full bottle of wine at a winery in Canberra.
4. Canberra is the capital of Australia.
5. My friends Jane and John visited me at work last week.
6. Jane and John are two generic names often used to disguise others' true identities.

Answers: E; S; E; S; E; S

Each time we learn a new piece of information, it is strongly tied to the specific context in which the learning occurred. In other words, all new memories begin as episodic. However, as we encounter the same

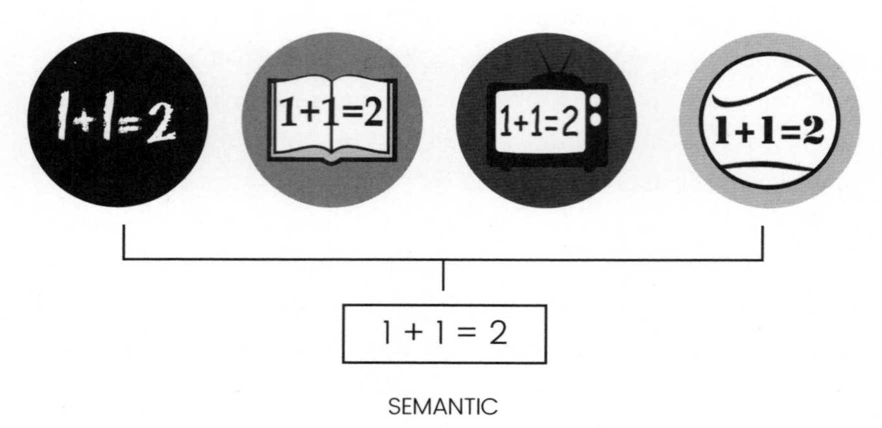

ILLUSTRATION 27. SEMANTIC MEMORIES CONTAIN ALL INFORMATION COMMON TO RELEVANT EPISODIC MEMORIES ...

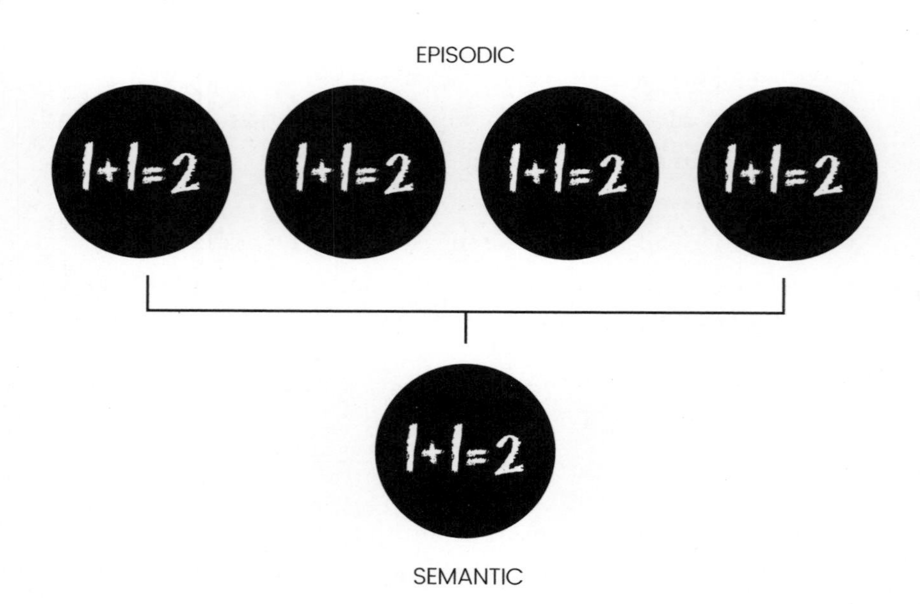

ILLUSTRATION 28. ... THE OPERATIVE WORD BEING ALL

piece of information across many and varied contexts, it can separate from any particular context and become a stand-alone fact. In other words, with repeated exposure across diverse scenarios, semantic memories will emerge.

As an example, imagine a child who undertakes four different maths practice sessions within four completely different environments: in a classroom, in the library, at home, and during gym class. Each of these sessions will create a unique episodic memory which includes relevant context and state details.

Eventually, this child will compare these different episodic memories, siphon out any features common to them all and use these similarities to construct a brand new, stand-alone semantic memory. In this instance, because the only commonality is the maths itself, her semantic memory will likely read, 'Maths is an isolated skill which can be freely accessed across any environment.'

Unfortunately, this process can backfire. Imagine the same child undertakes four practice sessions, except this time each session takes place only in a classroom — that is, in exactly the same environment each time. As before, each session will form a unique episodic memory and, eventually, these will be compared to filter out any commonalities. However, seeing as nearly *every* aspect of these memories is similar, her semantic memory will likely read, 'Maths is a skill which can be applied only within a particular classroom using a particular whiteboard.' These extra details serve only to *deepen* context and state-dependency and will make it much more difficult to apply these maths skills across different contexts in the future.

Returning to the introduction, this is why my great-uncle Mooney couldn't perform well when he stepped out onto an actual golf course. Seeing as he had only ever practised in a single location, his constructed semantic memory likely read, 'Chipping is a skill done in a backyard using a concrete incinerator and an old shovel.' Had he simply practised within different locations, utilized different targets and occasionally switched his shovel for a rake, he might have been able to dissociate the essential chipping skill from any particular context and perform just fine during the official competition.

Seeing the shift in action

Here's the story:

» If we study, train or practise only in a single location or circumstance, our learning will be intimately tied to this specific location or circumstance. For this reason, we can expect to perform well within this context, but poorly outside it.
» If we study, train, or practise across multiple locations or circumstances, our learning will decouple from any specific location or circumstance. For this reason, we can expect to perform well across a variety of contexts (even those we've never before encountered).

Perhaps the best real-world illustration of this comes from sports. 'Home-field advantage' refers to the performance boost teams get when competing on their home grounds. Interestingly, although home-field advantage exists in nearly every sport, the effect is rather small ... except when a new league is created. During the first two to three years of any new sports league, the impact of home-field advantage is quite large. Why is this?

The issue is not one of general skills (we can assume athletes know how to play their sport well). Rather, it is one of *team-specific* skills. Whenever a new league is formed, athletes must learn how to connect with teammates they've never met before, to perform plays they've never executed before, and to trust a coaching staff they've never worked with before. Of importance, much of this team-specific learning takes place on a team's home field.

As teams practise these skills in the same environment week in and week out, very strong context- and state-dependent connections begin to form. The layout of a stadium, the dimensions of a particular field, the advertisements surrounding the pitch, the air quality and the local food all become connected to the team-specific skills leading to a strong home-field advantage come game time.

However, after several years of playing 'away' games across multiple different fields, these skills begin to decouple from any specific ground. Eventually, the home-field advantage fades and teams begin to perform consistently across most circumstances and stadiums (even neutral grounds).

Implications for leaders, teachers and coaches

1. For discrete applications, match training context to performance context

A final exam in the high school gymnasium.
An end-of-year presentation in the main boardroom.
A big audition in the local theatre.

When the precise moment, location and circumstances of a performance are well known, it is worth matching the training context (as closely as possible) to the performance context. For instance, if a speech will take place in a room with red walls, ensure preparations occur in a room with red walls. In this way, only relevant context-related information (red walls) will become intertwined with new memories. Later, when it comes time to perform, this environment (red walls) can be used as a guiding cue to more easily access and apply relevant memories.

Study after study has revealed improved performance among workers who train on-site, students who study in the testing location and athletes who practise in the official venue. So steal a page from Uncle Mooney's playbook: help others hone their skills in the location they hope to perform in.

2. For flexible applications, mix up learning contexts

The ability to write a persuasive article on any topic.
A sales pitch delivered to dozens of clients.
A stage show going on a world tour.

When the circumstances of a performance are many, varied or largely unknown, it is worth training in as many different and diverse contexts as possible. Crowded rooms and empty rooms; private spaces and public spaces; small venues and large venues. The more variation encountered during training, the more dissociated ideas and skills will become from any particular context. This, in turn, will make relevant memories far easier to access and apply when in unexpected or unknown performance venues in the future.

Study after study has revealed improved performance within novel environments among employees who train across multiple settings, students who study across varied locations, and athletes who practise across diverse venues. Again, steal a page from Uncle Mooney's playbook: help others hone their skills in multiple locations if they hope to broadly apply those skills.

BURNING QUESTION 1:

QUANTITY

'How many times must a person encounter a new concept in order to "learn" it?'

Unfortunately, there is no precise or steadfast answer to this question. Sometimes people will learn a new concept after one exposure (think about grabbing a hot iron), while other times people won't learn a concept even after dozens of exposures (can you name all the European countries by heart?). In addition, the speed with which people learn new concepts depends heavily upon those concepts they already know. For instance, if I wanted to learn a new language, it would take quite a lot of exposure and practice just to learn the basic rules. However, once I had amassed a basic vocabulary, it would become easier and faster for me to learn new phrases as I would have a solid foundation to connect each idea to.

With that said, there is a rule of thumb: researchers can predict with 80 to 85 per cent accuracy whether or not people will learn a particular concept based purely on the number of times they encounter and interact with it. Those who engage with a new concept only once or twice typically won't recall it at a later time, while those who engage with it *three or more times* typically will.

You might therefore assume that if you simply repeat an idea three times it is bound to stick. Unfortunately, this isn't the case. Just think of the hundreds of radio commercials that repeat a phone number three times in quick succession; I doubt you remember the details from very many. This means pure repetition is not enough. In order for a concept to be learnt, each exposure must be *deliberate* and *explicit*. If people do not consciously think about and/or interact with information, they will never learn it.

BURNING QUESTION 2:

MEMORY STORAGE

'What happens to episodic memories once a semantic memory is formed?'

Good news — nothing! Just because episodic memories form the foundation of semantic memories, this does not mean we lose access to them once a semantic memory has formed. In fact, the two different types of memory work together, each serving as a guiding cue for the other.

As an example: Princess Diana passed away in 1997 following a car accident inside a Paris tunnel. You likely have this stand-alone information stored within a context-less semantic memory. However, as you read it, did you think back to where you were and what you felt when you first heard about this tragedy? In this instance, a semantic memory was able to cue an episodic memory.

Now: think about how you were feeling when you took your final high school exam. As you access this episodic memory, do you recognize any other information coming to mind? Perhaps you briefly thought about your final score, the university you ultimately attended, the vast number of exams people sit in their lives. In this instance, an episodic memory was able to cue a semantic memory.

3. Use senses to reinstate memories

If everything we see, hear, taste, smell and feel while learning becomes part of new memories, then we can leverage our senses to boost future performance.

The possibilities are infinite. If you chew a particular flavour of gum while training, you can use that same gum to make it easier to access relevant memories during performance. If you wear a particular soft shirt during training, you can wear the same shirt to make it easier to access relevant memories during performance. If you use a particular pen during training, smell a particular air freshener, hum a particular melody ... all of these simple and largely subconscious sensory cues can be used to assist future recall.

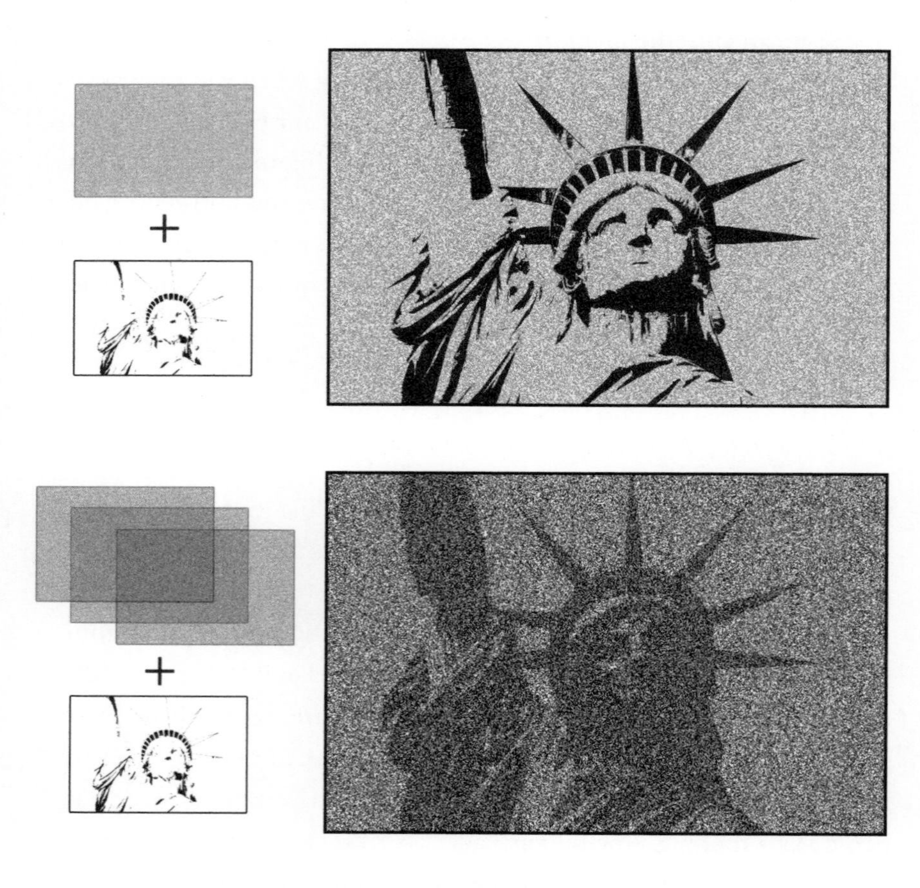

ILLUSTRATION 29. NOISE CAN SHARPEN STIMULI ... BUT NOT TOO MUCH NOISE!

BURNING QUESTION 3:

MUSIC

'Does listening to music while studying help or hinder learning?'

The answer depends completely on how that music is used.

To understand what I mean, we have to quickly explore the concept of *stochastic resonance*. This intimidating-sounding term is actually quite simple to understand. In essence, stochastic resonance states that when noise is added to a stimulus, it can make that stimulus easier to perceive.

As a simple example, take a look at the top image on the opposite page. Chances are you can see it, but it's not easy — everything is a bit faint and hard to make out.

Now, take a look at the second image and see what happens when we add one layer of noise (in this instance, the noise is simply that random static that used to come up between stations on old televisions). Incredibly, adding noise actually makes the picture easier to interpret.

Surely, if adding one layer of noise can boost clarity, than adding several layers of noise should make the picture crystal clear, right? Turns out, as you can see, when we add too much noise the image degrades and again becomes difficult to decipher.

What does any of this have to do with listening to music while learning?

As you may have guessed, music can serve as a source of stochastic resonance *inside the brain*. Essentially, as the music enters your ears and triggers patterns within specific areas of your brain, these patterns can begin to resonate through your attention networks, thereby making it easier to focus on and interpret relevant information.

However, there are two important caveats to remember. First, every person has a different threshold. This means there is no single 'correct' musical level that will work for everyone; the perfect amount of noise for some might be too little or too much for others. This is why some people have no problem studying in crowded cafés while others require a silent library. Second, music will only generate stochastic resonance so long as it remains *noise*. This means it must be predictable enough that you don't explicitly focus attention on it. As soon as music becomes surprising, it stops being noise and becomes a *signal* (something that grabs explicit attention and pulls you away from learning).

This does not mean music need be monotonous or boring; it need only be highly predictable. For instance, if you play an album you've listened to hundreds of times before, the music will almost certainly fade away into noise. However, if you set your iPod to shuffle and every three or four minutes an unexpected and unpredictable song pops on, then the music will become a signal, grab attention and impair learning.

BURNING QUESTION 4:

CLASSICAL MUSIC

'Will listening to Mozart make me smarter?'

No.

4. Apply context-dependent effects to help others recognize information

If you want others to quickly and easily recognize a piece of information (be it your company name, a specific product or a key concept), ensure you build a number of clear and consistent contextual elements around it. As you now know, even if people never consciously attend to these elements they will become intertwined with the material being learnt and the elements can be employed in the future as guiding cues to reinstate key information.

A consistent logo, colour scheme, webpage layout, musical jingle, announcer, commercial format, etc. These contextual aspects *will not* replace learning (people must still engage with your company, product or idea in order to form memories), but they will serve as support cues for future recognition and recall.

5. Be aware of state dependency when learning

It's often the case that people will procrastinate and put off preparing for a performance until the day before (according to some surveys, 99 per cent of students admit to only studying on the night before an exam ... and 1 per cent of students are liars). This practice typically leads to a cram session supplemented by caffeine, nicotine, alcohol, junk food, etc.

As we saw above, these chemicals will become part of the memories being formed. As such, when people return to a clean and sober state, minus the chemicals present during preparation, memory and performance can drop markedly.

Now I'm not your mother, so I'm not going to tell you what chemicals you should or should not be putting into your body. What I will say is that it's worth being cognizant of state-dependent effects. If you prepare while in a unique state, it might be worth mimicking that state come performance time. Conversely, if you know you will be in a unique state come performance time (say, delivering a presentation after cocktails and dinner), then it might be worth mimicking this state during preparation.

AT A GLANCE

Where people practice and *how they feel* during practice form an integral aspect of *what* they learn.

- » The external environment (physical and sensory) enters into all new memories (context-dependent).
- » The internal environment (chemicals and emotions) enters into all new memories (state-dependent).
- » *Episodic* memories are locked to a specific time and place.
- » *Semantic* memories are formed using similarities gleaned from relevant episodic memories.

APPLICATIONS

1. For one-offs, match training context to performance context.
2. For multiple applications, mix up training contexts.
   - » It typically takes three exposures to 'learn' an idea (form a semantic memory).
   - » Semantic memories *do not* replace episodic memories.
3. Leverage senses to reinstate memory.
   - » Music as *noise* can focus attention and boost learning.
   - » Music as *signal* can distract and impair learning.
   - » Classical music does not boost memory or intelligence ... sorry.
4. Use context to boost *recognition*.
5. Be aware of state-dependent effects during preparation.

1952

GET A-HEAD!

FOR ADULTS
AT
NO CHARGE

ADULT EDUCATION
CLASSES

MANY COURSES · · MANY PLACES

Intermission 2

Please take around 15 seconds to study and enjoy
this old adult education poster.

5.

Multitasking

Anyone who can drive safely while kissing is simply not giving the kiss the attention it deserves.

— *Anonymous*

Let's start this chapter with a little game. For this, you'll need something to write with, something to write on, and a timer.

Round 1

During this round, your goal is to try to complete two different tasks in under 10 seconds.

1. Divide your page into two vertical columns.
2. Set your timer to 10 seconds.
3. As soon as the timer begins, begin writing out the first twelve letters of the alphabet (A to L) vertically in the left column. Do this as quickly as you can.
4. Once finished with the letters, begin writing out the first twelve numbers vertically in the right column. Again, do this as quickly as you can.

See if you can write out all 24 letters and numbers within the 10-second window.

Ready … set … begin!

I'm guessing you either completely finished or got fairly far along that process before time ran out. Now let's play this game again, except this time let's change one small thing …

Round 2

During this round, your goal is to complete the same two tasks as above — except this time you will quickly alternate between each.

1. Divide your paper into two vertical columns.
2. Set your timer to 10 seconds.
3. As soon as the timer begins, write out the first letter in the left column (A), then the first number in the right (1), then the second letter in the left (B), then the second number in the right (2), etc.

Again, see if you can write out all 24 letters and numbers within the 10-second window.

Ready … set … begin!

If you're like most people, this time you probably only made it about two-thirds of the way through each list. More importantly, even though the tasks weren't particularly difficult, you might have found yourself getting flustered and making a few mistakes, perhaps repeating a number or needing to mentally run through the alphabet to remember the next letter.

So what happened? Why was the second round so much trickier than the first?

Attention filters

The world is a chaotic place.

As I write these words, I am sitting in a crowded coffee shop with dozens of customers streaming by my table, an espresso machine hissing in my ear and two girls boisterously debating the extracurricular activities of some guy named Chad. With all this stimulation it's an absolute wonder anyone can get anything done at all — yet, somehow, we can cut through the chaos and home in on those sights, sounds, tastes, smells and feelings that are meaningful to us in the moment.

This is the power of attention.

Perhaps the easiest way to understand how attention works is to think of a filter. Much like those 3D glasses we used to wear as kids that only allowed certain wavelengths of light to hit our eyes, attention allows only *relevant* information to pass into conscious awareness while blocking out *irrelevant* information. As we learnt in the last chapter, information deemed irrelevant still enters our memories (context and state dependency), but it's simply not *consciously* processed.

This leads to an important question: what determines if a piece of information is relevant? The answer changes depending upon the specific task we are engaged with. Just like a board game, every task we undertake — be it writing an email, tallying up bills or simply taking the dog for a walk — comes with its own unique set of rules that dictate what actions are required in order to 'succeed'. For instance, to successfully read these words right now, your reading ruleset dictates that you must move your eyes left to right over each line, hold each word in memory until you reach the end of a sentence, use your fingers to flip between pages, etc.

Whenever we engage with a task, the relevant rules must be loaded into a small area of the brain called the *lateral prefrontal cortex* (we'll call it the LatPFC). Whichever specific ruleset is loaded into the LatPFC will determine what information is deemed relevant or irrelevant. For instance, seeing as your reading ruleset is currently loaded into your LatPFC, this has tweaked your attention filter to allow these black squiggles into conscious awareness while blocking out the texture of these pages against your fingers, the chapter title at the bottom of this page, any noises going on around you, etc.

I often liken this entire process to those old video game systems from the 1980s. In this instance, each video game (task) has its own unique set of characters, controls and objectives (ruleset). Any time you wish to play a particular game, you must pop the relevant cartridge into the game system (LatPFC). Once a game is loaded in, the pixels on the television screen will display that game's heroes, villains, weapons, etc. (attention filter).

Who's in charge here?

Sticking with the video game analogy, who *selects* which game to play at any one moment?

The primary selector is you. Via a specific brain system called the *dorsal attention network*, your personal goals, desires and intentions are used to select relevant rulesets. Right now, seeing as you have personally chosen to read these words, your dorsal network has accessed your reading ruleset, loaded it into your LatPFC and set your attention filter accordingly.

However, imagine if an angry, snarling bear suddenly came running towards you. Technically, seeing as this bear is irrelevant to your chosen

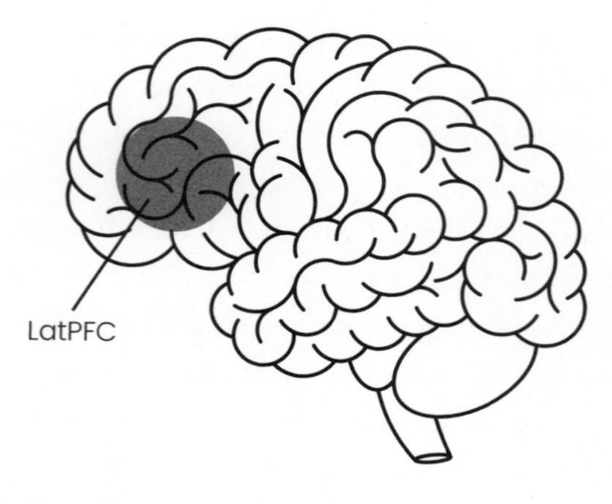

ILLUSTRATION 30. THE LATERAL PREFRONTAL CORTEX (LATPFC)

RULESETS

LatPFC

ATTENTION FILTER

ILLUSTRATION 31. YOU CAN ONLY LOAD ONE RULESET AT A TIME

goal of reading, your filter should block it out and you should never be consciously aware of it. Clearly this isn't the case. If a bear suddenly appeared, I imagine you'd be out the door before this book hit the floor. This means there must be a *secondary* selector somewhere within the brain.

Indeed, there is.

Churning away in the background is a system called the *ventral attention network* which continuously (and subconsciously) monitors all the information your attention filter deems irrelevant and blocks out. If something shocking or unexpected occurs — such as a bear running towards you — this secondary system will *automatically* take over, load up a new set of rules ('escape from a bear' ruleset) and change your attention filter accordingly.

An easy way to conceptualize how these two different networks operate is to consider one of those driving instructor's cars that has two different steering wheels. Most of the time, the car is being controlled by the student driver (the dorsal network), who is consciously focused on moving and turning in a specific manner. However, sitting quietly by is the ever-vigilant instructor (the ventral network), constantly aware of the surrounding world and able to take control should anything dangerous arise.

It's not multitasking — it's task-switching

Think back to the first chapter where we learnt that attempting to simultaneously read while listen to someone speak leads to a processing bottleneck. It turns out we have the same issue here. Much like a video game console, *the LatPFC can only hold onto one ruleset at a time.*

Put another way: we cannot multitask.

Wait a second — you've surfed the internet while writing an email; texted while attending a meeting; updated your Facebook status while reading. Isn't this multitasking?

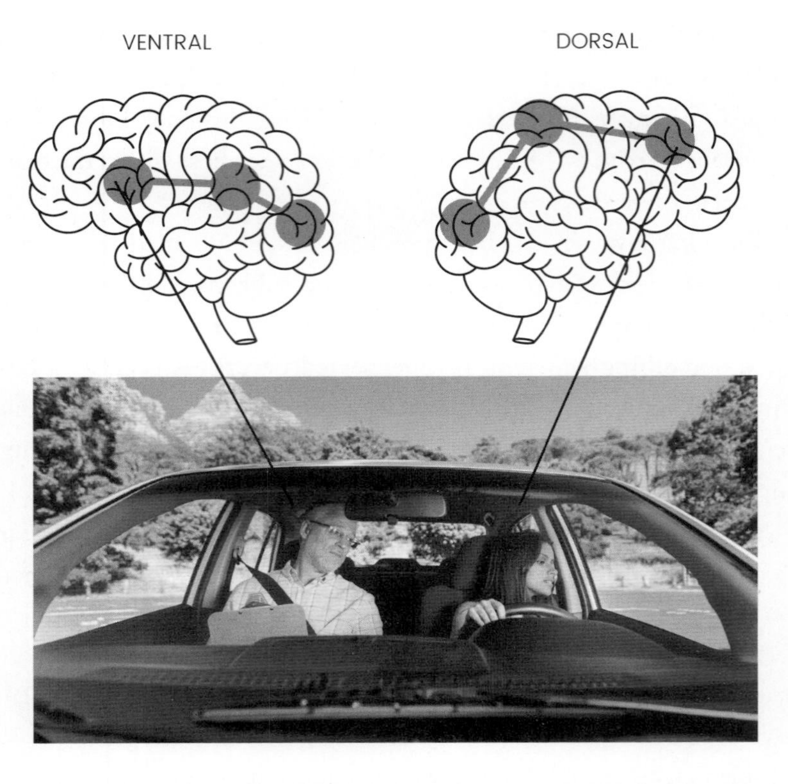

ILLUSTRATION 32. THE DORSAL & VENTRAL ATTENTION NETWORKS

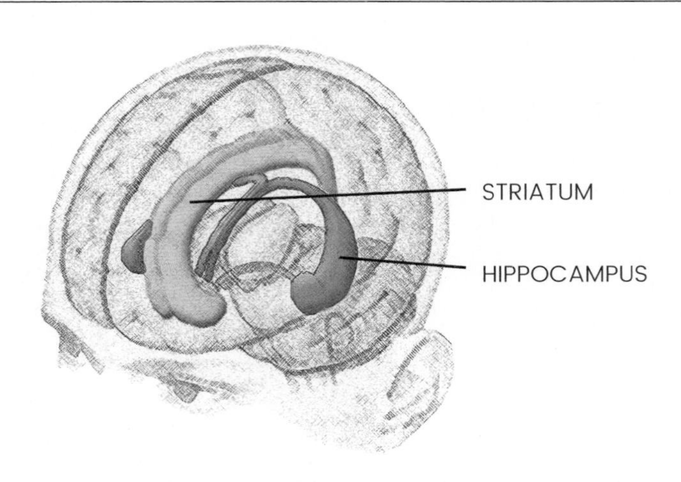

ILLUSTRATION 33. THE STRIATUM

Surprisingly, no it isn't.

Although we often *think* we're multitasking, never do we actually undertake multiple tasks simultaneously. Rather, we really quickly *jump back and forth* between tasks, swapping out rulesets within the LatPFC each time we do. Researchers call this *task-switching*, and it's a lot like trying to watch two different shows on a single television: sure, you can quickly flip back and forth between stations but you're only ever watching one show at a time.

Why does this matter? It turns out that jumping between tasks has three major consequences.

COST NO. 1: TIME

Task-switching is not an instantaneous process. As we jump from one task to another there is a brief period when our attention turns 'off' as the filter is updated. Researchers call this period the *attentional blink* and it is essentially a sensory dead zone: all external information stops being consciously processed.

Although a single attentional blink is relatively short (0.1 to 0.2 seconds), this occurs *every time* we switch between tasks. Accordingly, as the number of task-switches increases, so too does the amount of time we spend in this sensory dead zone. Thinking back to the game at the start of this chapter, this is why you could finish more during round 1 (uni-tasking) than you could during round 2 (multitasking).

COST NO. 2: ACCURACY

Task-switching is not a seamless process. As we jump from one task to another there is a brief period when the two rulesets blend. Researchers call this the *psychological refractory period* and during this time general performance suffers.

Have you ever tried to write an email while having a conversation and accidentally typed out the words you meant to speak aloud? Have you ever been rushing to prepare for work in the morning and accidentally poured coffee in your cereal bowl? Have you ever had to jump back and forth between writing letters and numbers (say, at the start of this chapter) and accidentally scribbled down the digits in the wrong order? This is the psychological refractory period in action.

COST NO. 3: MEMORY

At this point in the book, whenever you hear the term 'memory' there should be one brain region that immediately comes to mind: the hippocampus. Interestingly, during task-switching, activity within the hippocampus decreases. This means that attempting to multitask impairs memory formation.

To make matters worse, during task-switching, activity within the *striatum* increases; this is an area of the brain that subconsciously processes reflexive and repetitive skills (such as walking). This means that information learnt during multitasking is often stored as a habitual routine, making it incredibly difficult to consciously access and manipulate in the future (try describing the exact muscle movements you undertake in order to walk).

Task-switching in the real world

Imagine you're driving when suddenly a deer jumps in front of your car. How long do you think it would take you to react? If you were focused only on driving, it would take about one second to recognize the deer and slam on the brakes.

Interestingly, if you were drunk, this reaction time would slow to about 1.15 seconds. Seeing as alcohol dampens sensory processing and slows the speed with which people recognize and respond to the world, this leads to an estimated 275,000 motor accidents in the US every year: that's about one accident every two minutes.

Here's the scary part. If you were *reading* or *writing* a text message while driving, it would take you around 1.3 seconds to slam on the brakes. Every time you jump between your phone and the road, you must update your relevant ruleset. This process takes *twice as long* as the reflex lag caused by alcohol and leads to an estimated 1.6 million motor accidents in the US every year: that's about one accident *every 20 seconds*.

It's bad … and getting worse

On the scale of 0 (horrible) to 10 (incredible), how good would you say you are at multitasking?

Believe it or not, the better you rated your ability to multitask, the worse a multitasker you likely are. Researchers consistently find that people who consider themselves strong multitaskers are notoriously bad at recognizing just how poorly they perform when jumping between tasks.

Furthermore, the adage 'practice makes perfect' has little bearing on multitasking. In fact, people who frequently multitask almost always perform worse during task-switching than people who rarely multitask. To make matters worse, frequent multitasking strengthens people's confidence in their ability to task-switch … which leads to more multitasking … which leads to even higher confidence … and so on.

To be fair, if you spend time explicitly practising multitasking with two specific tasks (say, writing emails and sending texts), you will likely improve your switching speed between these. Unfortunately, this does not mean you will boost some general 'multitasking ability' which will help you jump between any and every task. In fact, as we saw above, any improved ability to jump between email and text will almost certainly be due to the striatum forming a habitual routine — meaning it will be a subconscious skill difficult to explicitly access and apply across other task-switching scenarios.

Enter the supertaskers

A small warning: it's possible you will read the following section and think to yourself 'That's me!' The truth is, for every 100 people who read this book, only one will fit this bill. To put that into perspective, more of you will have a small hole above your ear that's thought to be a remnant of gills from our ancient fish ancestors (the preauricular sinus); more of you will have two distinct hair whorls going in opposite directions on the back of your head (a double-crown); more of you will be able to bend your thumb backwards far enough to touch your wrist (hypermobility).

Just saying.

In a 2010 multitasking research study, people were asked to memorize word lists and mentally complete maths problems while undertaking a driving simulation. Of the 200 participants, the vast majority performed as expected: horribly. Their reaction time slowed by almost 20 per cent while their memory and maths skills dropped by nearly 30 per cent and 10 per cent, respectively.

Interestingly, five people showed no change whatsoever! These people showed no slowing of their reaction time and had no decline in memorization or mental maths ability. It was as if they weren't multitasking at all.

Further research has revealed there is a small subset of people dubbed 'supertaskers'. Just like normal people, supertaskers cannot actually do two tasks at one time; however, they can swap rulesets incredibly rapidly. This ability shortens their attentional blink and allows them to quickly recognize any ruleset overlap, thereby combating the psychological refractory period.

As I said above, supertaskers are quite rare and I wouldn't get my hopes up about being one. However, if you would like to check your status, you can go online and search for 'supertasker tests'. Even if it turns out you're a mere mortal like the rest of us, these tests will help demonstrate just how truly difficult and detrimental multitasking can be.

Implications for leaders, teachers and coaches

1. Don't invite multitasking

This one is simple: if you're at all interested in reducing effort while boosting efficacy and efficiency, do not invite multitasking. Every time we mention a web address, distribute practice problems or display a complex graph during a learning session, we encourage others to multitask which, ultimately, can impair comprehension, memory, and performance. To avoid this, we must ensure that every learning task has a clear focus, a step-wise trajectory (see Implication 2, below) and a devoted block of time to allow for engagement and completion.

In addition, ask others to turn off emails, put away their smartphones and keep only one internet tab open during sessions. Though this might cause a few grumbles, when people focus on a single task they will finish quicker, perform better and remember more.

BURNING QUESTION 1:

WALKING AND TALKING

'If it's impossible to multitask, then why can I walk and chew gum at the same time?'

Touché!

The truth is, we multitask every day. We hold conversations while eating. We sing while showering. We ponder work projects while jogging.

Interestingly, if you look closely at these examples, each includes a *habitual routine* mediated by the *striatum*. Chances are you have mastered the art of eating, showering and jogging — you can perform these skills on autopilot. This means we *can* perform two tasks at the same time, as long as one of those tasks is automatic and can be done with little conscious thought.

With that said, have you ever been so involved with a conversation during a meal that you forgot to eat? Or been so wrapped up in a song that you absentmindedly shampooed twice? Or been so concerned with a project that you accidentally tripped while jogging?

Even when one task is a habitual routine, this does not guarantee effective multitasking. Rulesets, filters and goals can still become mixed up, leading to impaired reaction speed, performance and memory. Furthermore, beyond a certain age, even automatic tasks like walking and talking can begin to interfere with one another (which is why many older people stand still when chatting).

So, walking and chewing gum is certainly possible — but this does not negate the multitasking story.

BURNING QUESTION 2:

BATTLE OF THE SEXES PART 1

'Women are better than men at multitasking … right?'

Although there is quite a bit of research exploring this issue, the results are all over the shop: sometimes women perform better, sometimes men perform better and sometimes there's no difference at all.

Whenever a body of research is this chaotic, there is typically a very simple explanation: individual differences. In this instance, it's highly unlikely that one gender is better at multitasking than another. Far more likely is that some people are better than other people at multitasking — regardless of gender. And, of course, when I say 'better', I really mean 'less worse'. Outside of the rare supertasker, everyone suffers.

BURNING QUESTION 3:

THE MIND WIPE

'Sometimes I walk into a room only to suddenly forget why. What's going on there?'

As we learnt earlier, whenever the ventral attention network registers a threat it will automatically drop our current ruleset.

When this occurs, any lingering information that has not been funnelled through the hippocampus will be effectively erased. It's as if every time you turned a page in this book you were to forget the last sentence you read. Researchers call this moment an *event-model purge*: but it's more commonly known as a mind wipe.

This process makes sense when a hungry bear is approaching (who cares what you were just thinking about if your life is suddenly in danger?), but why should it happen when we walk between rooms? It turns out, our ventral network sometimes interprets doorways as threats. Although no one is certain why this happens, it's commonly thought when the door jamb passes quickly in front of our eyes, danger is sensed, our ruleset is reset and whatever information we were just pondering is erased. This is called the *doorway effect*, and it's the same reason why we sometimes open the refrigerator and, as the door quickly passes in front of our eyes, we suddenly forget what food we intended to grab.

Luckily, if we return to the room we were originally in (or close the refrigerator door), we can use spatial-, context- and state-guiding cues to reconstruct our initial train of thought and remember our original intentions.

2. Break complex tasks into small bits

When confronted with a long-term, complex task, many people set their sights squarely on the final product. Unfortunately, when people form a singular goal that exists far in the future (known as a distal goal), this increases their tendency to multitask which, in turn, can delay project completion, decrease performance and diminish an individual's confidence in their own skills and abilities.

When large projects are broken down into small, discrete steps (known as proximal goals), you are more likely to persist with and effectively complete each individual step. Beyond curtailing multitasking, setting smaller goals has been demonstrated to hasten project completion, improve performance, boost confidence and deepen learning.

There is one issue to keep in mind when considering proximal goals: difficulty. If small goals are too demanding or impossible to accomplish (for example, writing 1000 words in one hour), this can make you feel incompetent and drive you to quit. Conversely, if small goals are too easy and require no real effort to accomplish (writing ten words in an hour), this can perpetuate a sense of pointlessness and kill creativity, innovation and performance.

As such, when breaking a large project into small segments, keep in mind the Goldilocks principle: not too difficult, not too easy — a solid mix of challenge and time is paramount.

3. Ensure technology is integral

Many people employ technology with little rhyme or reason. Every student gets a laptop; every session is streamed online; every discussion occurs via digital message-boards. The sentiment seems to be that 'If there's a computer involved, people must be learning'.

Unfortunately, this sentiment simply isn't true. Generally speaking, those who utilize technology more often during learning tend to remember *less* than those who don't.

This is largely because technology breeds multitasking. In fact, it's built into the very fabric of most programs: smartphones run dozens of apps simultaneously; laptops display several windows on a single screen; Twitter cycles multiple conversations concurrently. As such, if you choose to utilize a piece of technology to help others learn, ensure all background programs are switched off so that people can devote their attention completely to the task at hand.

Furthermore, only employ technology if it is *integral* to the learning task. A good rule of thumb: if you can run a session or activity in person using physical tools and interaction — do it! By ditching unnecessary technology, you can remove the temptation to multitask, keep others focused and boost learning.

However, if *learning* is not your ultimate goal, then much of this discussion is irrelevant. Technology is a great means to boost *engagement* and *enjoyment* — though, as we learnt earlier, engagement and enjoyment are not synonymous with learning (remember the Attenborough Effect?). Simply be clear on *why* you are using technology. If it's to get people involved and excited, then go to town. If it's to help others embody new ideas, then ensure the technology is essential, otherwise ditch it.

BURNING QUESTION 4:

MEDIA MULTITASKING

'Does watching TV while studying impact learning?'

I'm guessing you've already gleaned the answer to this one.

It's been estimated over 60 per cent of people engage with different forms of media while studying. Unfortunately, watching television, surfing the web or texting while learning are all forms of multitasking which require task-switching and can negatively impact on memory.

To make matters worse, when people use devices to media multitask while in a group setting, this not only impairs *their* learning but also the learning of *everyone within that person's immediate vicinity*. In other words, media multitasking has a detrimental radius and anyone caught up within it suffers.

As an interesting aside: think of all the television shows that actively encourage viewers to tweet or email during episodes. Though this might boost engagement, it will ultimately kill viewer memory which, in turn, might decrease willingness to watch future episodes.

4. One message at a time

As this mirrors the graphs and tables discussion from Chapter 2, I'll keep it short. When giving a presentation, you will only ever be able to verbally discuss one idea at time. Unfortunately, if your accompanying slide or handout contains multiple ideas, your audience will likely attempt to jump between them all and lose key information from each. This is simply to say make sure you and your slides impart *one* message at a time. If this isn't possible, employ signalling (see p. 69 in Chapter 3) to guide attention and curb multitasking.

5. Avoid unfinished problems and premature questions

Human beings hate (or love) unsolved puzzles. This is thought to spring from the fact that our brains are prediction machines and an incomplete puzzle represents a failed prediction that must be corrected.

Sometimes during a presentation, we will unwittingly leave concepts or ideas half-finished. Maybe we'll begin a story, only to run off on a tangent and never return. Or perhaps we'll begin drawing a diagram, only to get side-tracked and shift to a different topic. When information is incomplete, many people will feel compelled to complete it while still trying to listen to you — multitasking in action. Accordingly, try to remain cognizant of the flow of ideas and avoid leaving things unfinished (I know, easier said than done).

Similarly, if you supply handouts with practice problems or reflection questions meant to be addressed at a later time, guess what will happen? Drawn to unsolved puzzles, many people will begin immediately filling them in. This could cause them to miss key information and impair learning. As such, hold onto any questions or problems until they fit into the material you are presenting.

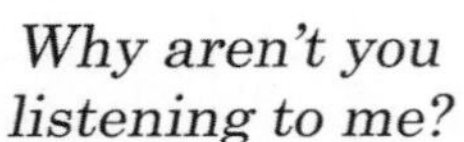

ILLUSTRATION 34. DON'T INVITE MULTITASKING!

AT A GLANCE

Human beings *cannot* multitask. Trying to do so impairs learning and memory.

- » We can hold onto one ruleset at a time. This ruleset determines what information our attention filter allows in.
- » Typically, *we* select which ruleset is active, but any threatening or surprising situation can automatically activate a different ruleset.
- » We don't multitask — we quickly jump between tasks. This takes time, kills accuracy and pushes memory into 'subconscious' networks.
- » Although some people can jump between tasks faster than others, nobody can truly multitask.

APPLICATIONS

1. Don't invite multitasking.
   - » People *can* perform two tasks simultaneously as long as one is habitual and automatic.
   - » Women are not better than men at multitasking.
   - » When a threat is sensed, people undergo a sudden mind wipe.
2. Break complex tasks into small bits.
3. Ensure technology is integral.
   - » Watching TV, surfing the net or texting while studying can impair learning/memory.
4. Focus on one message at a time.
5. Avoid unfinished problems and premature questions.

6. Interleave

> If you think adventure is dangerous, try routine: it is lethal.
>
> — *Paulo Coelho*

Imagine you're a tennis player undertaking a training session prior to a big match. The goal of this session is to get comfortable with three different shots: forehand, backhand and volley. Trick is, you've only got the court for an hour, so you can only face a total of 90 balls.

Which of the following breakdowns do you think would ensure you're best prepared for the upcoming match?

» Option A: 30 forehands; then 30 backhands; then 30 volleys.

» Option B: ten forehands, ten backhands, ten volleys; then ten backhands, ten volleys, ten forehands; then ten volleys, ten forehands, ten backhands.

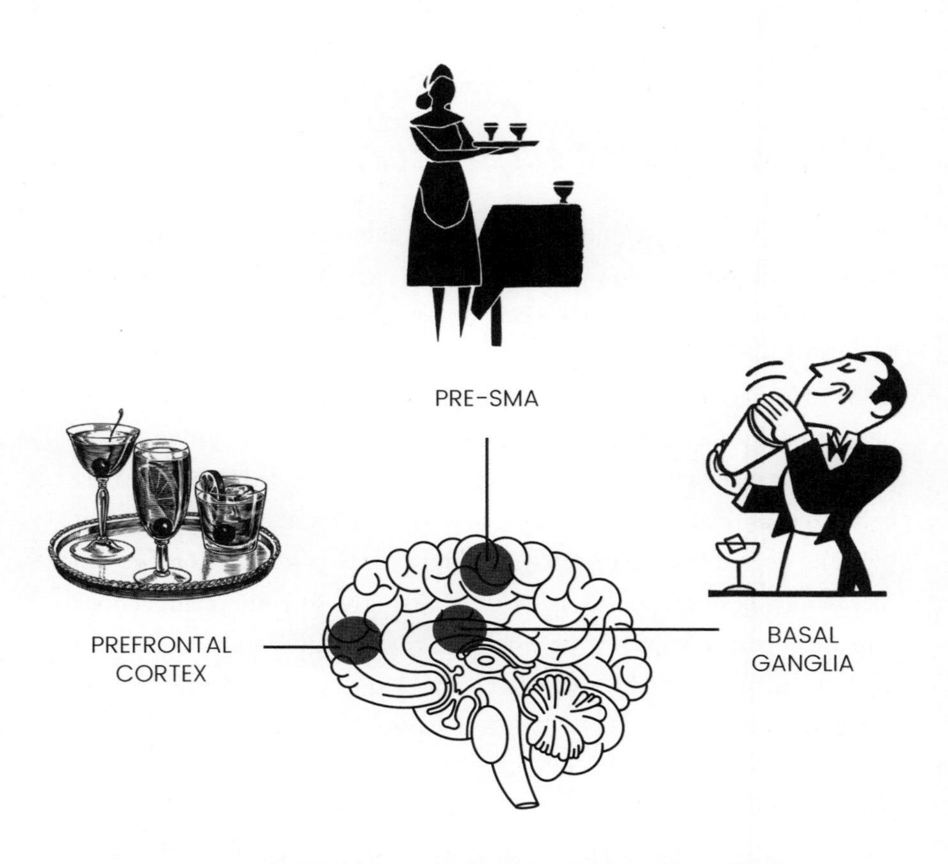

ILLUSTRATION 35. THE ACCESSOR AND THE SEQUENCER

Seeing as you face 30 of each type of shot in both options, it would be intuitive to assume they're equivalent.

Turns out, this isn't the case at all. In fact, only one of these options will lead to a truly strong performance come match-time. But which is it — and why?

Accessor, meet sequencer

Nearly every action we undertake is constructed from a well-organized sequence of smaller component actions. For instance, think about what it takes to tie your shoelaces: first you must grab each lace, then tuck right under left, then pull taut, etc.

Within the brain, component actions must be individually accessed by a network called the *basal ganglia,* then sent up to the *prefrontal cortex* in order to be enacted. Unfortunately, the basal ganglia is not the most organized of brain regions. When it sends actions up to be enacted, it typically does so in a completely random order. As such, before we can successfully perform an action, we must first arrange component actions into their proper sequence (it would do no good to pull the laces taut *before* you'd tucked right under left). This sequencing is largely the job of a brain region called the *presupplementary motor cortex* (or pre-SMA).

A simple analogy I use to clarify this process is that of a crowded pub. As drink orders flood in, the bartender must quickly make up each individual cocktail (basal ganglia). After each drink is complete, he pops it onto a serving tray to be distributed (prefrontal cortex). Typically, these drinks are placed randomly onto the tray; as such, it is the job of the server to sequence them and make sure each drink goes to the correct customer in the correct order (pre-SMA).

Using this analogy, you may have noticed a small problem: namely, we've got another one of those pesky bottlenecks. In this instance, a serving tray can only hold several drinks at any one time. This means that, regardless of how quickly the bartender can whip up cocktails, he can only ever send them out in small batches. Furthermore, he must wait for the server to sequence and deliver each set of drinks before he can reload the tray with the next batch.

Unfortunately, this same bottleneck exists within the brain. Just as with the serving tray, there appears to be a limit to the amount of information the prefrontal cortex can hold onto at any one time. To experience this, see if you can memorize these thirteen letters in under 10 seconds:

F P Q C V O I Y M R F S A

As my father used to say: it's like trying to squeeze 10 pounds of dirt into a 5-pound bag.

Although the basal ganglia can access dozens of component actions incredibly quickly, the prefrontal cortex simply cannot hold onto all of them at once. This means that the basal ganglia must divide actions into small batches and wait patiently for the pre-SMA to sequence each before the next batch can go out.

As you can likely guess, this process of loading, sequencing and reloading can take a bit of time. This is why it usually takes young children quite a while to tie their shoelaces. However, as skilled adults we can tie shoelaces incredibly quickly, with little-to-no conscious thought. This means there must be more to the story.

Indeed, there is.

Sequencer, meet accessor

I have re-arranged the thirteen letters from above. See if you can now memorize them in under 10 seconds:

F Y I R S V P F A Q C O M

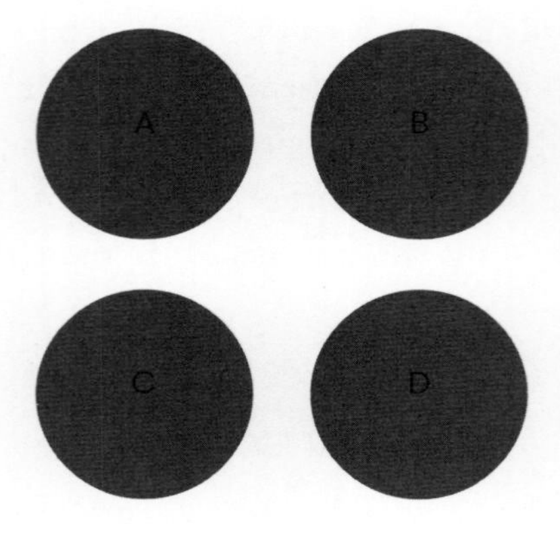

PRACTICE

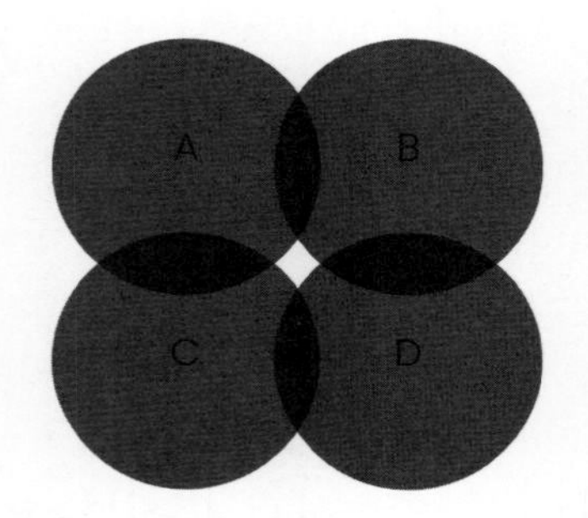

PRACTICE

ILLUSTRATION 36. WITH PRACTICE, INDIVIDUAL ITEMS CAN BE COMBINED INTO A SINGLE CHUNK

I'm guessing this was much easier as the individual letters were organized into coherent acronyms. This process of grouping discrete items into a unified concept is called *chunking*. Importantly, chunks are held as a single unit within the prefrontal cortex. In other words, rather than trying to hold onto thirteen individual letters (impossible), you now need only maintain four chunks (easy).

This is how we squeeze 10 pounds of dirt into a 5-pound bag.

The more we practise the same component skills in the same order, the more we come to understand those skills as a singular process. After enough repetition, the *sequencer* (pre-SMA) can send a message back to the *accessor* (basal ganglia) telling it to group those actions into a single chunk for future use. Returning to our analogy, it's as if the server, after several nights of delivering the same drinks in the same order, pulled the bartender aside and said, 'From now on, why don't you just pour those four drinks into a single large pitcher? This will save me the hassle of having to sequence them, plus it'll free up space on the serving tray so I can pump out drinks more quickly.'

Here is the most important thing to remember: embedded within every chunk is a relevant sequence.

> The smpile fcat taht you can raed tihs pragasrph wtih miinaml eforft is an eamxlpe btoh of yuor ailbity to cunhk and of the inrehent sueenqce embdeedd whiitn ecah cunhk. In tihs insatnce, as you nocite the frsit and lsat letetr of ecah wrod (and plcae tehm wtihin the cotnxet of tihs disisucsoin), you actatvie yuor 'cunhk' for taht wrod. Raehtr tahn hainvg to oganrzie the letrtes yuorelsf, the cunhk *auoatmcallity* seucenqes tehm for you.

Chunking is the reason why you can tie shoelaces with little-to-no explicit effort. Although you originally needed to access and sequence

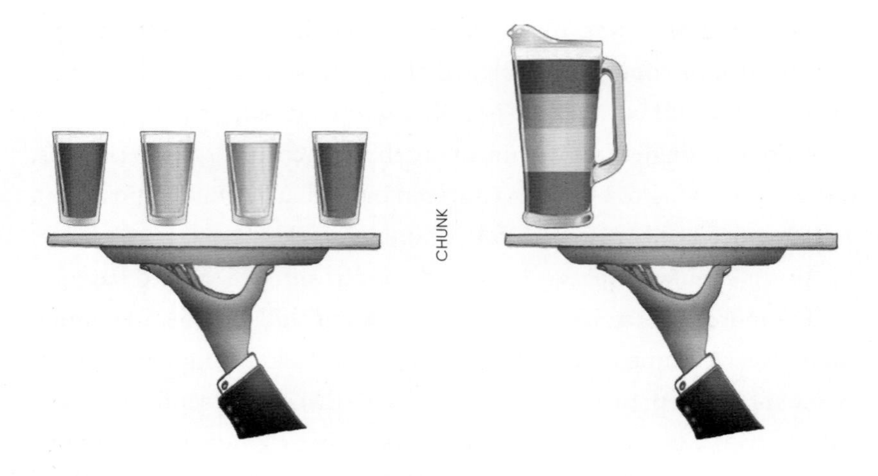

ILLUSTRATION 37. CHUNKING FREES UP SPACE

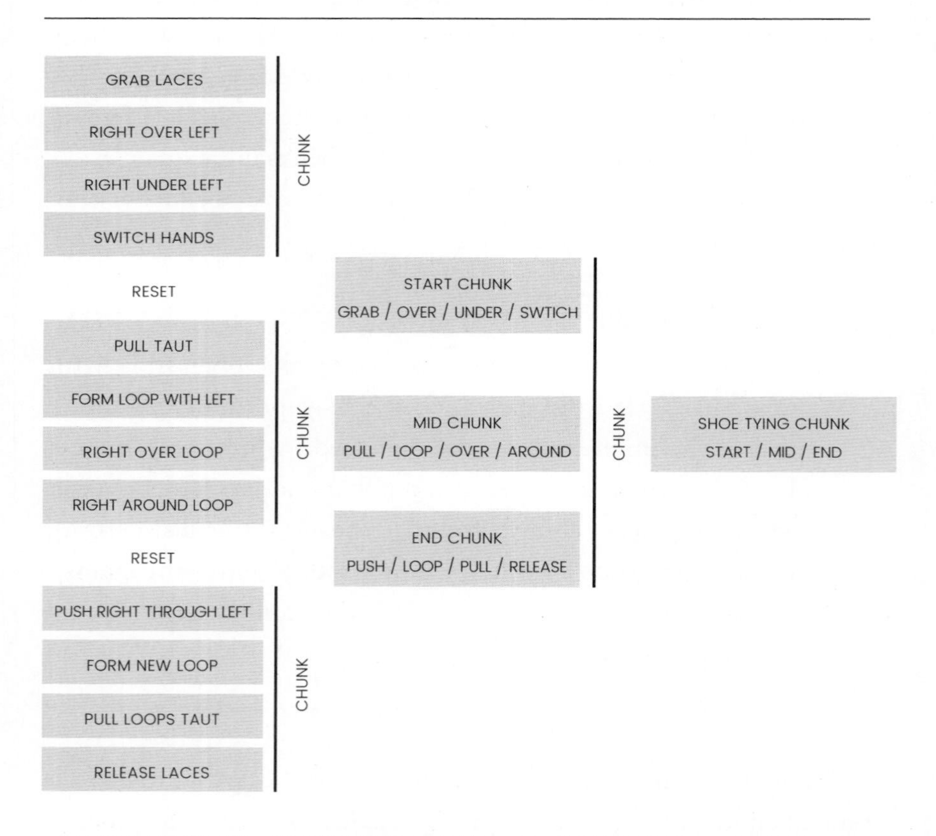

ILLUSTRATION 38. TYING YOUR SHOES – FROM ISOLATED ACTIONS TO UNIFIED CHUNK

each component action, with practice you were able to pool these into a single 'shoe-tying' chunk that takes up minimal space within the prefrontal cortex. Now, you need only activate this chunk and allow the sequence to play out as you ponder more important issues (such as what's for breakfast).

This leads to an important question: when does chunking stop? Believe it or not, under the right circumstances it never will. As long as the same skills are practised in the same order, chunks will keep growing without ever taking up more space within the prefrontal cortex.

Have you ever zoned out while driving? Your keys hit the ignition and the next thing you realized you were pulling into your garage with no memory of the intervening 20 minutes? This is likely because you've driven the same route so many times that you were able to create a single, large 'driving home' chunk. Once accessed, you could sit back and let the sequence roll with almost no conscious effort.

What's the catch?

Here's the problem with chunks: they are incredibly durable. Once a chunk is formed, that sequence becomes locked down and it can be extremely difficult to access individual component actions.

As an example, what are the last three digits of your telephone number? I'm guessing you just quietly recited your entire number from the start. This is because you've sequenced those digits so many times in the past that they are now stored as a single 'phone-number' chunk. Seeing as chunks are incredibly durable, rather than simply jumping to the last few digits, you had to work your way through the complete sequence.

To see this on a larger scale, watch pro basketballers shoot free throws. Before taking the shot, players will run through a sequence of highly personal and highly consistent physical motions (dribbling the ball several times; touching various body parts; dipping into an exaggerated squat). Although these pre-shot routines likely started as a way to calm the nerves, after enough repetition each dribble, touch and squat entered into the players' unique 'free-throw' chunks. Just like your phone number, they must run this entire sequence each time they take a free throw. In fact, when players are not allowed to work through their complete pre-shot routine, shooting accuracy drops significantly.

For most purposes, the durability of chunks is a blessing — would you really want to access and sequence each component skill every time you tied your shoelaces? However, sometimes the durability of chunks can prove a liability.

The accidental chunk

Let's return to the thought experiment at the start of this chapter. Drawing on what we've just explored, what do you think might happen if you practised the same exact sequence (30 forehands, then 30 backhands, then 30 volleys) across several consecutive training sessions? Just as with the basketball players, there's a very strong chance this sequence will coalesce into a single *accidental chunk*, whereby forehands always precede backhands, which always precede volleys.

Although this might not be a problem during training (where you're sure to face these same 90 shots in this exact order every day), this will wreak havoc come game time (where this pattern won't exist and you'll need to jump randomly between different shots). The unpredictability of an actual tennis match means you will have to expend conscious effort breaking down your accidental chunk which, in turn, will cause your performance to suffer.

So how do we avoid forming accidental chunks?

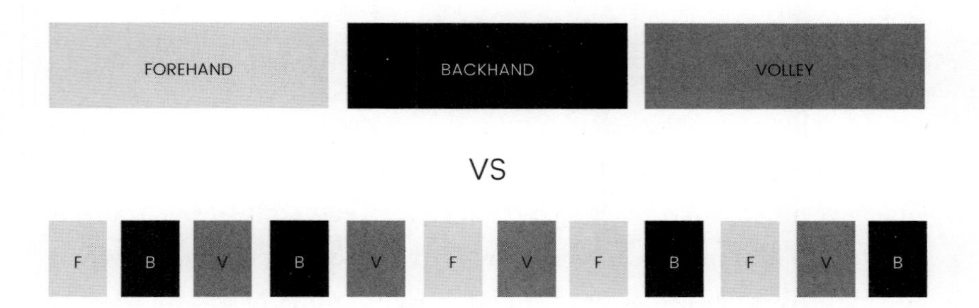

ILLUSTRATION 39. INTERLEAVING IN ACTION

Interleaving

Remember in Chapter 4 when we learnt that training across a number of different contexts can help decouple a skill from any particular location or circumstance? This same principle applies here: to avoid creating an accidental chunk we must practise in a manner that embraces randomness and does not allow for extended sequences to emerge.

Cue interleaving.

The idea is simple: during training, you frequently and randomly *switch between different skills* so that you experience accessing and applying each across a number of shifting and unpredictable scenarios. This continual mixing-and-matching ensures that no larger pattern will emerge and individual chunks will not blend into a single, extended sequence.

Beyond avoiding accidental chunks, interleaving helps people access individual chunks faster and apply them more accurately. The reason for this involves *reconstruction*. When we practise a single skill for an extended period of time (say, 30 forehands in a row) we need only access that chunk once, hold it in the prefrontal cortex and then return it when we're done. Conversely, when skills are mixed together, we might access, hold and return the same chunk *dozens* of times during a single training session. This continual recycling helps to solidify and strengthen each chunk, making skills easier to access and more reliable in the future.

Returning to the start of this chapter, and with this new knowledge in mind, what do you think might be the outcome if you practised in an *interleaved* fashion across several consecutive training sessions? Although this might prove tricky during training (where you can never get into a 'groove' and must continually stay on top of a constantly changing situation) it will work wonders come game time, where randomness and unpredictability rule the day.

But wait … there's more!

During an actual tennis match it's likely you'll face a shot you didn't prepare for — say, a lob. It turns out, interleaving *increases flexibility*. Though you may not have a 'lob-shot' chunk in your repertoire, your ability to quickly jump between skills will allow you to rapidly access and test out related chunks to determine which combination makes the most sense in this novel scenario. Researchers call this process *transfer* (the ability to adapt previously formed chunks to perform similar but never-before-learnt skills), and interleaving boosts transfer far more than practising skills in isolation.

Considerations

Before diving into the applications, there are four issues to consider.

First, the benefits of interleaving do not truly show up until it comes time to perform. In fact, people who mix and match skills will often look worse during training than people who follow a consistent and predictable routine. For this reason, interleaving requires no small amount of faith. Arguably the only way to confirm that the technique is working is to dive head-first into a performance: a less-than-thrilling proposition for many. Unfortunately, beyond knowledge and experience, there is no simple way around this.

Second, interleaving is only effective when the ultimate

performance will be *unpredictable*. If you were a musician preparing to play Beethoven's *Symphony No. 5*, where every note is clearly defined and sequenced, it makes more sense to practise in a manner that will allow you to generate extended sequences and form larger chunks.

Third, although most of this chapter has explored physical skills, interleaving appears to work equally well for cognitive skills. For instance, students who interleave maths skills during homework often show better performance and transfer on final exams. Similarly, doctors who interleave study material often show higher diagnostic accuracy and flexibility in the clinic.

Fourth, interleaving requires you to change *between* chunks — not simply adjust difficulty within one chunk. If you were to simply change your forehand speed (mixing fast and slow shots), this wouldn't be interleaving; it would be much more akin to a process called *deliberate practice*. As we'll see below, although this is a very important form of training, it leads to very different outcomes than interleaving.

Implications for leaders, teachers and coaches

1. Teach first, interleave second

When first introduced to interleaving, some people try to apply it directly to instruction. Rather than devoting ample time to teaching a single skill ('Today, I will show you how to tie shoelaces') they jump back and forth between different topics ('Today, I will show you how to tie shoelaces, fly a kite and cook an omelette!').

Unfortunately, this is not a great idea. Seeing as the primary purpose of interleaving is to maintain the integrity and flexibility of individual chunks, it is important that people first be allowed to *form* these chunks. In other words, people must first learn a skill before they can meaningfully interleave it.

To be fair, there is *some* evidence to suggest that interleaving during the learning phase might help people better differentiate between concepts, but this is largely subconscious and individuals have difficulty explaining exactly what it is they understand. Accordingly, if you want others to have conscious control over skills and their application, employ interleaving during rehearsals, homework and scrimmages — not during lessons.

BURNING QUESTION 1:
DIVING RIGHT IN

'Should we start interleaving from the moment a new skill is learnt?'

Only after skills have reached a certain level of fluency (whereby people no longer need to reload different batches of component skills into the prefrontal cortex) does interleaving begin to make sense. As such, this technique has been shown to work best when it is introduced slowly and ramped up over time as skills become more automatic. Building up interleaving ensures people must continue to expend conscious effort applying skills which will strengthen chunks and make them easier to access in the future.

2. Embrace mock performances and track growth

Seeing as the benefits of interleaving are typically not apparent until performance, try to establish a number of mock-performance scenarios. For instance, create practice tests that mirror final exams; run drills that mimic game conditions; conduct intimate shows in front of small groups. As long as these scenarios remain low- or no-stakes, people can experience the unpredictable nature of performance without any undue stress or pressure.

Beyond experience, mock performances will also help others recognize improvements born from interleaving. Explicit awareness of these improvements will inspire them to continue embracing this technique and work through sometimes difficult training sessions. As such, include relevant measures in mock performances that will help others compare/contrast their growth over time.

3. Interleave only when performance is unpredictable

I know I said this earlier, but it is important enough to reiterate here. Interleaving is effective when the ultimate performance is largely *unpredictable*. If the precise sequence of an upcoming performance is well known and unlikely to change, practise in a way that will allow the formation of larger and larger chunks. For instance, when preparing to perform Shakespeare (where scene II will *always* follow scene I), be sure to practise this ordered sequence. In this way, come performance time people will be able to access extended chunks and let them roll out with minimal conscious effort (freeing up cognitive resources to focus on specifics within the moment).

BURNING QUESTION 2:

BREADTH

‘Does interleaving only work when we mix up similar skills (such as forehands and backhands), or can we mix up totally different skills (such as forehands and calculus)?’

Seeing as the primary benefits of interleaving come from the repeated accessing and returning of chunks across varied situations, this technique should work regardless of how similar or dissimilar the intermingled skills are. As an added bonus, when you mix and match wildly disparate skills, it's possible you will begin to recognize unobvious connections between each (the hallmark of creativity). For instance, mixing up poetry with cooking might lead to the creation of a novel metaphor or a fresh recipe.

Unfortunately, transfer (the ability to adapt chunks to never-before-learnt skills) appears to be dependent upon *similarity*. The more similar interleaved actions are, the more interference will arise between them; the more interference, the more effort will be required to differentiate between each; the more effort, the more flexible and transferable each skill will become.

As an example, seeing as kicking a ball and flying a kite use very different muscle movements, there is little chance of confusing these skills as you jump between them. However, seeing as a forehand and a volley use similar (but distinct) muscle movements, there is a high chance of confusing these two skills as you jump between them. This interference requires conscious effort to combat, and it is this effort that drives transfer.

As such, if your goal is to make skills easier to *access* and *apply* in the future, interleave any chunks. However, if your goal is to make a skill *transferable*, interleave similar chunks.

4. Use deliberate practice within skills; interleave between skills

Deliberate practice is a very specific form of training that involves drilling *a single skill* for extended periods of time. The goal here is to subtly tweak component actions *within* a chunk so as to push performance beyond current limits. For instance, imagine you wanted to add speed to your tennis serve. Deliberate practice dictates you repeat your serve again and again for hours, each time making minor adjustments based on feedback (twist your hand 3 centimetres to the right; angle your hips 5 degrees to the left; etc.). Over time, this repetition and tweaking should slowly boost your serve speed.

Here's the rub: deliberate practice kills transfer. The more you drill a specific skill in isolation, the more automated that skill will become — and once a skill becomes deeply automated, it becomes incredibly difficult to access, analyze and adapt to novel situations.

As you can tell, interleaving and deliberate practice serve very different purposes: the former aims to keep multiple skills accessible and transferable while the latter aims to incrementally improve and automate single skills. For this reason, both techniques are useful and worth employing depending upon your desired outcome. Some elite coaches will play the two against each other: using deliberate practice to tweak a specific skill, then quickly interleaving that skill in order to maintain flexibility.

BURNING QUESTION 3:

BRAIN TRAINING PART 1

'Can I really increase my memory capacity and become super-smart?'

Put simply: no. Brain training games do not do what most people think (nor what most companies claim) they do. To make sense of this, there are two points to consider.

First: as we saw above, there is a limit to the amount of information you can hold within your prefrontal cortex at any one time. Luckily, this limit can be circumvented. Remember this:

FYI RSVP FAQ COM

Let's crank it up a notch. Can you memorize these letters?

A B C D E F G H I J K L M N O P Q R S T U V W X Y Z
A B C D E F G H I J K L M N O P Q R S T U V W X Y Z
A B C D E F G H I J K L M N O P Q R S T U V W X Y Z
A B C D E F G H I J K L M N O P Q R S T U V W X Y Z

That is over 100 letters you can *easily* hold within your prefrontal cortex.

But don't be fooled! Just because you can chunk information does not mean you've increased your prefrontal cortex limit. If that were the case, you should have no problem memorizing these eight letters:

א ת ט ג ל ש ץ ף

Uh oh.

After playing a brain training game for some time, your score will likely increase. Unfortunately, just as with the letters above, this does not mean you have boosted your memory: it simply means you are getting better at chunking information within that brain training game.

This leads us to point two: brain training games are a form of deliberate practice. As we learnt above, if you drill one game for weeks on end, your ability to *transfer* skills from that game will diminish. This wouldn't matter if your ultimate goal was to master brain training — but I imagine most people want

ILLUSTRATION 40. BRAIN TRAINING MAKES YOU BETTER AT … BRAIN TRAINING

to improve their ability to remember names, mentally calculate numbers or hold complex arguments in mind. Do you see the problem? In a very real sense, the better you get at brain training games, the *less* likely you'll be able to apply those skills to any meaningful, real-world situation.

To combat this, many brain training programs now employ interleaving and jump between different games. Unfortunately, this misses the point. Transfer is commonly narrow and typically only occurs between similar skills (between, for example, a forehand and a lob shot). As such, interleaving games might improve your ability to tackle new brain training games in the future, but it won't improve your ability to comprehend classic literature or write persuasive essays, as these skills are simply too far removed from the brain training format.

My purpose here is not to scare anyone away from brain training games. My goal is simply to ensure that you understand what you can (and cannot) meaningfully expect to gain from them. If you enjoy these games, then keep it up! However, if you have a more specific goal in mind (say, to improve maths skills) you'd be better off dedicating time and effort to explicitly addressing that goal.

5. Breaking accidental chunks takes time and effort

Breaking a chunk is hard. It takes time, intense struggle and frequent failure. However, with enough effort and dedication, chunks can be deconstructed and reconstructed.

Just look at professional golfer Tiger Woods. In 2003, after being ranked world number one for over four years, Woods decided to change his golf swing. I don't mean the small tweaks characterized by deliberate practice — I mean a *complete* swing overhaul. In order to break down and rebuild his 'golf-swing' chunks, Woods had to struggle through twelve hours of practice a day for nearly two years. During this period he failed to win any major golf tournaments and his world ranking dropped. However, by 2005 he had successfully constructed new chunks and once again rose to world number one.

There are three things required to break a chunk. First, you must explicitly deconstruct a chunk into its *component actions*. For instance, with shoelace tying you must recognize and delineate every minor movement involved, from first grabbing the laces to tightening the final bow.

Next, you must drill component actions *in isolation*, tweaking them until you can perform each differently. For instance, you would need to practise *only* grabbing your laces in the absence of any other motions.

Finally, you must battle through *chunk re-formation*. Once conscious effort stops, chunks have a tendency to spontaneously re-form. For this reason, it's smart to avoid performing the complete action until each component action has been reworked in isolation. This might mean you go months without ever completely tying shoelaces as you focus on tweaking each movement in isolation.

As I said above, this process is long, arduous and difficult … but it is ultimately doable.

AT A GLANCE

Interleaving skills *during practice* can boost performance and skill transfer.

- » To perform an action, component skills must be accessed and sequenced.
- » With time and practice, component skills can merge together to form chunks.
- » Interleaving is a practice technique that mixes and matches chunks to ensure they do not accidentally blend and are easier to access in the future.

APPLICATIONS

1. Teach first, interleave second.
   - » Interleaving is most effective when introduced slowly and built up over time.
2. Embrace mock performances and track growth.
3. Interleave only when performance will be unpredictable.
   - » Interleave any chunk to boost skill access and application.
   - » Interleave only similar chunks to boost skill transfer.
4. Use deliberate practice within skills; interleave between skills.
   - » Brain training games do not boost memory or intelligence; they simply make you better at chunking brain training games.
5. Breaking chunks takes time and effort.

1959
THIS IS AN
ADULT WORLD
ITS PROBLEMS
ARE UP TO You!
FREE
Enroll: FEDERAL ADULT SCHOOLS
MANY COURSES • MANY PLACES • INFORMAL TEACHING

1959
THIS IS AN
ADULT WORLD
ITS PROBLEMS
ARE UP TO You!
FREE
Enroll: FEDERAL ADULT SCHOOLS
MANY COURSES • MANY PLACES • INFORMAL TEACHING

1959
THIS IS AN
ADULT WORLD
ITS PROBLEMS
ARE UP TO You!
FREE
Enroll: FEDERAL ADULT SCHOOLS
MANY COURSES • MANY PLACES • INFORMAL TEACHING

1959
THIS IS AN
ADULT WORLD
ITS PROBLEMS
ARE UP TO You!
FREE
Enroll: FEDERAL ADULT SCHOOLS
MANY COURSES • MANY PLACES • INFORMAL TEACHING

Intermission 3

Please take around 60 seconds to study and enjoy these old adult education posters.

7.

Error

I never lose —
I either win or I learn.

— *Anonymous*

Pop your thinking cap on, because we're going to open this chapter with a few questions randomly selected from a 'general knowledge pub quiz' booklet.

Questions

1. How many senses do human beings typically have?
2. Who invented the lightbulb?
3. In naval lingo, what does the Morse code SOS stand for?
4. Bulls commonly become enraged at the sight of what colour?
5. Oxygenated blood is red. What colour is de-oxygenated blood?

And now, the answers:

Answers

1. Five (vision, hearing, smell, taste, touch)
2. Thomas Edison
3. Save Our Ship
4. Red
5. Blue

Finally, the reveal.

Each answer in the box above … is completely and utterly wrong. If you gave any of these answers, you have just committed an error.

Take a moment to experience what you're physically and mentally feeling in this moment. Do you feel as if the forward momentum of your thinking has ground to a halt? Maybe you feel a sharpened sense of awareness? These visceral sensations represent the human *error alarm* and they can be leveraged to guide and enhance our influence.

The error alarm

Back in Chapter 3 we learnt that the brain implicitly forms mental maps reflecting the physical layout of different environments. These maps are used to make predictions and guide future behaviours.

It turns out that this concept goes way beyond physical layouts. In truth, the brain implicitly creates representations for space, sight, smell, taste, touch, sound, motion, behaviour, emotion, cause-and-effect … essentially, everything!

We call these *mental models* and, just like the simpler mental map, we use these models to make predictions about the world around us in order to guide our behaviours. In fact, the reason you can read and understand this paragraph right now is because you have a mental model that is accurately predicting the sequence of these words, the flow of these ideas and the structure of the argument being made.

ILLUSTRATION 41. THE PARIS TRIANGLE

Each time a prediction proves correct, the relevant mental model strengthens. However, sometimes mental models can become too strong. When this happens, we run the risk of trusting our predictions more than the actual world. This is the reason why many people fail to notice the second 'the' in the triangle above: because their mental models for 'reading' have proven so effective in the past, they quickly predict what that sentence *should* say and read that prediction instead of the actual words.

Seeing as the world is forever changing, it is important that we frequently update our mental models to ensure our predictions accurately reflect reality. This leads to a very important question: how do we know when a mental model has become outdated and needs an upgrade?

Errors! Errors alert us that there is a discrepancy between our predictions and reality.

It's important to note that an *error* is different than simply *not knowing*. For instance: what is the natural spin of a fermion? If you're anything like me, 'fermions' don't exist anywhere within any of your mental models. As such, when you learn that fermions typically demonstrate a half-integer spin, you don't feel any sense of surprise because no error has occurred.

Now: how many knees does an elephant have? This time, you almost certainly have a mental model which predicts that any mammal with four legs must have four knees. As such, when you learn that elephants only have two knees you might feel stunned and focused. This is the error alarm signalling a problem with your mental model.

To understand how this works, let's turn to the brain.

Any time there is conflict between a prediction and reality, a small blip called an *error positivity* is generated within the *anterior cingulate cortex* (a brain area deep behind your forehead). The size of this blip changes depending upon the size of the conflict: small errors generate small blips; large errors generate large blips.

Here's the important part: only large error positivities will trigger an error alarm. When discrepancies are minor, people typically will not become consciously aware that something is amiss. This means your brain *did* spot the second 'the' in the triangle opposite but the conflict was too small to alert you.

Once an error alarm is triggered, two things happen. First, the ventral attention network activates. As we learnt in Chapter 5, this network subconsciously monitors all the information blocked by our attention filter and can take over control whenever something dangerous or unexpected occurs (remember the driving instructor?). Second, the body and brain slow down: heart rate decreases, breathing slows and any information being held within the prefrontal cortex is abandoned. These processes force our attention towards the error and free up resources so that we can analyze the conflict and update our mental model accordingly. This is why most people feel hyper-aware and hyper-focused after committing an error.

Of course, the error alarm is merely a signal. What we choose to do with it is up to us.

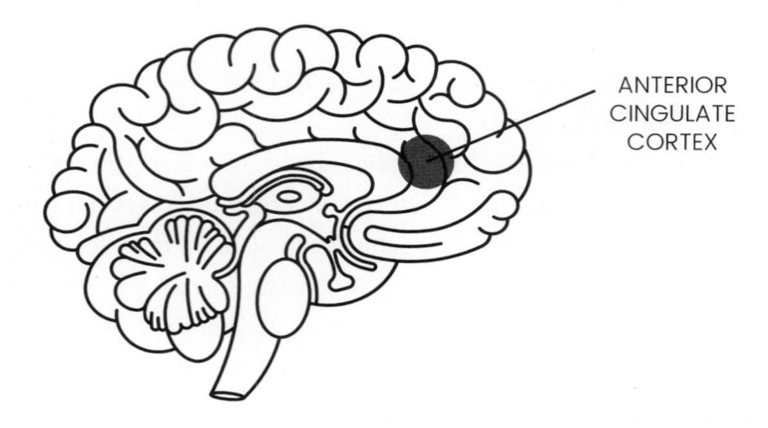

ILLUSTRATION 42. THE ANTERIOR CINGULATE CORTEX

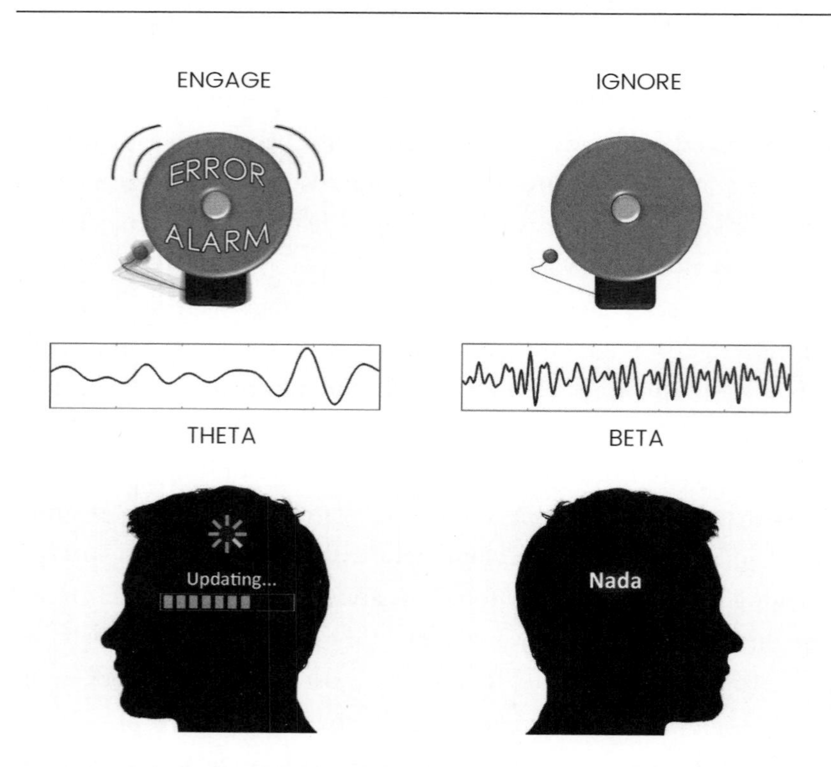

ILLUSTRATION 43. ENGAGE OR IGNORE — THE CHOICE IS YOURS

Fight or flight

There are two common responses to the error alarm: engage or ignore.

If you choose to engage with an error, two things occur. First, communication throughout the brain shifts into a pattern called *theta*. This pattern reflects your brain physically changing as it assimilates new information and updates your mental model. In other words, theta is a sure sign that you are *learning* from an error. Next, activity within the areas of the brain that process reward *decreases*, while activity within areas of the brain that guide attention *increases*. This means that, after engaging with an error, you become less focused on success and more focused on sussing out additional errors that might signal the need to further adjust your mental model.

If you choose to *ignore* an error, two different things occur. First, communication throughout the brain shifts into a pattern called *beta*. This pattern is essentially a 'status quo' signal that tells the brain everything is fine and there is no need to change any mental model. In other words, beta silences your error alarm and impedes learning. Next, activity within areas of the brain that guide attention *decreases* while activity within areas of the brain that process reward *increases*. This means that, after ignoring an error you effectively block out additional errors and become deeply focused on successfully upholding your prediction.

So what dictates whether we choose to engage with or ignore a particular error? Although there are dozens of factors, the primary driver is *personalization*. When we do not take errors personally (such as with the elephant knees example) we typically have no problem engaging with and learning from them. However, when we interpret errors as a threat to our personal identity, not only do we typically ignore that error but we also avoid situations that could trigger the same error in the future.

Let's see what this looks like in real life.

Error-free existence

Ever since the IQ test was invented there has been a fascination with measuring and ranking young children's intelligence. Those who achieve high IQ scores are typically singled out and labelled as 'gifted', 'advanced' or (in some extreme cases) 'geniuses'.

Here's the rub: research has consistently demonstrated that these labels may be detrimental to many children. In fact, some estimates suggest that up to 50 per cent of children saddled with the term 'gifted' begin to lose confidence, underperform and ultimately fail to live up to academic expectations.

Why would this be? Personalization of error.

Once singled out, many children come to deeply embody the concept of 'gifted' and use it to anchor their identity. Unfortunately, embedded within this concept is an expectation of success: gifted people are too intelligent to screw up and must always perform at the highest level. For this reason, many gifted children come to interpret the error alarm as a direct threat to their selfhood. They quickly learn to avoid any situation that might lead to failure and gravitate only towards those that match their current mental models and guarantee success.

Unfortunately, when we surround ourselves with things we already understand, growth is stifled and innovation dies. In other words, by avoiding situations that may trigger the error alarm, many gifted students self-handicap and, in the interest of self-protection, stunt their own learning.

On the flip side, students who interpret error as separate from and unrelated to their personal identity come to view learning as a *process* driven by effort rather than a birthright driven by IQ. As such, they tend to seek out difficult situations that will trigger the error alarm. When we surround ourselves with things that challenge and confuse us, short-term success may be stifled, but long-term growth and innovation flourish.

I am not saying we should stop labelling children: that debate is rife with danger and is way beyond anything I want to tackle here. I simply wish to demonstrate how personalization can morph the error alarm from an *opportunity* into a *liability*.

Error-full existence

It would be amazing if, after every error we made, our mental model was automatically updated. Although this does happen on occasion (think about the first, and likely last, time you grabbed a hot iron), learning from errors typically follows a four-stage process.

Stage one is *awareness*. Unless we consciously recognize that an error has occurred, there is no way to address it. Unfortunately, as we learnt earlier, the more deeply ingrained a mental model is the *less* likely we are to recognize discrepancies between predictions and the real world. As such, awareness is far from trivial and can benefit greatly from the support of a teacher or mentor (see 'Feedback' on p. 162).

Stage two is *categorization*. Within most fields, errors can be organized according to a relatively small set of functional groups. For instance, although there are millions of specific errors I could make during a maths exam, almost all of these will fall under the categories of miscalculation (I multiplied incorrectly), misunderstanding (I used the wrong equation), misapplication (I didn't follow all the steps of an equation) or sloppiness (I read the question incorrectly). Categorization makes it easier to recognize any error-making patterns and identify underlying causes; it helps us move beyond *what* things are going wrong and towards *why* things are going wrong. Again, this stage can benefit greatly from the assistance of a teacher or mentor.

Stage three is *correction*. Once an underlying cause has been identified, we can work to address and amend it. Although the specifics will necessarily differ across circumstances, the concepts and suggestions throughout this book are all solid techniques to employ during this stage. Once again, since correcting errors typically requires knowledge and practice, this stage can benefit greatly from the guidance of a teacher or mentor.

Stage four is *autonomy*. As people develop expertise within a particular field, the errors they commit will slowly shift from the *known* into the *unknown*. These are errors that occur at the cutting edge of a field; errors no person has previously made; errors that signal the need for a creative leap. When unknown errors occur, there is no simple guidance or support — you must be ready to push forward and innovate on your own. For this reason, it is important that teachers and mentors eventually step away and allow others to learn how to run this error-analysis cycle independently. Only through self-diagnosis, self-classification and self-intervention will novel ideas, concepts and knowledge be created.

One last thing

So what about that quiz at the start of this chapter? How many senses *do* human beings have? Who *did* invent the lightbulb? As you think back on these questions, you might start to feel a sense of anticipation, an internal tingle, an almost visceral pull: you *need* to know the answers.

Believe it or not, this feeling is what is meant by *curiosity*. If the error alarm signals a gap in our knowledge or understanding, curiosity is the recognition that this gap can (and must!) be filled.

Television shows exploit this beautifully. During an episode they will help us construct a mental model that leads to a simple prediction ('Philip is the hero and will certainly save the day!'). Then, at the end of the episode, they will do something to break that prediction and trigger an error alarm ('Oh my — Philip just drove his car off a cliff!'). Finally, they will ensure you're aware that this gap will soon be filled ('Tune in next week!)'. That pull to watch just one more episode is curiosity in action.

Unfortunately, although it seems like a universally wonderful emotion, there is a dark side to curiosity.

ILLUSTRATION 44. WHAT ARE THESE BLACK BLOBS?

The real answers

Q: How many senses do human beings typically have?

A: Seventeen. Vision, hearing, smell, taste, touch, pain, balance, joint perception, kinesthesis, heat, cold, blood pressure, blood oxygen content, cerebrospinal fluid acidity, thirst, hunger, lung inflation.

Q: Who invented the lightbulb?

A: Warren la Rue. Although Thomas Edison commercialized the lightbulb, he did not invent it.

Q: In naval lingo, what does the Morse code SOS stand for?

A: Nothing. SOS was selected as the emergency code because it is the easiest pattern to type and recognize in Morse code.

Q: Bulls commonly become enraged at the sight of what colour?

A: None. Bulls are dichromatic and cannot detect the colour red (at least, not as we see it — to them, red likely looks green). Bulls become enraged at the threatening motions made by the matador and his or her cape.

Q: Oxygenated blood is red. What colour is de-oxygenated blood?

A: Red. Veins look blue due to the way light reflects off our skin and interacts with the oxygen molecules within blood cells.

Now that you've read the real answers and filled that gap in your knowledge, how do you feel? I'm guessing slightly deflated, underwhelmed, maybe even disappointed.

Many of us assume excitement resides in the solution. Unfortunately, this is rarely the case. In truth, excitement resides in the process of *finding* the solution. In other words, the thrill of curiosity exists in the knowledge-gap itself. Once that gap is filled, the pull of curiosity fades and we return to the hum-drum world of mental models and predictions. Just think of all those times you excitedly sat down to watch the next episode of a television show, only to immediately feel let down ('Oh … Philip jumped out of the car before it went over the cliff … clever.').

I often liken curiosity to a car race. When the drivers cross the finish line, that signals the end of the race: the day is done and it's time to go home. All the exhilaration and emotion take place on the track as the drivers fight to reach the finish line. The more people come to recognize this concept, the more willing they will be to seek out errors and engage with the error-analysis cycle.

P.S. Those black blobs on p. 155 are a frog sitting on a log. Take another look … and there goes your curiosity.

ILLUSTRATION 45. FAREWELL CURIOSITY

Implications for leaders, teachers and coaches

1. Foster a culture of error

Within businesses, schools and teams there are two different cultural orientations: *outcome* and *process*. Outcome orientation stresses the importance of the finished product and runs according to a success–reward system. This often leads to the personalization of error and can foster risk aversion, peer competition and isolation. Conversely, process orientation stresses the importance of effort, failure, growth and mastery. This often leads to the de-personalization of error and can foster risk-taking, collaboration and loyalty.

If you wish to cultivate a process-orientated culture (not everyone does), it is important to take steps that ensure errors and error analysis are explicitly featured and encouraged across all levels. Openly discuss any errors that influenced specific decisions; ask people to identify and categorize errors during review sessions; highlight the effort and failures that led to successful outcomes. Only when errors are transparent and accepted will people intrinsically seek out knowledge-gaps, chase curiosity and embrace process.

BURNING QUESTION 1:

OUT WITH THE OLD

'Do we lose old mental models each time we update them?'

Learning is *constructive*, not *destructive*. This means we don't replace mental models — we simply expand upon them.

To understand what I mean, think back to your childhood. There was likely a time when you believed in Santa Claus; your mental model accepted him and your predictions accounted for his existence. At some point, however, you came to recognize he was fictitious and you updated your mental model accordingly. At that moment, you didn't suddenly forget everything about Santa Claus. To this day, you can still recognize him, speak of him and embrace young children's belief in him. In other words, you didn't destroy your old mental model, you simply added new information to it.

By building upon (instead of deleting) old mental models we are able to maintain ties to the past, foster a deeper understanding of concepts and develop an ever-expanding pool of information to draw upon in order to continually adapt to an ever-evolving world.

2. Use misconceptions to boost learning

When people receive new information without first activating a mental model and generating a prediction, they come to understand that information in *isolation* without connecting it to previously learnt concepts or ideas. For instance, had I simply said 'Bulls are dichromatic' this fact might never have become tied to or influence the relevant mental model and you'd likely still believe that bulls hate the colour red.

However, when people activate a mental model and generate a prediction *prior to* receiving new information, they come to interpret that information through their current understanding. By first leading you to predict that bulls hate the colour red, I was ensuring that the relevant mental model was activated. Later, when you learnt that 'Bulls are dichromatic' you were able to incorporate this information into your existing mental model and update accordingly.

Rather than avoiding common mistakes or misconceptions, try to embed them within your sessions. Prior to a presentation, ask people to discuss what they currently understand about a particular topic; conduct a demonstration meant to contradict common assumptions (such as dropping two differently weighted balls and guessing which will hit the ground first); or deliver a multiple-choice pre-quiz that includes typical misunderstandings in the answer choices. Only when a mental model is active and a prediction made will new ideas be linked to old and updating occur.

BURNING QUESTION 2:

HYPERCORRECTION

'Why do I remember some error fixes (elephants only have two knees, for example) but quickly forget others?'

Researchers call this phenomenon *hypercorrection* and it largely boils down to confidence.

When we have only a *basic* understanding of a particular topic, our mental models will be quite weak and we'll have little confidence in our predictions. As an example, what is my favourite sport? Though you've probably gleaned enough information throughout this book to make a guess ('He references golf quite a bit, so I'll guess that'), you wouldn't bet money on this prediction. As such, when I reveal that my favourite sport is ice hockey, no error alarm will be triggered, curiosity will be minimal and you won't feel any pressing need to engage with the error-analysis cycle. This means if I ask you this same question next week, you'll likely make the same incorrect prediction ('Golf?').

Conversely, when we have a *deep* understanding of a particular topic, our mental models will be quite strong and we'll have high confidence in our predictions. As an example, how were witches traditionally executed during the Salem witch trials? You have probably come across this story many times in the past, so will feel quite confident in your prediction ('They were burned at the stake'). As such, when I reveal that no witch was *ever* burned in Salem, your error alarm will ring loudly, your curiosity will pique and you will feel deeply compelled to update your mental model (they were hanged). If I ask you this same question next week, you're likely to recall this error and make the correct prediction.

Of course, this all hinges upon your willingness to engage with the error. As we learnt earlier, if you chose to ignore the error alarm, this all becomes null and void.

3. Develop error categories for your field

As we saw above, many errors will slot neatly into a small group of functional categories. Delineating these categories means that, rather than addressing 100 individual errors we might only need to address one underlying cause.

As much as I wish I could type up a universal list, error categories will necessarily differ across fields. For this reason, you may need to construct your own list relevant to whatever material you are presenting. Remember: the key is to focus on underlying processes. You don't want to simply highlight *what* is going wrong ('You failed that maths test'). You want to be able to organize dozens of mistakes so as to find any underlying pattern and discern *why* things are going wrong ('You misread every question; let's work on slowing down your reading'). Share these categories with others and work with them to address errors and build autonomy.

4. Feedback: your shortcut to the error alarm

As we learnt earlier, only large errors will generate an error positivity strong enough to trigger the error alarm. This means many small errors are overshadowed by our predictions and never reach conscious awareness.

Luckly, there is a simple way to ensure that even the smallest of errors will be recognized: feedback. Whenever an error is explicitly pointed out to us (such as me pointing out that the word 'luckily' at the start of this paragraph is misspelled), this will generate a signal in the brain called the *feedback-related negativity*. Of importance, this signal will always and immediately trigger the error alarm.

BURNING QUESTION 3:

EFFECTIVE FEEDBACK

'Surely there must be more to feedback than simply pointing out a person's error?'

Indeed, there is.

In order to be effective, most feedback requires three pieces of information.

1. Where am I going?
   Effective feedback first explicitly clarifies the goal or standard meant to be achieved. This information ensures the proper mental model is activated and a relevant prediction is made.
2. How am I going?
   Next, effective feedback explicitly highlights any discrepancy between an individual's performance and the intended goal in order to trigger the feedback-related negativity. This bit of information must reflect a specific aspect of an individual's performance; anything vague or relative will not be enough to trigger the error alarm.
3. Where to next?
   Finally, effective feedback will suggest what steps to take to address the discrepancy. With novices, this might require much detail. However, as people gain expertise and autonomy over their own correction, this might require less detail (a simple reminder or nudge may be enough).

ILLUSTRATION 46. WHERE AM I GOING? CLARIFY THE GOAL

ILLUSTRATION 47. HOW AM I GOING? DELIVER SPECIFIC (NOT VAGUE) PERFORMANCE INFORMATION

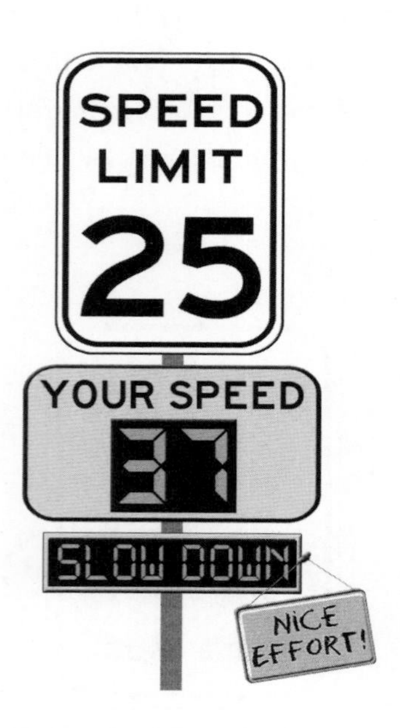

ILLUSTRATION 48. WHERE TO NEXT? SUGGEST RELEVANT ACTIONS (AND DON'T FEAR PRAISE!)

There's one final thing to point out: feedback only works if it has been *received*. If a person chooses to ignore the error alarm, all the feedback in the world will be for naught. If you notice someone frequently blocking feedback, it might be worthwhile addressing the issue of personalization and taking steps to build a more *process*-oriented culture.

BURNING QUESTION 4:

PRAISE

'I've heard we should never praise others as this will stunt their learning. Is this true?'

This one always leaves me shaking my head.

Praise is not feedback. It does not incorporate the three elements outlined above, it does not trigger an error alarm, and it does not guide people towards updating their mental models. In other words, praise does not drive learning.

But it is not meant to!

Praise is a tool meant to acknowledge an individual's effort and progress. This, in turn, can boost confidence, reignite motivation and inspire people to continue along the oftentimes difficult journey of learning.

Praise is only dangerous when it is mistaken for and used to replace feedback. When praise and feedback are used for their respective purposes, we typically see great results.

5. Explicitly practice error analysis

Like every skill, the ability to engage the error-analysis cycle will improve with practice. As such, be sure to explicitly employ this process with others. Embed common but not-too-obvious errors within reports, readings or presentations and work with others to recognize, categorize and address each. With time, as people gain competence, make these errors less explicit and ask people to run the error-analysis cycle on their own. As an added bonus, the more others see you commit and embrace errors (even intentionally), the less likely they will be to personalize related errors in the future.

ILLUSTRATION 49. A WOMAN AND HER WINE

AT A GLANCE

Embracing errors can lead to improved learning, memory and predictions.

- » Our brain creates mental models and uses these to form predictions about how the world works.
- » The error alarm signals a discrepancy between a mental model and the real world.
- » We can either *embrace* (and learn from) errors or *avoid* (and ignore) errors.
- » The error-analysis process involves awareness, categorization, correction, and autonomy.

APPLICATIONS

1. Foster a culture of error.
   - » Old mental models are never erased, they're simply added to.
2. Use misconceptions to boost learning.
   - » *Hypercorrection* suggests people are more likely to correct high-confidence errors.
3. Develop error categories for your field.
4. Feedback is the shortcut to the error alarm.
   - » Like a GPS device, effective feedback must help others recognize *where they are at, where they are going* and *what the next step is.*
   - » Praise can boost confidence and motivation.
5. Explicitly practise error analysis.

8.

Recall

> We don't think about the things we remember; we remember the things we think about.
>
> —*Jared Cooney Horvath*

Here we are: Chapter 8. A perfect spot to take a look back at where we've been.

I imagine some of you might feel compelled to skip this bit, but stick with it! Though it might seem pedantic, I assure you there is a larger purpose for my doing this here.

Over the last seven chapters, we've learnt about a number of important brain regions. Here are some of the biggies.

- The Broca/Wernicke network allows us to process language and can 'bottleneck' when we are trying to listen and read simultaneously.
- The hippocampus is our gateway to memory: all new information must pass through this structure to be remembered (though memories aren't stored there).
- The parahippocampal place area subconsciously encodes the physical aspects of our surrounding environment.
- The presupplementary motor cortex acts as a sequencer and works with the basal ganglia to form chunks.
- The anterior cingulate cortex contains a region that compares mental models to reality and can trigger an error alarm.

Over the last seven chapters, we've also explored a number of interesting psychological phenomena. See if you can select the correct answers to the following questions.

- Which of the following is the term used to describe text written in a single, continuous line without spaces or punctuation?
  a. scriptura continua
  b. block writing
  c. stream of consciousness

- When the words we hear change as a result of the particular face we are looking at, this is an example of what?
  a. synaesthesia
  b. cross sensation
  c. the McGurk Effect

» The act of staring at the region of space where information used to be (but no longer is) in order to remember that information is called:
a. looking at nothing
b. the method of loci
c. re-staging

» Declarative memories can be divided into two distinct categories — what are they?
a. personal vs impersonal memory
b. episodic and semantic memory
c. explicit vs implicit memory

» The ability to adapt a known skill to perform a similar but never-before-learnt skill is called:
a. transfer
b. application
c. translation

Answers: A; C; A; B; A

Finally, before we dive into this chapter, I've got one final question …

» Without flipping back or stealing a peek, what are the titles of the first seven chapters of this book? (Honestly — give it a minute or two and try to recall each.)
1. ______________________
2. ______________________
3. ______________________
4. ______________________

5. ______________________________
6. ______________________________
7. ______________________________

Now, flip back through the book and check to see how you did …

Each of the above boxes taps into a completely different memory process. Of importance, only one of these boxes will lead to the formation of deep, durable and long-lasting memories for the content contained within: can you guess which one?

The memory triumvirate

Why is it so easy to remember that radio jingle you heard a couple of times as a kid, yet so hard to remember those maths equations you spent years studying in high school? So easy to remember your first kiss yet so hard to remember last week's board meeting? So easy to remember episodes from popular TV shows yet so hard to remember chemical elements from the periodic table?

People typically account for these memory discrepancies by arguing that we tend to better remember those events that are personally relevant and highly emotional. Although this is true, it doesn't really explain the above examples. Of what possible relevance could a song describing hamburger ingredients be to your personal life? Similarly, you likely experienced very strong emotions when learning maths equations (stress; fear; accomplishment; relief).

Clearly, there must be more going on here. To understand what this is, we need to take a closer look at memory and how it works.

In its simplest form, memory can be understood as a three-step process:

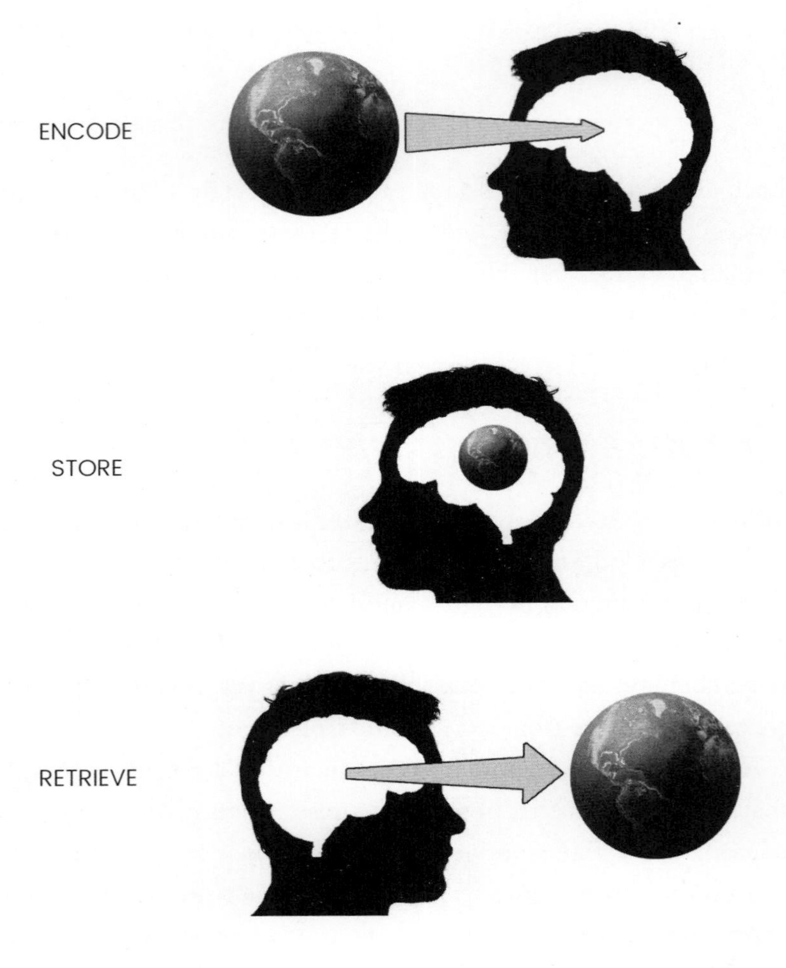

ILLUSTRATION 50. THE THREE STAGES OF MEMORY

1. encoding: information must *get into* the brain
2. storage: information must *stick in* the brain
3. retrieval: information must *come back out of* the brain.

When it comes to influencing, many people focus on the first two steps. The assumption is that the more times people come across a piece of information (encoding), the better chance it'll have of finding a permanent home in their brain (storage). However, if this assumption was correct, then surely your first kiss (which only happened once) should have faded away long ago while the periodic table (which you've likely seen dozens of times) should be alive and well.

It turns out that focusing on encoding and storage leads to the formation of shallow, fleeting memories. This isn't a problem if your goal is to remember something for a short time and apply it only in the immediate future — but what if you want to create deep, lasting memories that can be applied throughout your lifetime? In this instance, you must shift your focus to the most overlooked step in the memory triumvirate: retrieval.

Within the human brain, retrieval is *constructive*. This means every time you retrieve a memory it becomes deeper, stronger and easier to access in the future. An easy way to visualize this is to imagine each of your memories as a small hut within a dense jungle. The first time you travel to a particular hut, you need to forge a path by hacking through tree limbs and undergrowth. However, the more you travel this path the more obvious and etched into the landscape it becomes. With enough retrieval, this path can become like a super-highway leading straight to the memory with no impeding foliage in sight.

This is the reason why many people can remember details from popular TV shows despite only watching (*encoding*) each episode once. Every time they discuss the show with friends, search for fan theories online or visualize their favourite scenes, they are *retrieving* relevant memories and making each deeper and easier to access in the future. This is also the reason why many people can't remember last week's board meeting. Without water-cooler discussions or dinner-time debates, this memory is never retrieved and quickly becomes overgrown and lost in the jungle.

I want to write this out again because I honestly believe this single sentence has the potential to shift your entire perspective on influencing (as it did mine):

Retrieval is the key to forming deep, lasting and accessible memories.

Unfortunately, if you've made it this far into the book you know things are never *that* easy. It turns out there are three different methods we can use to retrieve a memory: review, recognition and recall.

Before we dive into these, we've got to quickly come to terms with what memories are.

The metaphor

Imagine the brain as an orchestra and each of the different brain regions as a specific instrument. Maybe the visual cortex is a violin, the auditory cortex an oboe, the hippocampus a harp, etc.

Whenever information enters our brain, it does not trigger off a simple melody confined to a single instrument; rather, it triggers a cascading symphony that includes every instrument. For instance, when you look at the duck opposite, that image will drive your violin to play a specific melody … which will drive your oboe to play a specific melody … which will drive your harp to play a specific melody … etc. Ultimately, your memory for this duck will be the *global symphony* being played by your entire brain at the moment of encoding.

In order to *retrieve* a memory, we must get the entire orchestra (or, at least, most of it) to play back the complete memory symphony. In other words, if you were to close your eyes right now and think about the duck, your brain would look incredibly similar to how it looked at

ILLUSTRATION 51. A SWEET DUCKLING

the moment you encoded it. This is why we often feel as though we 'relive' memories: in a very real sense, our brains return to the past each time we replay a memory symphony.

One last thing: for any orchestra to play in unison, there must be a conductor who coordinates all the different instruments and cues the right melodies at the right time. Within the brain, this conductor is thought to reside within a small area of the right prefrontal cortex. Whenever we see strong activity within this region it's a sure sign someone is working hard to retrieve and play back a memory.

With this metaphor in mind, let's explore the three different methods of memory retrieval.

REVIEW (PURELY EXTERNAL)

The easiest way to get our neural orchestra to play a particular memory symphony is to simply re-listen to that symphony. Just like hitting repeat on a CD player, each time we return to the original source of information and simply allow it to flow back into our brains, it will trigger off the same (or, at least, an incredibly similar) melody.

This type of memory retrieval is called *review*. It relies exclusively upon the external world to activate memories. Re-reading book chapters, re-watching recorded lectures and re-scanning a set of notes are all examples of review.

ILLUSTRATION 52. THE RIGHT PREFRONTAL CORTEX — OUR CONDUCTOR

"GERMAN CAPITAL"

ILLUSTRATION 53. RECOGNITION MEMORY PART I — CUEING RELEVANT INTERNAL MELODIES

Unfortunately, seeing as review doesn't involve the conductor, it requires almost no effort and does little to strengthen memories.

To get a sense of what I mean, *without closing the book or stealing a peek*, try to describe what the cover of this book looks like. What image/s are there? What writing is there? What colours are used? How is everything arranged? Try to be as specific and comprehensive in your description as possible.

Now, shut the book and take a look.

If you're like most people, you did worse than expected ... maybe a lot worse. This is despite the fact you've likely looked at (*reviewed*) the cover dozens of times. Although review feels like it *should* be beneficial, it rarely is.

If you want to create deep memories, you need to ramp up the effort a notch.

RECOGNITION (EXTERNAL/INTERNAL MIX)

Can you pick out the names of Snow White's seven dwarves from the options below?

Sleepy	Grumpy	Inky	Blinky
Sneezy	Laughy	Hangry	Nervey
Oopsie	Dopey	Cheerie	Drowsy
Doc	Droopy	Happy	Khalesi
Trixie	Bashful	Pinky	Clyde

This type of memory retrieval is called *recognition*. Unlike review, which relies exclusively on external input, recognition combines external and internal processes in order to access memories. Here's how it works:

What is the capital of Germany?

After reading this question, your conductor (right prefrontal cortex) comes to life and gets to work. Using information from the question, it will begin to cue relevant melodies within different parts of your brain. In this instance, it might cue the cellos to start playing 'Germany', and the flutes to start playing 'capital'.

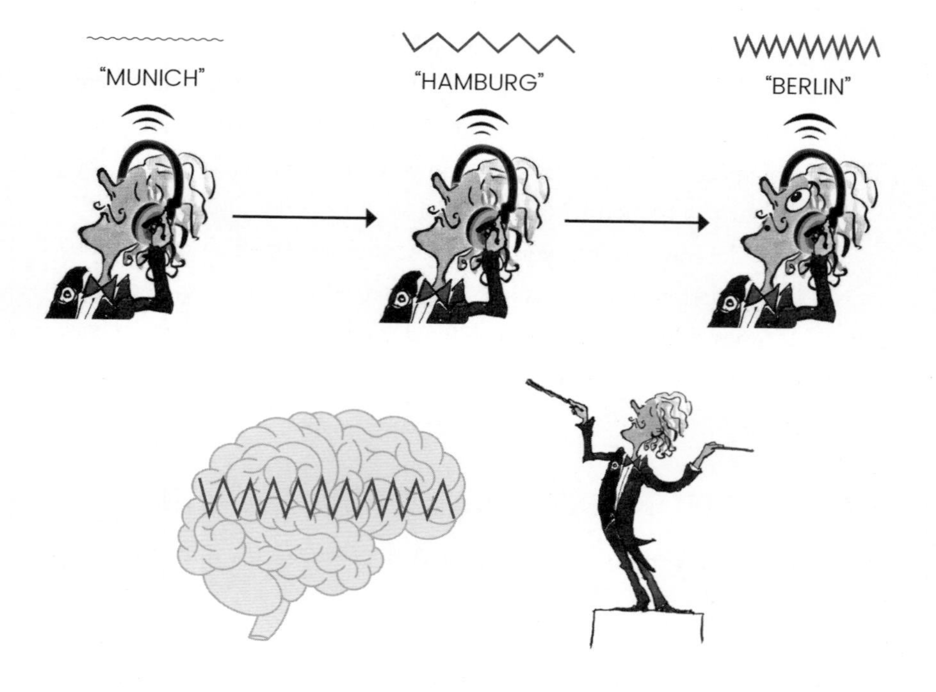

ILLUSTRATION 54. RECOGNITION MEMORY PART II — SELECTING THE MATCHING EXTERNAL MELODY

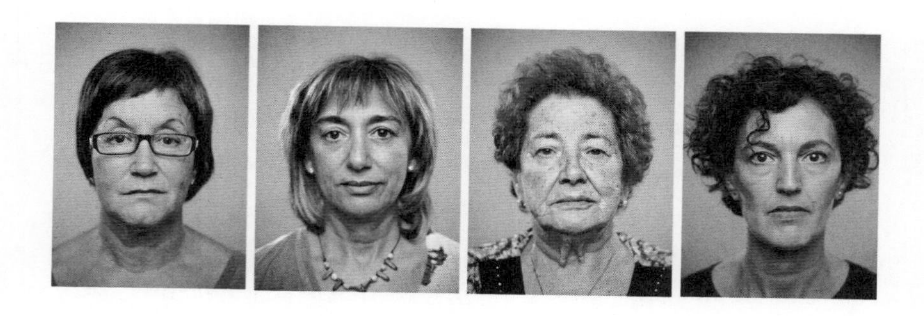

ILLUSTRATION 55. MUGSHOTS

Unfortunately, at this point, only some instruments are playing the 'German capital' melody. As we learnt earlier, we must get the entire orchestra to play the complete symphony in order to retrieve a memory.

Take a look at these three possible answers:

a. Munich
b. Hamburg
c. Berlin.

As you read these options, each triggers a specific pattern within your brain. Meanwhile, your conductor listens closely to these incoming patterns and compares each to the 'German capital' melody it is maintaining. As soon as it hears a match, it will cue the entire orchestra to play the complete 'Berlin is the capital of Germany' symphony.

Recognition is the form of memory retrieval employed during police line-ups. In these instances, witnesses hold onto aspects of the 'crime' melody within parts of their brain as they scan the faces of possible criminals. As soon as they find a match, the conductor cues the complete orchestra and we have our perpetrator!

Let's try it out. At the end of the last chapter, I included a picture of a woman in her kitchen sipping some red wine. *Without flipping back or stealing a peek*, see if you can pick that woman out of the line-up opposite.

Now flip back to p. 166 and have a look.

If you're like most people, you mistakenly selected the woman in the first photo. Herein lies the problem with recognition. When incoming information is *close enough* to a certain melody, the conductor can misinterpret it, incorrectly cue the orchestra and unwittingly create a false memory. In fact, estimates suggest that this type of witness misidentification plays a role in nearly 70 per cent of all wrongful convictions.

Problems aside, recognition will certainly create deeper memories than review — but watch what happens when we ramp the effort up even more …

RECALL (PURELY INTERNAL)

What are the seven deadly sins? (Honestly — give it a minute or two and try to recall each.)

1. ____________________________
2. ____________________________
3. ____________________________
4. ____________________________
5. ____________________________
6. ____________________________
7. ____________________________

Now, flip to the last page of this chapter (p. 192) and check to see how you did …

This type of memory retrieval is called *recall.* Unlike review and recognition, which draw upon the external world for assistance, recall is a purely *internal* process. Here's how it works:

What is the capital of Germany?

As before, after reading this question your conductor will cue the 'German capital' melody within parts of the brain. However, since this time around it has no outside help, it will start cueing various melodies around the brain that it hopes will *guide it* to the memory symphony it's looking for. In this instance, it might cue that German novel you once read; that German film you once saw, that German song you once heard, etc. These related melodies are called *associations*, and the hope is that, by cueing enough associations, the conductor will be able to gather enough clues to piece together the complete 'Berlin is the capital of Germany' symphony by itself.

Every association activated when trying to recall a particular memory will become strongly tied to that memory. This means that, in the future, it will be much easier to recall *'Berlin'* as you will have forged a number of strong association pathways to that

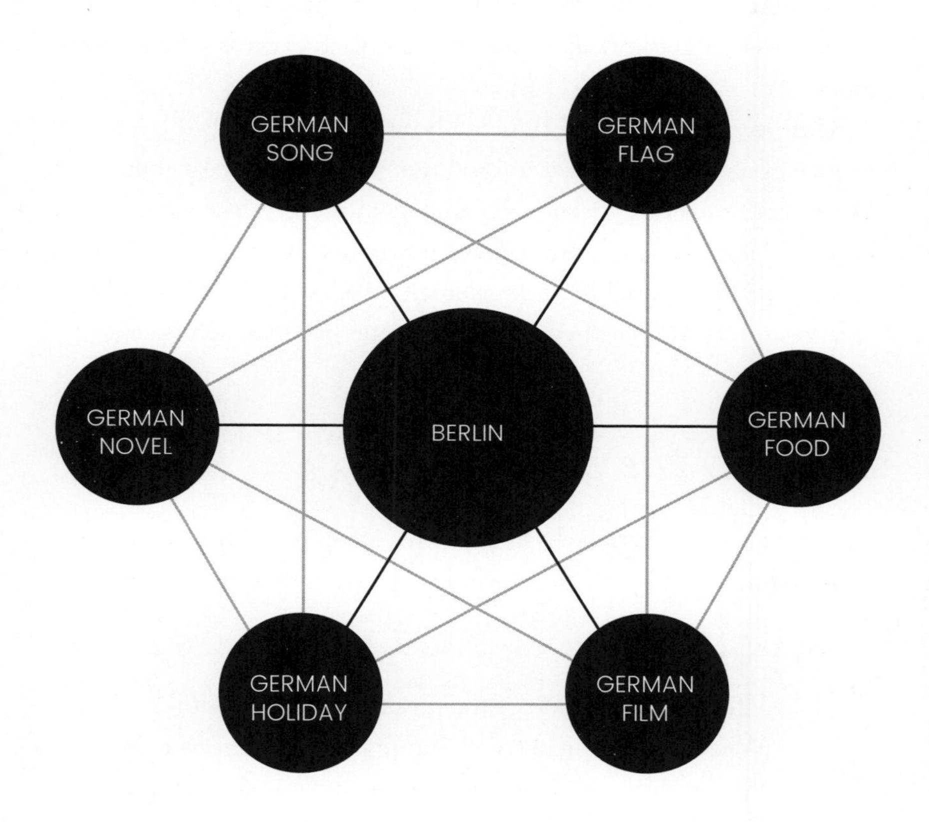

ILLUSTRATION 56. AN ASSOCIATION NETWORK

memory. More importantly, however, every association will also become strongly tied to *every other association*. The German novel, film and song will also become strongly tied together, making each of these memories easier to recall in the future as well. With time (and enough recall) we can create vast, interconnected networks of associations that allow us to quickly and easily access an enormous amount of information.

Unfortunately, just as with the police line-ups, there is the very real chance of recalling incorrect information and creating false memories. When false memories become entangled within a web of associations, entire networks of ideas can become corrupted. As such, it is always a good idea (when possible) to supplement recall with feedback. If recall creates *deep* memories, then feedback creates *accurate* memories.

Back to the beginning

Let's finish as we started — albeit with a small twist. *Without flipping back or stealing a peek*, try to answer the questions below.

» What is one key job of the presupplementary motor cortex?
» What is the name of the brain region that detects errors?
» Where in the brain are environmental stimuli thought to be mapped?

» Episodic and semantic are two forms of which type of memory?
» whatistheancientnamegiventothestylethissentenceis writtenin
» The McGurk Effect refers to which psychological phenomenon?

» What are the titles of the first seven chapters in this book?

1. ______________________________
2. ______________________________
3. ______________________________
4. ______________________________
5. ______________________________
6. ______________________________
7. ______________________________

How'd you do this time around?

If you're like most people, you probably struggled a bit with the first set of questions … despite the fact that you re-read that exact information not a dozen pages ago. This is the impact of *review*: by using purely external support to retrieve information at the start of this chapter, the resulting memories were quite shallow and difficult to access here at the end.

Did you perform a bit better on the second set of questions? This is the impact of *recognition*: by marrying internal and external processes to retrieve information at the start of this chapter, the resulting memories were deeper and somewhat easier to access here at the end.

Finally, if you're like most people, you probably did quite well with the third set of questions. This is the impact of *recall*: by relying on purely internal processes (combined with feedback) at the start of this chapter, the resulting memories were deep, accurate and easy to access here at the end.

Implications for leaders, teachers and coaches

1. Embed retrieval (especially recall) into sessions

Many people assume retrieval is a trivial process only relevant during final performance.

Now that you understand the essential role retrieval (especially recall) plays in memory, you can guess the negative impact this assumption might have. Rather than postponing retrieval, find ways to embed it within lessons and practice time. Ask people to verbally explain a process or topic; include low- or no-stakes quizzes before, during and after presentations; select a specific fact or concept and brainstorm relevant associations.

Ensuring there are ample opportunities to retrieve information during and between sessions will deepen memory, improve understanding and boost performance.

BURNING QUESTION 1:

SUPPORT

'Is it okay to offer hints when people can't recall an idea, or is it better to leave them struggling?'

There are two distinct types of recall: *free* and *cued*.

Free recall is when we are left to our own devices to access a specific memory. Cued recall is when we are supplied with external guidance to help lead us to a specific memory.

Cued recall is different than recognition. During recognition, people are supplied with the correct answer (Berlin, in our earlier example) and need only identify it. During cued recall, people are supplied with *associations* (remember that German film you saw last week?) and must still come up with the correct answer themselves. For this reason, cued recall leads to deeper memories than recognition (though free recall beats them both).

A good rule of thumb is to embrace cued recall when people are first learning new material. In this way, you can highlight the importance of associations and help others *build* effective association networks. As learning progresses, however, begin to pull back and move into free recall. This will ensure they *strengthen* associations and form truly deep memories.

BURNING QUESTION 2:

TIP-OF-THE-TONGUE

'Sometimes, when writing or speaking, I know what word I want to say … I simply can't come up with it. What's up with that?'

This phenomenon is called the Tip-of-the-Tongue Effect and although nobody yet knows the exact reason why it happens, most theories revolve around recall.

As we learnt earlier, to recall a memory (in this case, a specific word) the conductor will cue a set of associations with the hopes they will guide it to the correct symphony. When Tip-of-the-Tongue occurs, people can typically remember the first letter of the word they want to say ... what the word sounds like ... the last book they read it in ... etc. These are all associations the conductor is using to try to access the correct word — unfortunately, none are working.

To address this, many people shift into *recognition*; essentially playing charades with the hopes that someone else will guess the word, say it aloud and externally trigger the symphony.

If you are ever alone when Tip-of-the-Tongue occurs (say, when writing a book), there are three steps to address it. First, quickly write down a list of all the associations you can activate (What does the word rhyme with? How many letters are in it?). Second, move on to something else. When you stop focusing on the word, it will likely pop into your mind five to ten minutes later. Third, once you've got the word, write it down next to the association list. In this way, you can explicitly re-link the word to the relevant associations, thereby making it easier to access in the future.

2. Open-book exams don't lead to deep memories

When people are allowed to consult notes, textbooks or the internet during an exam or performance, they are not learning how to internally *maintain* and *recall* information. Instead, they are learning how to externally *locate* and *recognize* information.

Don't get me wrong — the ability to locate and recognize information is an incredibly important skill and, in fact, might be exactly what you hope to pass along to others. For instance, rather than asking customer service reps to memorize hundreds of standard responses to common questions, it might make more sense to train them how to quickly locate each on a digital system.

As such, I am not arguing for one form of exam over another. I am simply saying that, if your ultimate aim is to help others internalize a specific set of ideas and form deep, lasting memories, then open-book exams work in opposition to this goal.

BURNING QUESTION 3:

DIGITAL DEMENTIA

'Is technology killing our memory?'

Here's an experiment that will only work for readers of a certain age. First, answer this question:

What was your childhood phone number?

Now answer this one:

What is your current best friend's phone number?

I have no problem rattling off a dozen numbers from my youth, despite the fact I've not dialled any of them for decades. Yet, I have no idea what numbers are in my smartphone contact list, despite the fact I sent texts to half of them yesterday.

Though it would be easy to interpret this as 'technology killing memory', that doesn't appear to be the case (if it were, why haven't those childhood phone numbers disappeared?). In reality, technology simply appears to be changing *how* and *what* we remember.

Digital devices cater to *review* and *recognition* memory. Rather than bringing up internal information, we need only sift through external information. Importantly, the ability to organize and search through external information requires an incredible amount of internal memory (we must remember where to look, how to search, what purpose the information will serve, etc.). As such, though we might not be able to recall a specific fact, we certainly can recall how to access and engage Google in order to quickly and easily bring it up, and recognize the fact when we see it.

I realize this is a highly charged topic so I won't dive any deeper here. My intention is not to praise or vilify technology — it's merely to point out that technology engages a different form of memory retrieval than we have historically favoured.

3. Utilize flashcards with recall and feedback

Flashcards. One of the oldest study techniques is still one of the greatest ... as long as it's done correctly. The secret is to create flashcards that embrace *recall* and *feedback.*

FLIP OVER

ILLUSTRATION 57. USE NOTECARDS WITH FEEDBACK TO EXERCISE RECALL

On each card, write a free-response question on one side and the relevant answer on the other. As people read each question, this will trigger specific melodies, cue relevant associations and strengthen memory symphonies. Afterwards, when they flip over the card and read the correct answer, this will protect against false memories.

BURNING QUESTION 4:

DROP-OUTS

'When using flashcards, should I drop questions I get correct and only continue with questions I missed?'

Many people see flashcards as 'one-and-done'— if I successfully recall a fact once, why waste any more time studying it? Unfortunately, dropping cards is a bad idea for two reasons.

First, remember the jungle path? The more we recall a memory, the easier it will be to access that memory in the future. As such, ditching each flashcard we get correct will reduce the number of times that particular information is recalled, which may hurt our ability to access it later.

Second, when we study a set of ideas together we begin to form an association network between those ideas: the backbone of recall. When we drop cards we get correct (and continue to study only those facts we get wrong) we essentially pull a node out of this network and reduce the number of associations we can use in the future to access each fact.

So don't ditch facts as you learn them. Keep flashcards together in order to construct a large, reliable web of associations.

4. Employ recall post-meetings

It's never too early to start recalling.

Immediately after a presentation, meeting or training session, ask people to put away their notes and spend a few minutes free-recalling key information and ideas from the preceding lesson. Not only will this help to solidify memories, it will also allow you (as the leader, teacher or coach) to quickly judge which concepts are sticking and which may require additional coverage.

Additionally, ask people to pair up and discuss/compare *what* they recall and *how* they understand this information. This will allow people to begin constructing an association network around newly learnt material.

Compared to simply standing up and leaving, a short recall and discussion session can lead to deeper memories, greater understanding and broader connections.

BURNING QUESTION 5:

HIGHLIGHTING

'Is it worthwhile highlighting as I read?'

Absolutely. Highlighting text is a great technique to help guide your eyes, focus your attention on key topics and locate key ideas.

Unfortunately, highlighting won't deepen your memory.

Typically, people highlight with the intention of returning to and reviewing material at some point in the future. The operative word in that sentence is 'review'. As you now know, when you simply go back and re-read a piece of text this will do almost nothing to strengthen memories for that material.

A better idea would be to return to highlighted text, translate that information into your own words, then develop a set of free-response questions (flashcards) using that material. As you can guess, this shift from review into recall can generate the learning and memory boost most people seek through highlighting.

5. If learning and memory aren't your goal, embrace recognition

Sometimes, recall is unimportant. User interface design; office organization; website development. In these instances, ensuring others can quickly and easily locate items is far more important than ensuring they can recall those items.

When forming deep, accessible memories is not a primary goal it makes more sense to embrace recognition. Clearly label important items; use icons to represent the function of particular buttons; employ cues to help people recognize where they're at (and where they're going). In addition, when employing recognition to boost ease of use, maintain consistency across variations, versions and iterations of a particular program or device. Using the same labels, icons and cues will ensure people will always be able to quickly access whatever tool or function they require.

Just remember: if you embrace recognition, do not expect others to be able to recall specific details in the future. To see what I mean, ask yourself: does the top of the Apple logo have a stem, a leaf, or a stem and a leaf?

ILLUSTRATION 58. EMBRACE RECOGNITION WHEN RECALL IS UNIMPORTANT

The seven deadly sins

Envy
Gluttony
Greed
Lust
Pride
Sloth
Wrath

AT A GLANCE

Recall leads to stronger, deeper and more accessible memories.

- » The more a memory is retrieved, the more memorable it will become.
- » Memories can be retrieved via review, recognition or recall.
- » Review leads to shallow memories. Recognition leads to decent (if fleeting) memories. Recall leads to deep memories.
- » Recall is facilitated by association networks: links between related ideas or concepts.

APPLICATIONS

1. Embed retrieval (especially recall) into sessions.
   - » Cued recall helps people build association networks while free recall helps strengthen associations.
2. Open-book exams don't lead to deep memories.
   - » Technology is not killing memory, it is simply changing *what* and *how* we remember.
3. Utilize flashcards with recall and feedback.
   - » Don't discard flashcards once you get them correct.
4. Employ recall post-meetings.
   - » Highlighting text while reading doesn't help strengthen memories.
5. If learning and memory aren't your goals, embrace recognition.

1952

GET A-HEAD!

FOR ADULTS
AT
NO CHARGE

ADULT EDUCATION
CLASSES

MANY COURSES · · MANY PLACES

Intermission 4

Please take around 15 seconds to study and enjoy this old adult education poster.

9.

Priming

> Once an idea gets into your head, it's probably going to stay there.
>
> — *Eliezer Yudkowsky*

I'm not usually a huge fan of riddles. I tend to file them under the same category as dad jokes, reality TV and high school: fun at the time, but embarrassing to look back on.

With that said, I came across a riddle a couple of years ago that I've not been able to shake.

What's wrong with this scenario?

A boy and his father have been exposed to a disease. Sadly, the father rapidly develops a tumour and dies. The boy survives but desperately needs an operation and is rushed to the hospital. A surgeon is called. Upon entering the room and seeing the patient, the surgeon exclaims, 'Oh no! I can't do the operation. That's my son!'

To understand why this riddle has stuck with me, we need to explore a concept called priming.

What's happening?

ILLUSTRATION 59. TOILETRIES

In the last chapter we learnt that every memory is bound to a number of associations that can be activated in order to support recall.

What I failed to mention is that once associations are activated *they do not immediately shut down*. Instead, much like a plucked guitar string, associations continue to resonate throughout the brain for an extended period.

To get a sense of what I mean, try to complete the word below:

S _ _ P

You could have selected *ship*, *soup*, *slap*, *stop* or any other number of words. But I'm guessing you selected *soap*. This is because the echoes of the towel, shampoo and shower head images above were still reverberating within your mind and you used these as a lens through which to decipher the word.

This is priming in a nutshell. As you're now well aware, the brain is an advanced prediction machine. One prediction it frequently makes is that whatever *has occurred* in the recent past will be relevant to whatever *will occur* in the near future (cause-and-effect). For this reason, the brain holds onto recent patterns of thought and uses these as a guide to perceive and understand new incoming information.

Let's see this in action:

Which planet is seventh from the sun?

As you read that question, activity throughout your brain likely increased. This isn't because the question was particularly difficult; it's simply because the question had absolutely nothing to do with any topic we've recently been discussing. This means you (and your brain) had to invest conscious effort into recalling Uranus. In other words, you were not primed.

Now try this one:

Roast Most Host Ghost Post
What food goes into a toaster?

As you read that question, activity throughout your brain likely decreased. Again, this isn't because the question was any easier; it's simply because the echo from the preceding list of words quickly and easily guided you to the answer without any additional effort required. In other words, you were primed.

Here's the rub: did you incorrectly answer 'toast' for the question above … or did you correctly answer 'bread'? This is the trick with priming: it works even when the activated associations are not ideally suited for the task at hand.

Although priming comes in dozens of unique flavours, there are three distinct categories highly relevant to influencing.

CONCEPT PRIMING

Can you fill in the blanks to determine this common word?
_ E X _ G _ _

Arguably the easiest (and most utilized) form of priming is called concept priming. This is when specific facts or categories are activated in order to guide how others interpret and comprehend new information.

If you're like most people, you probably had a bit of trouble solving the word puzzle above. Now, let's do some concept priming:

Circle   *Triangle*   *Square*   *Pentagon*

Returning to the word puzzle, does it now seem to solve itself? Of course, the word is 'hexagon'. This is the power of concept priming. By activating relevant facts and allowing them to echo throughout your mind, you can more easily decipher seemingly difficult material. This is why many school teachers spend the first 10 minutes of each class reviewing material learnt in previous lessons: they are conceptually priming students in order to make new ideas easier to situate and remember.

Concept priming is the cornerstone of advertising. In fact, the next time you're watching television pay close attention to how each commercial is sequenced. Rather than jumping straight into the product or service, most will open with a blatantly emotional scene: maybe a happy family laughing around the dinner table, an intimate couple kissing in a hot air balloon, or a dusty man fishing in a wild river. This short vignette is a *concept prime* meant to trigger a specific emotion. Later, when the product being sold is finally revealed, you can't help but interpret it through the lens of that emotion resonating throughout your brain ('I never knew an internet service provider could bring me so much joy!').

EXPECTANCY PRIMING

> *It's a scientifically established fact that males have a larger 'calculation' region of the brain than females. This is why men typically outperform women on tests of maths ability.*

You've probably heard this statement before (or something similar to it). It certainly sounds compelling … too bad it's complete and utter nonsense. Believe it or not, there is no single 'calculation' region in the brain and (as long as they undergo similar schooling) both sexes will perform equally well on maths exams.

Here's the twist: if people hear this statement immediately before taking a maths exam, everything changes. Reminding women they are supposed to be poor at maths can greatly impair their performance, while reminding men they are supposed to be good at maths can greatly boost theirs. In a very real sense, a demonstrably false argument can quickly morph into a self-fulfilling prophecy.

This phenomenon is called expectancy priming and it serves to activate specific expectations or beliefs in order to guide how others perceive, understand and react to various circumstances.

In this instance, activating the 'maths/gender' expectancy doesn't cause anyone to suddenly remember or forget basic maths facts. Rather, this prime changes how people respond to difficulties. Women primed with low expectations will be more likely to interpret struggle as a sign of their natural shortcomings and quit at the first sign of challenge. On the other hand, men primed with high expectations will be more likely to interpret struggle as a call-to-arms and ramp-up their efforts at the first sign of challenge.

Importantly, this process is a two-way street. Although expectations can be *internally* directed and used to understand our own thoughts and behaviours, they can also be *externally* directed and used to understand the thoughts and behaviours *of others.*

As an example, ask two different groups of people to read and evaluate the exact same student essay. Beforehand, tell the first group the essay was written by a highly intelligent student who always earns top marks. Conversely, tell the second group the essay was written by an extremely lazy student who is barely passing. Can you guess what will happen? Despite everyone reading identical words, those primed to believe the essay comes from a star student will almost certainly rate it higher than those primed to believe it comes from a slacker.

External expectancies are the reason why food tastes better when we're told it was prepared by a celebrity chef; why wine tastes sweeter when we're told it was bottled by a famous vintner; why water tastes fresher when we're told it was collected from a pristine Arctic glacier. And don't underestimate the power of this type of priming within journalism ...

COURT OVERTURNS ARSON VERDICT

MELBOURNE - A Federal judge has overturned his previous 'guilty' verdict from a 2014 arson case. After reviewing the case, the judge deemed the evidence too '*circumstantial and ambiguous.*' Thomas Jones, originally convicted of setting a bush-fire that destroyed two homes, will be released from prison having served three years of his original 5-year sentence.

VS

CONVICTED ARSONIST ON THE LOOSE!

MELBOURNE - A Federal judge has overturned his previous 'guilty' verdict from a 2014 arson case. After reviewing the case, the judge deemed the evidence too '*circumstantial and ambiguous.*' Thomas Jones, originally convicted of setting a bush-fire that destroyed two homes, will be released from prison having served three years of his original 5-year sentence.

ILLUSTRATION 60. HEADLINES ARE EXPECTANCY PRIMES

ILLUSTRATION 61. I SUPPOSE I SHOULD EAT MORE CHIPS

STRATEGY PRIMING

Can you solve this problem without using a calculator?
(Reminder: volume = length x width x height.)
If you dig into the mud a rectangular hole that is 2 metres (6½ feet) wide by 3.5 metres (11½ feet) long and 5 metres (16½ feet) deep, what is the total volume of mud in the hole?

In a simple experiment, researchers divided people into two different groups, gave each a large bowl of potato chips and sat everyone down to watch a couple of hours of television. The first group watched programs interspersed with generic commercials (cars, banks, clothing, etc.), while the second group watched the same programs interspersed with commercials featuring people happily munching away on potato chips. Believe it or not, those people who watched the snack food commercials ate more potato chips than those who watched generic commercials.

Okay, before you file this away under the 'common sense' category, let's quickly explore why this happened. The phenomenon being investigated here is called strategy priming. Unlike concept priming (which activates facts) and expectancy priming (which activates expectations), strategy priming serves to activate a very specific *procedure* or *approach* to guide how people tackle future tasks. In this instance, the act of watching people on television eat potato chips primed the strategy 'when you see potato chips, eat them'— which is precisely what people did.

As with all primes, this process can go astray. Looking at the hole-digging question above, the strategy being primed was 'multiplication'. Chances are you mentally calculated the volume of the hole (35 cubic metres/376 cubic feet). However, take another look at the question without this prime:

If you dig into the mud a rectangular hole that is 2 metres (6½ feet) wide by 3.5 metres (11½ feet) long and

5 metres (16½ feet) deep, what is the total volume of mud in the hole?

This time, you likely noticed that there's no need to multiply anything; in fact, the numbers are quite meaningless. By definition, a hole has no mud in it, so the correct answer is 'zero'.

Back to the start

Let's return to the riddle at the start of this chapter. The reason I find this so intriguing is that it employs each of the three types of priming explored above. Re-read it now and see if you can pick out each prime:

What's wrong with this scenario?

A boy and his father have been exposed to a disease. Sadly, the father rapidly develops a tumour and dies. The boy survives, but desperately needs an operation and is rushed to the hospital. A surgeon is called. Upon entering the room and seeing the patient, the surgeon exclaims, 'Oh no! I can't do the operation. That's my son!'

Concept prime: The riddle opens by repeating the words 'father' and 'boy' twice in close proximity. These words serve to activate the 'male relationship' association. For this reason, when people read the word 'son' at the end of the riddle, many interpret it as referencing this masculine connection.

Expectancy prime: Though it is slowly changing, medicine has historically been a male-dominated field. The word 'hospital' in the middle of the riddle serves to activate this 'masculine' expectation. For this reason, when people read the word 'surgeon' at the end of the riddle, many interpret it through this masculine lens.

Strategy prime: The riddle opens by asking 'What is wrong?'. This phrase suggests there is a problem somewhere and serves to activate an 'error-seeking' strategy. For this reason, when people read through the riddle, many actively search for flaws in logic, language, grammar, etc.

Once you strip away all these primes, it quickly becomes clear that this is no riddle at all: it's just a simple story about a boy, his father and his mother.

The catch

When you are in complete control of a meeting or session, you can use priming to quickly and easily guide learners along whichever path you wish them to travel. Unfortunately, rarely (if ever) are we in complete control. In reality, people are constantly activating their own concepts, expectancies and strategies, which may contradict any primes you try to establish. This is why many researchers are quick to point out that, although primes may work well in heavily controlled, artificial laboratory settings, they can prove quite fragile and unpredictable in messy, real-world situations.

As such, there are two important things to keep in mind when considering how best to apply priming to boost influence. First: never depend on a prime. Because they are finicky and may not always work, do not use primes to replace other, more reliable strategies explored throughout this book. Instead, use primes to support and supplement these strategies. Second: be clear about what you want a prime to achieve. Knowing the specific outcome you desire will ensure that, should a prime fail, you will be ready to jump in and employ other methods to guide learners.

By all means, have fun with priming — just don't put all your eggs in this one basket. It's best to think of this as a secondary strategy which adds icing to your primary strategy cake. A cake without icing is still a cake; it just might not taste as sweet.

Implications for leaders, teachers and coaches

1. Feel your way through first impressions

Love them or hate them, first impressions exist. After being introduced to a new person or situation, it typically takes people less than 30 seconds to make a judgment and activate relevant expectations. Interestingly, a peek at the brain reveals that first impressions are rarely influenced by logic or conscious deliberation; rather, they are driven by the amygdala — the emotional epicentre of the brain. This means that, when it comes to making a first impression, we need to consider which *feelings* will best guide others along the path we desire.

As an example, when presenting I typically wear casual clothing and begin with a free-flowing, full-group conversation. I do this because the feeling (first impression) I desire to generate is one of safety: I want everyone to feel secure enough to participate and confident that their voice will be heard.

Once I was asked to wear a suit and tie when working with a group of young children. As you can guess, the first impression set was one of authority which, in turn, caused the students to feel intimidated and sit quietly throughout the entire lesson. Regardless of how hard I tried, the die had been cast and I couldn't break their silence or inspire them to interact. In the end this didn't stop anyone from learning, but it did lead them to interpret everything through a more didactic, academic lens than I desired.

BURNING QUESTION 1:

MAKE IT AND BREAK IT

'Is it true that first impressions last forever?'

Good news: first impressions can be broken — though perhaps not in the manner you might expect.

It's intuitive to assume that first impressions naturally fade with time; that if you spend enough time with people you initially dislike, you will slowly come to recognize their strengths and eventually grow to like them. Unfortunately, impressions don't gradually melt away like candle wax. Instead, they flip on a dime.

Seeing as first impressions are formed via an emotional reaction, breaking an impression requires a stronger, *counter*-emotional reaction. For instance, if your first impression of me is one of fear, then months of me telling you I'm not a scary person would do very little to change this. However, if I slipped on a banana peel, this might flip your impression to silliness. If I wrapped a shivering dog in a warm blanket, this might flip your impression to comfort. If I told you a heartbreaking story from my past, this might flip your impression to sympathy.

Feelings to make an impression; feelings to break an impression.

2. Get on the same page; get on the right page

It would be a mistake to assume that everyone will enter a meeting, presentation or practice session with the same associations echoing through their minds. Some people might be thinking about breakfast, others about an upcoming deadline, and others about a new TV show. If we know that these lingering associations will impact how people interpret and remember new information, then it makes sense to devote time to ensuring everyone is on the same page and is thinking about the same facts.

Beyond this, it's equally important to ensure everyone is thinking about the *right* facts. If you open a meeting by allowing people to vent their frustrations over the pitiful vending machine selection, then everyone will no doubt be on the same page — but this likely won't be the best page to guide their understanding (lest you want them to view your material through a slightly negative lens).

As such, it's not a bad idea to steal a play from the 'good teacher's handbook' and devote the first five to ten minutes of a session to reviewing and activating *relevant* facts. Importantly, this review need not be boring: in fact, this is a wonderful opportunity to implement recall strategies (deliver a game-show style quiz, for example), error strategies (build common misconceptions), narrative strategies (weave a compelling story), etc.

It's worth noting, however, that there might be times when you *do not* want others on the same page. For instance, if you're interested in facilitating an exchange of opinions, engendering novel connections or helping others put a personal spin on different ideas, then concept priming may actually hinder these goals. Only lead others down a particular path when that path serves your intentions.

3. Warm-ups drive performance

Just as with facts, the first strategy we activate can influence how others interpret and tackle future tasks. If you open a session with a debate, people will be more inclined to take a critical stance towards the information you present. If you open with a compare/contrast discussion, people will be more inclined to look for broader patterns and connections within the information you present. If you open with a memorization task, people will be more inclined to focus on the minute details of the information you present.

Being clear with the strategy you want others to utilize during a presentation, lesson or training session will help you determine and design initial (review) tasks accordingly.

4. Embrace blind assessment

As we have learnt, external expectations can influence how we understand and judge the work of others. Simply being aware that a disliked colleague is involved in a particular project might lead us to reject potentially incredible ideas. Similarly, simply being aware that a beloved friend is involved in a different project might drive us to accept less-than-stunning ideas.

Whenever possible, strive to assess material in a 'blind' fashion. Skip over cover pages, block out prominent names, ignore letterheads. By keeping secret the authors, affiliations and/or origins of a particular piece of work, you can reduce the chance of activating an external expectancy prime and increase the chance of more accurately judging the merits of an idea.

BURNING QUESTION 2:

BATTLE OF THE SEXES PART 2

'Wait … do men and women have different brains or not?'

One of the brains on the next page is from a man, the other is from a woman. Can you pick which is which?

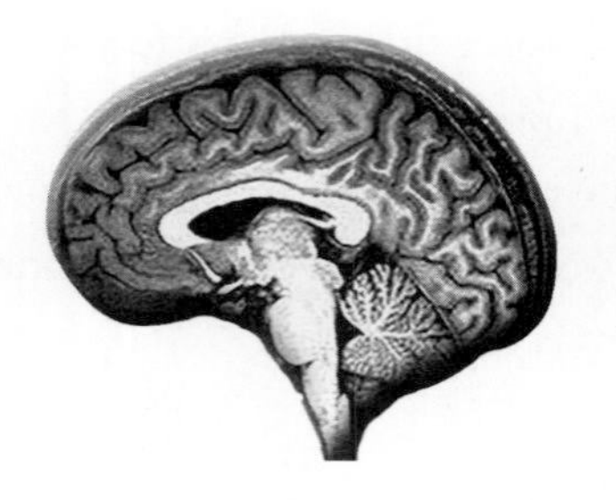
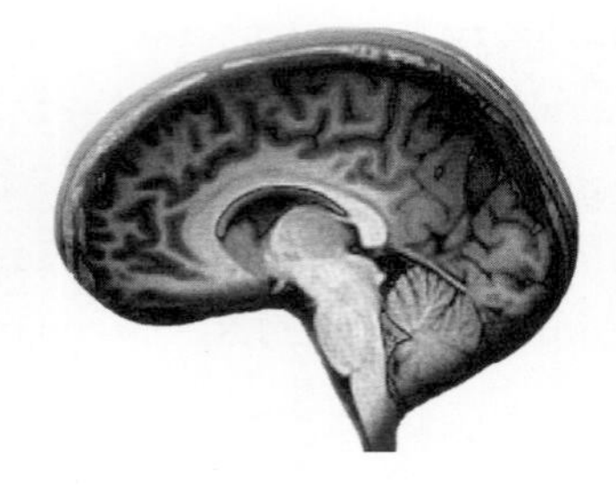

ILLUSTRATION 62. MALE VS FEMALE BRAIN — WHICH IS WHICH?

Here's the joke: neither can anyone else! In fact, if you ask 100 brain scientists to play this game, exactly *zero* will be able to consistently and accurately differentiate between male and female brains.

Back in Chapter 5 we learnt that different sexes aren't better or worse at multitasking — different individuals are (regardless of sex). The same is true here. Brains are not organized along gender lines. Rather, they morph and change according to emotions, environments, experiences, etc. Just like fingerprints, each brain is wholly unique and individual.

For this reason, it makes little sense to speak of a 'male brain' and a 'female brain': the singular term 'brain' will suffice.

5. Demonstrate cognitive strategies

We tend to think of strategies as something we *do*. For this reason, when demonstrating a particular process or procedure, most people focus on the physical motions. The goal is simple: when people see how an expert completes a particular task, they will be able to mimic and learn it themselves.

Without a doubt, physical demonstration is one of the most effective teaching techniques available — so use it often and liberally. However, it's important to recognize that strategies are not only physical; they are also *mental.* As such, it's an equally good idea to explicitly highlight the *thinking processes* that underpin different strategies.

As a simple example, imagine I was teaching you multiplication. Rather than only walking you through the behavioural process of multiplying numbers down and across, I could also verbalize how I mentally approach and assess these types of problems. For instance, I might explain: 'First, I look for any mathematical signs to determine which procedure to utilize (in this instance, I see a "cross" sign so know I will be doing multiplication). Next, I ensure the two columns are lined up correctly ...' and so on.

Knowing how to *think about* a process can help people apply and adapt it across varied situations.

As an added bonus, many people never explicitly consider what they are thinking when undertaking particular tasks. The act of verbalizing and explicitly teaching an otherwise subconscious thought process can actually help you (as a leader, teacher or coach) to better understand, tweak and evolve your own practices.

BURNING QUESTION 3:

AWARENESS

'Is priming permanent, or is there an escape?'

It is ridiculously easy to break a prime. All it takes is awareness.

Remember the 'roast–toast' rhyming prime we saw earlier? With that in mind, take a look at this:

Joke Poke Smoke Soak Broke

What's the white of an egg called?

I'm guessing you didn't say *yolk*, even though the prime was leading you down that path. This is because simply knowing that a prime was in play was enough to allow you to recognize and negate it. Luckily, awareness appears to work for all types of primes. For instance, women who recognize the 'maths/gender' expectancy prime typically perform just fine on maths exams.

Be careful though: awareness can lead people to react against a prime and swing the pendulum in the opposing direction. For instance, some people who are aware that the name of a fancy chef is being used to make a meal taste better will actually rate the food worse than if they had never been primed at all. As mentioned above, don't ever overestimate the power of primes: they are fragile and can backfire if you over-rely on them.

BURNING QUESTION 4:

INOCULATION

'Sure, if someone explicitly points out a prime I can break it … but what about primes I'm not consciously aware of? Is there a way to protect against those?'

The secret to inoculating yourself is to predict what potential influence/s a future prime might have and develop a specific plan to address this *before it occurs*. We typically refer to this process as building an 'if–then' plan.

The concept is simple: once you've set a goal (for example, 'I want to deliver a 30-minute presentation'), spend a few minutes projecting into the future and consider any potential impediments to that goal ('I might become distracted and lose my train of thought'). Next, decide upon a specific set of actions you will undertake if these impediments occur ('*If* I lose my train of thought, *then* I will ask the audience to remind me of the last sentence I spoke').

By creating this 'if–then' plan, you will become almost hyperaware of any primes that may lead to distraction and cause you to lose your train of thought (such as the expectancy prime of someone reminding you of a poor presentation from your past). As we saw above, once you're aware of a prime, that prime will no longer work. This means that the very act of developing a contingency plan *in case* a prime occurs is typically enough to negate and inoculate you against primes.

AT A GLANCE

Pre-activate facts, expectations and strategies to influence others' learning.

- » The brain holds onto recent associations and links them to new information (cause-and-effect).
- » Exploiting this pattern is called *priming.*
- » *Concept* primes activate facts and guide comprehension.
- » *Expectancy* primes activate expectations and guide perception and/or reaction.
- » *Strategy* primes activate procedures and guide performance.

APPLICATIONS

1. Feel your way through first impressions.
   - » Feelings to make an impression; feelings to break an impression.
2. Get on the same page; get on the right page.
3. Warm-ups drive performance.
4. Embrace *blind* assessment.
   - » We have yet to find consistent differences between male and female brains.
5. Demonstrate cognitive strategies.
   - » Knowledge of a prime can break its influence.
   - » Use 'if–then' plans to anticipate and negate possible primes.

10.

Story

> Disconnected facts in the mind are like unlinked pages on the web: they might as well not exist.
>
> — *Steven Pinker*

In a chapter dedicated to story, it would only make sense to open with a compelling narrative; perhaps a tale from my childhood that weaves together pulse-pounding action and heart-wrenching sorrow in a way that rekindles humanity's faith in the power of love …

By now, you've probably realized that I rarely take the 'traditional' route. As such, rather than *me* trying to come up with the perfect story, I'm going to ask *you* to do the heavy lifting.

For these activities, you'll need a timer and (eventually) something to write with and to write on.

Round 1

Below is a list of words. Your job is to spend 60 seconds trying to memorize as much of this list as possible. During this round, as you study, try to visualize each word in your mind's eye.

Set your timer and begin!

ball	house	boat
bicycle	dog	flowers
movie	child	chair
hand	goose	glasses
phone	bottle	book

Great. Now let's quickly play another round, except this time I'm going to switch one small thing:

Round 2

Below is a new list of words. As before, your job is to spend 60 seconds trying to memorize as much of this list as possible. However, during this round, rather than visualizing each word I'd like you to try to link each word together into a coherent story. If you read 'caterpillar', 'hat' and 'apple' you might create the simple story, 'The hungry caterpillar wearing a cowboy hat ate through the juicy apple.'

Set your timer and begin!

restaurant	car	vase
witch	candy	table
lizard	suit	laptop
tooth	foot	hat
leaf	heart	lamp

Awesome. We will come back to this experiment a bit later. For now, just let those lists percolate away in your subconscious as we switch gears and focus on something new …

Memory landmarks

Throughout this book, I've shared a number of stories. There was the one about scuba divers memorizing words underwater; the one about Henry Molaison having his hippocampus removed and never again forming a new declarative memory; the one about me watching Abba sing *Dancing Queen* for the very first time.

Sure, these anecdotes were interesting and (hopefully) enjoyable to read — but there's a deeper reason why I chose to include each. To understand, let's take a quick jaunt through the world of urban design.

Back in the days before pocket maps and GPS, people needed a quick and easy way to navigate ever-expanding and increasingly confusing towns. The solution: erect an incredibly tall tower, spire or statue in the middle of the city. As long as this monument was taller than the surrounding buildings, anyone could easily spot it and use it as a simple landmark to orient themselves, determine where they were at, and work out which direction they were heading.

It turns out, memory isn't much different. As you're now well aware, every memory is tied to a number of associations. As association networks grow and expand, it can become increasingly difficult to locate and organize information. As such, to help navigate these networks, we need landmarks: incredibly prominent memories that help us orient ourselves and make sense of linked facts.

Cue stories.

Stories are like mental Eiffel Towers: they create prominent, indelible impressions within our minds, making them ideal *memory landmarks* around which to construct and organize association networks.

This is why I told you about my great uncle chipping golf balls with an old shovel. Sure, the story may have been interesting in its own right — but I was using it as a landmark to arrange and link subsequent concepts. My great uncle is now a central hub granting easy access to the concepts of context-dependent learning, state-dependent learning, episodic memories, semantic memories, etc.

Before we dive into *why* stories are so memorable, it's worth first defining precisely what a story is.

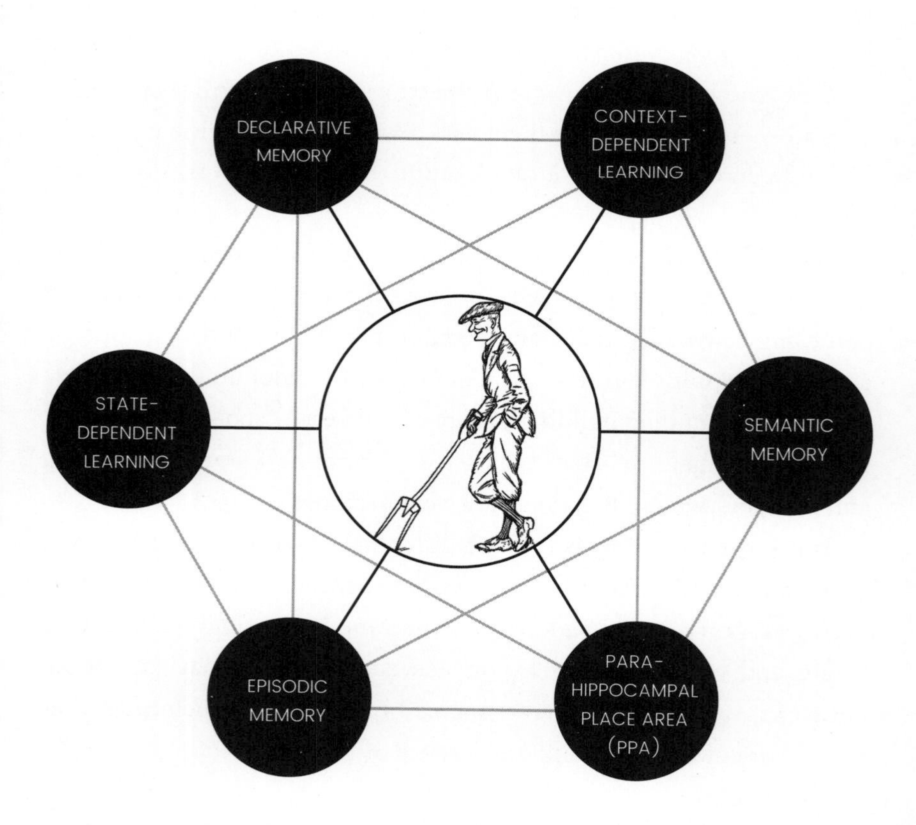

ILLUSTRATION 63. ASSOCIATION NETWORK TIED TO MY GREAT UNCLE

Sto ... ree?

The debate over what is and is not a story has been raging for thousands of years. From Aristotle to Stephen King, it seems everyone has an opinion and no one can agree on a single definition. Luckily, there are several commonalities we can siphon out to help clarify this tricky term. By no means will this solve the millennia-long debate, but it should suffice for our modest purposes.

In its simplest form, a story must contain three elements:

1. a physical thrust
2. a psychological thrust
3. an audience.

A PHYSICAL THRUST

Stories are largely composed of actions: these are isolated events, moments or facts. For instance, *the dog barked*; *the cat climbed a tree*; *the squirrel fainted*. These are all actions.

As you can see, simply listing several actions does not make a story. Rather, these actions must be linked together into a clear *cause-and-effect* sequence called a *plot*. For instance, 'Because the dog barked, the cat climbed a tree which, in turn, made the squirrel faint'. Now we're building a story.

A PSYCHOLOGICAL THRUST

A story must also contain mental and emotional elements that either reflect or drive the plot. This psychological thrust gives rise to characters, motives and meaning. For instance, 'Because the angry dog barked, the cat became scared and climbed a tree to escape. Thinking the cat was going to eat it, the squirrel fainted in a melodramatic fashion to trick the cat into thinking it was dead.' Now we've got a story!

It is worth noting that these psychological elements allow for exactly the same plot to take on a myriad of variations. For instance, 'Because I didn't make the sale, I *ashamedly* quit my job' and 'Because

I didn't make the sale, I *begrudgingly* quit my job' share the same plot but are vastly different stories. In fact:

Which book, film or television program is this plot describing?

- The lead character realizes s/he has lost (or desperately needs) a particular object …
- Because of this, s/he leaves home and goes searching for this object …
- During this search, s/he encounters many different people and situations …
- Due to these encounters, s/he learns a lot about her/himself and discovers her/his own capabilities …
- By the time the lead character finds the object of desire, s/he has already evolved into a new and different person.

This *physical thrust* is the backbone of stories ranging from *The Odyssey* to *Finding Nemo*; from *Alice in Wonderland* to *Dumb and Dumber;* from *The Lord of the Rings* to *The Walking Dead: Season 1*. However, there is very little chance anyone would confuse these different stories because the *psychological thrust* of each is different and unique.

AN AUDIENCE

Finally, a story must be shared or passed along in some fashion — be it orally, visually, physically, etc. An untold story is not a story; it is only an idea. For this reason, stories are largely a *social* phenomenon.

Now, let's see how each of these elements works together to make stories such incredible memory landmarks.

LINKS (THE PHYSICAL THRUST)

In the last chapter we learnt that the brain holds onto the echoes of recent events and uses these as a lens through which to interpret and understand upcoming events. In other words, the brain is always working to meaningfully link successive moments together. Think about dreaming. Awake and in the light of day, it's clear that dreams are a chaotic mishmash of disconnected moments (one minute you're flying over some mountains, the next you're taking an exam at school?). However, asleep and in the dark of night, dreams make perfect sense (*of course* you'd be taking an exam after flying over some mountains!). This is your brain working to build a coherent cause-and-effect chain between sequential actions.

Sound familiar? The primary element of any story is a plot that connects sequential actions into a coherent cause-and-effect chain.

This is one reason why stories are so memorable: they mimic the way the brain naturally works. When you are presented with isolated facts, you must devote time and effort to explicitly linking them together. However, when those same facts are woven into a story, no additional effort is required: the narrative can simply ride the cause-and-effect rails already laid down within your brain.

To see this in action, let's return to the activity at the start of the chapter.

Round 3

---

1. Without flipping back, spend 30 seconds recalling and writing down as many words as you can from Round 1. Set your timer and begin!
2. Again, without flipping back, spend 30 seconds recalling and writing down as many words as you can from Round 2. Set your timer and begin!

Now, flip back and see how you did.

It's intuitive to assume that visualizing each word (Round 1) would boost memory. In truth, this strategy served to *isolate* individual words. Conversely, building a story (Round 2) served to *link* each word into a cause-and-effect chain. Seeing as this is how the brain naturally works, chances are you remembered more words from the second list than from the first.

It's not metaphorical to say we think in stories.

SIMULATION (THE PSYCHOLOGICAL THRUST)

Whenever you perform a specific action (say, throwing a ball) your brain fires off in a very specific pattern. Interestingly, whenever you *imagine* yourself performing this same action, your brain fires off in almost the same pattern. This is why mental rehearsal is such a prominent technique in sports training: the brain doesn't draw a strict distinction between the real and the imagined.

Here's the best bit: whenever you hear a *story* about a person performing this same action (throwing a ball) your brain will fire off in almost the same pattern as above. This doesn't happen when you encounter this action in isolation ('The man threw the ball'). But as soon as it's embedded within a narrative your brain will respond largely as though *you* were performing the action.

This means we do not simply listen to stories — we experience stories. They are the original (and arguably still the best) virtual reality tool.

This holds true for the psychological and emotional aspects of a story as well. When involved with a story, we mentally simulate thoughts, ideas and feelings. Importantly, our brains respond to these simulations as though they were real. This means we don't merely *feel* what characters feel: we actually *learn from* these feelings as well.

Much like flight simulators help pilots mentally prepare to navigate the skies, stories help people mentally prepare to navigate life. Though it's highly unlikely I will ever be accused of a crime I didn't commit and forced to use a small rock-hammer to tunnel my way out of prison, there is a very good chance at some point in my life I will experience

ILLUSTRATION 64. STORIES DRIVE PSYCHOLOGICAL AND EMOTIONAL SIMULATION

persecution and feel the desire to strike out on my own. In this way, *The Shawshank Redemption* has helped me to psychologically and emotionally prepare for this potentiality.

SYNCHRONY (THE AUDIENCE)

There is an interesting chemical produced within the brain and released throughout the body called oxytocin. Although no one yet understands its complete function, this chemical is most commonly released when mothers are nursing or when couples are physically intimate. For this reason, many researchers believe this chemical helps people form close, kinship-type bonds.

I bring this up because oxytocin is also released whenever we become deeply involved with a story. This is likely one of the reasons why we sometimes become extremely attached to particular characters. More importantly, however, this is also likely one of the reasons why we sometimes become extremely attached to particular authors.

Here lives the social nature of stories I alluded to earlier. Across continents, oceans and centuries, stories can foster a strong bond between the storyteller and the listener. When employed during a presentation or session, this bond can help people feel safe and greatly boost their desire to learn. In fact, when people become deeply involved with a story, their brain patterns actually begin to mimic those of the storyteller. This phenomenon is called *neural coupling* and in these moments people not only learn *from* each other, but also *like* each other.

Not so fast ...

Before we explore how to employ stories to boost influence, there is one important thing to note: *stories do not always work.*

ILLUSTRATION 65. NEURAL COUPLING BETWEEN STORYTELLER AND AUDIENCE

When people have no previous experience with a topic, the right story can help them construct a memory landmark around which to understand, organize and link new information.

However, when people have a deep understanding of a topic, chances are they *already* have a memory landmark around which they've built relevant association networks. For this reason, experts typically prefer to receive pure information, devoid of any narrative. In fact, stories are often considered 'redundant' by experts and might actually cause them to disengage.

As such, it's important to be cognizant of *when* and *with whom* you employ different stories. Do not take this to mean you should completely ditch stories when working with highly knowledgeable individuals. In my experience (though this is circumstantial), stories that are sufficiently complex and nuanced can still be used to influence how experts understand and integrate cutting-edge concepts.

Implications for leaders, teachers and coaches

1. Open with a story

There are three benefits you can reasonably expect from beginning a presentation, lesson, or practice session with a story.

First, as we learnt in the last chapter, ensuring people are on the same page (and the right page) can guide how everyone interprets and remembers new ideas. One of the greatest methods to achieve this is to tell a compelling (and *relevant*) story that weaves together previously learnt ideas with upcoming concepts.

Second, due in part to oxytocin, a story can help others feel more at ease and willing to learn from you. Furthermore, thanks to neural coupling, this can also improve the chance of others understanding novel concepts in the manner you desire.

Third, mental simulation has been shown to boost engagement. As we've seen before, *engagement does not equal learning* — as such, we can't expect stories to carry the entire burden. However, if a story is followed up by solid teaching (possibly underpinned by techniques explored throughout this book), then this enhanced engagement can motivate people to devote time and energy to learning.

BURNING QUESTION 1:

EFFECTIVE STORIES

'We've seen what elements make up a story … but what elements make up a *good* story?'

I am not exaggerating when I say that hundreds (perhaps thousands) of books have been written on this topic … and here I am, stuck with a measly few pages.

C'est la vie.

As we learnt earlier, stories must have a plot: that cause-and-effect chain that pushes physical actions forward. It turns out, there is a common plot structure that many 'good' stories follow:

This structure swings between *stability* and *instability*. At the beginning of a story (baseline) there is stability: characters have a routine and the world is in balance. Unfortunately, an action or event occurs that breaks this balance and throws the world into uncertainty (turning point). The remainder of the story (rising action) is the struggle to re-establish balance. Finally, there is a culminating event (climax) that re-establishes stability — albeit one that is different than at the start (resolution).

This progression can be summed up in six sentences:

Once there was … (baseline)

And every day … (baseline)

Until one day … (turning point)

Because of this … (repeated many times: rising action)

Until finally ... (climax)
And ever since that day ... (resolution)

What's the story?

Using the six sentences below, see if you can guess the following story.

Once there was ... a young girl.
And every day ... she scrubbed the floors for her evil stepsisters.
Until one day ... she was invited to a ball.
Because of this ... she was given a dress and carriage, danced with the prince and ran home at midnight leaving her glass slipper behind.
Until finally ... the prince put the slipper back on her foot.
Ever since that day ... she has lived happily ever after.

You can repeat this process for just about every story.

This takes care of the physical thrust, but what about the psychological thrust? Is there a common mental or emotional trajectory that effective stories follow? According to Kurt Vonnegut, there are several — but one in particular Vonnegut called 'the most popular story in our civilization':

This structure is based on the interplay between ill fortune and good fortune. Typically, at the start of a story everyone is okay; there is a simplicity to life, though characters yearn for more. Following a turning point, fortune begins to shift; characters become bolder, braver and happier. Right before the climax, however, fortune drops precipitously. In this moment, everything goes belly-up and it feels as though life has reverted to the start and nothing will ever really change. However, after the climax things *do* change and fortunes soar.

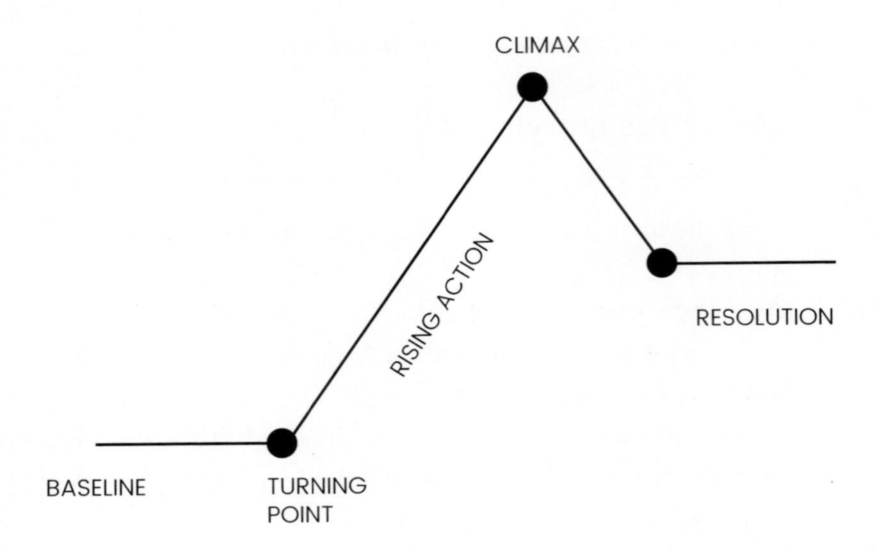

ILLUSTRATION 66. THE PHYSICAL THRUST

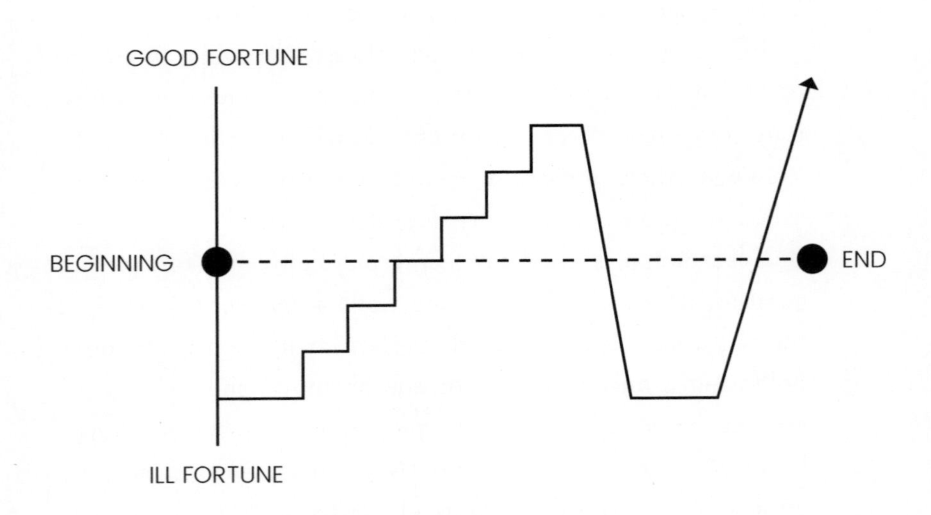

ILLUSTRATION 67: THE PSYCHOLOGICAL THRUST

Let's return to Cinderella. At the start of the story, she is sadly resigned to her less-than-stellar life. However, after she receives the invitation to the ball, things start looking up. She begins to feel more alive as she prepares for, meets and dances with her prince. Everything is going great … until the stroke of midnight. Suddenly, she is rushed home and returns to her normal, depressing life: surely, nothing will ever change. But then, the prince re-appears, the shoe fits and the rest is history.

BURNING QUESTION 2:

STORY TYPES

'What different types of stories are there?'

The impact of a story will depend entirely upon your purpose in telling it. Here are a few of the more prominent story types and their primary purpose.

The Origin

These stories focus on the birth of a particular fact, idea or process. For instance, one day there was no Pythagorean theorem and the next day there was — so what happened? Every good origin story focuses not only on the *how* (a cult-like group of mathematicians developed it together) but also the *why* (this group believed numbers *were* God, and were trying to commune with the heavens through their work).

This type of story can be used to drive interest in and deeper personalization of a topic. In addition, understanding the birth of an idea will guide people to organize ideas according to the 'foundations' of a particular topic.

The Controversy

These stories focus on a major conflict or contradiction that is not easily reconciled. For instance, a story about a dozen soldiers sent behind enemy lines to save a single prisoner-of-war. Often morally ambiguous with no right or wrong answer, this type of story can inspire people to question their own assumptions, expand their understanding of a topic, and connect seemingly disparate ideas.

The Application

These stories focus on how a person has used (or is using) a particular body of knowledge to address real-world problems. For instance, a story of someone repurposing fishing gear to clean rubbish from the oceans. This type of story can inspire people to personalize material, consider how academic issues impact real life, and drive creative problem-solving.

The Humanizer

These stories are personal and drawn from the life of the presenter. This type of story serves to build a connection with the audience to boost engagement, willingness to learn and the personalization of material.

The Cliff-hanger

Cliff-hangers work with every type of story. Begin a narrative, build to the climax ... then leave the conclusion a mystery (either to be revealed later or discovered by the audience). Just as in television, this type of story will drive curiosity and inspire others to fill gaps in their knowledge.

BURNING QUESTION 3:

STORYTELLING

'I've got the right story picked out ... any tips for presenting it in a compelling manner?'

The amount of advice doled out to help people become better storytellers is staggering.

Some people recommend you physically act out the story as you speak — which makes little sense if you're on the radio or recording a podcast. Other people suggest you modulate your voice to match each character — which feels silly if you're telling a deeply personal and emotional story.

In the end, there is no simple recipe to telling a good story. In fact, the only advice I'm willing to give is this: try to *feel* your story.

If neural coupling drives a resonance between storyteller and listener, then how *you* feel when telling a story will influence how *your audience* feels when listening. I've heard my father tell the story of how he lost his pocket watch dozens of times. Each time he tells this story, he genuinely laughs ... which means I can't help but laugh as well. Compare this to a former colleague of mine who was clearly bored with telling the same stories time and again during his lectures. Since he was disconnected, so too were his students.

Your emotional connection to a story will dictate how others sync with *it* and with *you*. Everything else is just decoration.

2. First stories can be everlasting

Being a child of the 1980s my first experience with *Star Wars* was the original trilogy. When the prequels came out in the late 1990s, I couldn't help but compare them (quite negatively) to the first films I'd seen. No Chewbacca? No good.

My nephew was born in the new millennium. His first experience with *Star Wars* was the prequels. When he finally got around to watching the originals, he couldn't help but compare them (quite negatively) to the first films he'd seen. No Jar Jar Binks? No good.

Since stories build the landmarks around which we organize later associations, the very first story we hear has the potential to drive how we interpret and come to understand entire bodies of knowledge. As such, ensure the story you use to introduce a particular topic is relevant and intriguing. If the initial story is overly didactic or dull, it's quite possible others will interpret the entire field as difficult and boring.

3. Beware early freedom

There is a growing trend (especially amongst online programs) called 'exploratory learning'. Essentially, individuals are presented with a wealth of information and left to their own devices to determine how it all fits together. The idea seems to be that if people are free to explore ideas on their own, then they can create their own stories and develop a rich, personal comprehension of the material.

To understand the problem with this, imagine I hand you a sack containing 5000 puzzle pieces and nothing else: you've got no clue what the final picture should be, what the final shape should be or even if all the pieces belong to the same puzzle (it could be a combination of several puzzles).

To someone who already has a strong understanding of how puzzles work (and solid memory landmarks to guide their thinking), this might be an excellent exercise. However, to someone who has never before seen a puzzle and has no idea what is expected of them, this will be a giant, confusing waste of time. To make matters worse, for those who *do* persist, there is no guarantee the puzzle they ultimately construct will be accurate or complete. Heck, it's possible they might end up gluing all the pieces together into a giant stack: sure, they will have created something, but they'll still have no idea what a puzzle is or how it works.

This is all to say that, when working with novices it makes far more sense to use narratives to help them build clear and coherent frameworks through which to approach and understand a topic. Only after the proper foundation has been laid does it make sense to step back and begin introducing freedom into the learning process.

ILLUSTRATION 68: THAT'S ONE WAY TO BUILD A PUZZLE

4. Ask others to share their own stories

Nothing trumps personal experience. You could spend years studying the flu, learning about its common symptoms and discussing possible remedies. However, once you *get* the flu, *feel* those symptoms and *try* those remedies yourself, these concepts take on a new level of meaning and importance.

When people recognize how various concepts are reflected in their own lives, they begin to *personalize* narratives. This, in turn, can boost motivation and ultimately deepen learning. As such, it's never a bad idea to encourage others to share personal stories that reflect and relate to the information being explored.

5. Match your story to your audience

I mentioned this earlier, but it's worth reiterating here.

When people are new to a topic, using stories to help them construct memory landmarks is extremely important. However, when people are highly knowledgeable and have long-established (and effective) memory landmarks, then stories can be redundant, stir resentment and ultimately impair learning.

For this reason, adjust your stories to your audience. Again, since we think in narrative it makes little sense to ditch stories completely. Instead, consider ways to add depth and subtlety so that stories match the experience of others. For instance, telling the story of Pearl Harbor to a group of World War II historians may not be a great idea … however, telling a little-known story of how a single soldier mounted a daring escape from an obscure POW camp might be just what is required to help this group integrate new information into their mental models.

AT A GLANCE

Use stories to guide understanding, memory formation and thinking.

- » *Association networks* are constructed around prominent *memory landmarks.*
- » Stories make ideal memory landmarks for three reasons:
  1. stories mimic the way the brain naturally thinks (cause-and-effect).
  2. stories allow for mental and emotional simulation.
  3. stories release oxytocin and drive storyteller–listener bonding.

APPLICATIONS

1. Open with a story.

- » Stories contain three elements: a physical thrust, a psychological thrust, and an audience.
- » The most common plot structure swings between stability and instability.
- » The most common mental structure swings between ill fortune and good fortune.
- » Common stories include Origin, Controversy, Application, Humanizer and Cliff-hanger.
- » When telling a story, how *you* feel will be how *your audience* feels.

2. First stories can be everlasting.

3. Beware early freedom with new learners.

4. Ask others to share their own stories.

5. Match your story to your audience.

1952

GET A-HEAD!

FOR ADULTS
AT
NO CHARGE

ADULT EDUCATION
CLASSES

MANY COURSES · · MANY PLACES

Intermission 5

Please take around 15 seconds to study and enjoy this old adult education poster.

11.

Stress

The dose makes the poison.

— *Paracelsus*

You may have seen the image opposite before. Called the inverted U, this graph teaches us three important principles about the relationship between stress and learning:

1. High levels of stress can impair learning.
2. Moderate levels of stress can improve learning.
3. Low levels of stress can impair learning to the same degree as high levels of stress.

Although I don't imagine you will be shocked with the first principle, it's possible the second and third might catch you off-guard. In a world that often emphasizes the 'pressure-free, hassle-free and effort-free' aspects of life, it can be surprising to learn that stress may not always be a bad thing.

Before exploring how stress can boost memory and learning, there's an important distinction we first need to make.

Body and mind

People often use the terms 'emotions' and 'feelings' interchangeably. But believe it or not, these two words refer to two very different things.

Emotions are the *physical sensations* that occur throughout the body in response to a particular moment or event. Driven by internal chemicals, emotions are things like butterflies in the stomach, tingling of the skin, shortness of breath, etc. Feelings, on the other hand, are the *psychological interpretation* of these bodily sensations. Driven by subjective perception, feelings are the mental experience of physical emotions.

Because this can be somewhat confusing, let's dig a bit deeper.

Emotions are mediated by two small structures located deep within the brain: the amygdala and the hypothalamus. The amygdala receives signals from each of our seventeen senses (!) and uses these to select an emotion relevant to each situation. The hypothalamus, in turn, triggers

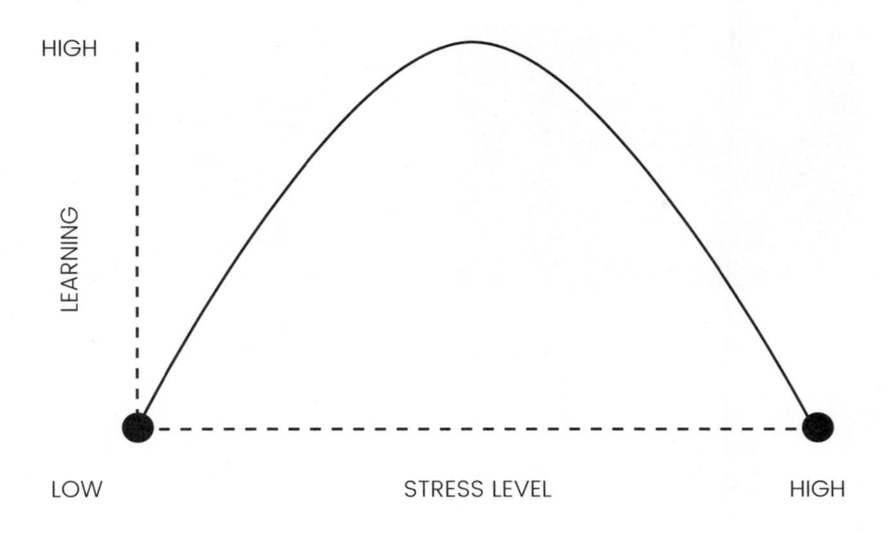

ILLUSTRATION 69. THE INVERTED U

ILLUSTRATION 70. THE SIX BASIC EMOTIONS

the release of chemicals into the body to manifest that emotion. For instance, if you were surrounded by snarling wolves, your amygdala would subconsciously analyze the situation and might select the emotion 'fear'. Your hypothalamus would then release chemicals into your body to speed up your heart rate, dilate your pupils, shorten your breathing, etc. These physical sensations *are* the emotion of fear.

Interestingly, there are only so many chemicals our bodies can produce. For this reason, many researchers believe that the amygdala/hypothalamus combination can really only generate six basic emotions — looking at the babies opposite, can you guess what they are?

Once you recognize that we have a rather limited set of fundamental emotions (joy, fear, anger, surprise, sadness, and disgust), a question arises: where does everything else come from? Humility, nostalgia, embarrassment, jealousy ... how do these manifest?

This is where feelings come into play.

Although the body may be restricted in how it can respond to the world, there is no limit to the ways in which we can mentally interpret these physical sensations. Returning to the example above, depending upon your prior wolf knowledge and experiences, you might interpret your racing heart negatively (leading you to feel scared, anxious, foreboding), positively (excited, exhilarated, intrigued), actively (enraged, furious, frenzied), passively (resigned, abandoned, powerless) or any combination of these.

Put simply, thanks to mental interpretations, the six basic emotions can give rise to a nearly infinite array of feelings.

Here's the most important part: the relationship between emotions and feelings is a two-way street. In other words, psychological interpretations can feedback to and alter physical sensations. For instance, if you interpret the wolves as threatening, this mental label can cause the release of additional chemicals that further speed up your heart rate. Conversely, if you interpret the wolves as funny, this mental label can cause the release of different chemicals that slow down your heart rate. In other words, *feelings* can exacerbate or diminish *emotions*.

So what?

This is all well and good, but what does any of this have to do with stress?

Simply put, stress is a feeling — not an emotion. For an event to be stressful, it must be psychologically interpreted as such.

Some people parachute out of an airplane, get a rush of chemicals (adrenaline, endorphins, etc.) and interpret this as 'excitement'. This feeling will feedback, alter the chemical flow and generate specific physical and mental changes. Other people parachute out of an airplane, get exactly the same rush of chemicals (adrenaline, endorphins, etc.), and interpret this as 'stress'. This feeling will feedback, alter the flow of chemicals in a different way and generate different physical and mental changes. Same situation, same chemicals, same physical sensations — but the interpretation changes everything.

This is all to say that if a person does not interpret a specific emotion as stressful, then everything we explore below will become null and void.

ILLUSTRATION 71. THE STORY OF STRESS — CAST OF CHARACTERS

It's showtime

To understand the impacts of stress there are several key players we must become acquainted with.

CAST OF CHARACTERS

Hippocampus: The gateway to memory. Composed of billions of specialized cells called neurons that process new information and lead to the formation of new memories. We can imagine neurons as trees and the hippocampus as a dense forest.

Amygdala: The selector of emotions. Heavily connected to and in constant communication with the hippocampus. We can imagine the amygdala as a castle tasked with protecting the hippocampus forest.

Cortisol: The primary stress hormone. In the body, it elevates blood sugar and regulates blood pressure. In the brain, it kills neurons within the hippocampus. We can imagine cortisol as a barbarian driven to cut down the hippocampus forest.

Norepinephrine: A secondary stress hormone. In the body, it increases heart rate and respiration. In the brain, it alerts the amygdala that cortisol is present. We can imagine norepinephrine as a messenger tasked with sending out a warning whenever the barbarian arrives.

ARC-proteins: **A**ctivity-**r**egulated **c**ytoskeleton-associated proteins. Developed in the amygdala, they have two jobs: to combat cortisol and to strengthen neurons. We can imagine ARC-proteins as a knight driven to fight the barbarian *and* as a gardener driven to help the hippocampus forest flourish.

FGF2: **F**ibroblast **g**rowth **f**actor **2**. These proteins lead to the growth of brand new neurons. We can imagine FGF2 as seeds which will (eventually) sprout into new trees.

Let's dim the lights and start the show …

ACT I: DR JEKYLL

Sometimes stress can be sudden, acute and short-lived. For instance, those ten minutes before you step on stage to deliver a presentation. During these periods of short-term stress, here's what happens:

Raise curtain

Scene I: When stress begins, cortisol floods into the hippocampus and begins attacking neurons.

Scene II: This attack triggers the release of norepinephrine which flows into the amygdala, signalling the need for back-up.

Scene III: The amygdala releases ARC-proteins into the hippocampus. These proteins begin to combat cortisol.

Scene IV: The battle between ARC-proteins and cortisol triggers the release of FGF2. This protein embeds itself throughout the hippocampus.

Scene V: As the stressful situation draws to a close, cortisol flees the hippocampus and ARC-proteins begin repairing the damaged neurons, making each thicker and stronger than before the battle.

Scene VI: Approximately two weeks later, FGF2 comes to fruition and new neurons sprout throughout the hippocampus. These neurons immediately take up the task of processing new information (learning).

Lower curtain

Thinking back to the inverted U at the beginning of this chapter, it should now make a bit more sense why *moderate* stress can boost memory and learning.

ILLUSTRATION 72. ACT I — THE RESPONSE TO ACUTE STRESS

First, during short-lived stress, ARC-proteins strengthen neurons within the hippocampus leading to the formation of deeper memories for that moment. It's as if ARC-proteins tell the hippocampus, 'Whatever caused that cortisol release must be important; please remember it.'

In addition, moderate stress triggers the release of FGF2 which leads to the formation of new neurons in the hippocampus. Unfortunately, these neurons take about two weeks to sprout. So how does this improve learning?

In the short-term, it doesn't. If you experience moderate stress today, this might improve your learning two weeks from now but will do nothing for the present moment. However, in the long-term, this process begins to make sense. If you experience moderate stress every day (triggered by errors, failed predictions and unexpected events) you will have new neurons sprouting *all the time*. Since these new neurons are dedicated to processing new information, general learning will be greatly enhanced.

However, despite these benefits, stress is not always rainbows and sunshine …

ACT II: MR HYDE

Sometimes stress lasts for a prolonged period. For instance, if you've got 30 days to complete an important project, you might spend weeks worrying about the impending deadline. During these periods of long-term stress, here's what happens:

Raise curtain

Scene I: When stress begins, cortisol floods into the hippocampus and begins attacking neurons.

Scene II: This attack triggers the release of norepinephrine which flows into the amygdala, signalling the need for back-up.

Scene III: The amygdala releases ARC-proteins into the hippocampus. These proteins begin to combat cortisol.

Scene IV: The battle between ARC-proteins and cortisol triggers the release of FGF2. This protein embeds itself throughout the hippocampus.

Scene V: As the stressful situation continues, more cortisol is pumped into the hippocampus. Eventually, stores of ARC-proteins run dry and cortisol begins *killing* neurons once and for all.

Scene VI: As neurons die, stores of FGF2 run dry and no new seeds are planted. Cortisol continues killing neurons and, since no new ones sprout to take their place, the hippocampus begins to wither away.

Lower curtain

ILLUSTRATION 73. ACT II — THE RESPONSE TO PROLONGED STRESS

Thinking back to the inverted U, it should now make a bit more sense why *high* stress can impair learning.

As ARC-proteins and FGF2 die away, cortisol has free reign to damage and destroy our gateway to memory. To make matters worse, as the hippocampus withers away our ability to access previously formed long-term memories becomes impaired. This means that prolonged stress not only makes it difficult to learn *new* information, but also cuts us off from *old* information learnt in the past.

Although this process might seem illogical, it actually serves an important purpose. Imagine you're trapped in a very bad situation and have no way to escape — say, stuck in a bear-trap deep in the woods and help won't arrive for three days. In this instance, you don't really want to make deep, vivid memories. Rather, seeing as you're helpless and there's no continuous lesson to learn, it makes far more sense to block out as much negativity as possible and simply survive until the ordeal is over. This is what the long-term stress response does: it helps prevent memories from forming during helpless situations.

However, rarely in the modern world do we get stuck in bear traps. More often than not, we experience prolonged stress within our jobs, families and responsibilities. In these instances, the long-term stress response can prove a dangerous liability leading to lost jobs, conflicting families and shirked responsibilities.

One last thing

We've learnt why high stress can be bad and why moderate stress can be good, but what about the third principle of the inverted U? How could no stress be just as bad as excess stress?

In the absence of stress, cortisol *does not* flood into the hippocampus. In the absence of cortisol, the amygdala *does not* release ARC-proteins. In the absence of ARC-proteins, FGF2 *is not* released and new neurons *do not* form. In other words, without stress, all those chemicals that bolster memory and facilitate learning simply lay dormant. This means that in a perfect world without errors, failed predictions or unexpected events, the hippocampus slips into pause mode.

Although this might not sound horrible, it's important to remember that *everything* degrades with time. As such, the longer the hippocampus remains on 'pause', the more susceptible it becomes to the natural ravages of time. Without ARC-proteins, neurons within the hippocampus will naturally deteriorate and die away. Similarly, without FGF2 no new neurons will be formed to replace the old. As neurons fade away, so too does our ability to remember and learn.

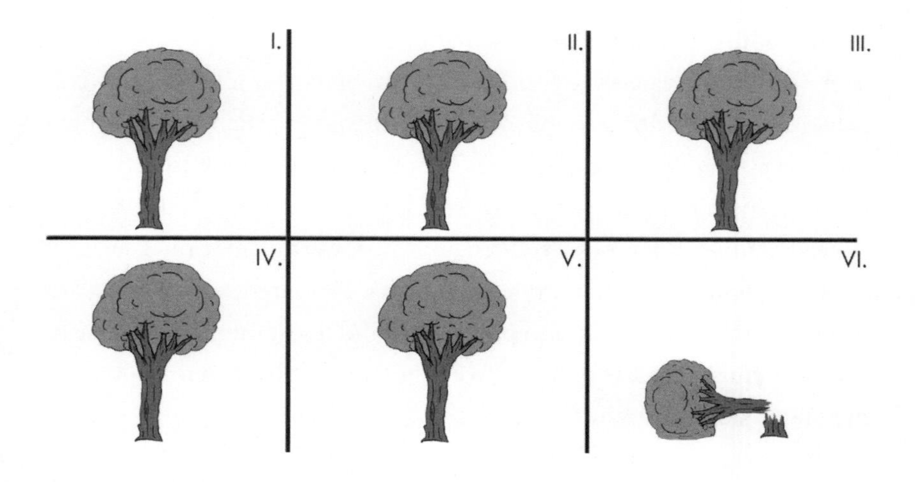

ILLUSTRATION 74. ACT III — THE RESPONSE TO ZERO STRESS

Implications for leaders, teachers and coaches

1. Leverage emotional shifts to boost memory

You may have heard that emotions enhance memory. Although this is basically true, there is a bit more to the story.

Since emotions are simply chemicals flowing throughout your body, it is impossible to ever turn them off (unless you somehow manage to rid your body of all chemicals ... which, I worry, might be fatal). This means *every* memory has an emotion attached to it. For this reason it can't be emotions *per se* that enhance memories; rather, it's one specific feature of the emotional process that does it.

As we learnt earlier, norepinephrine triggers the release of ARC-proteins into the hippocampus which, in turn, strengthen newly formed memories. Here's the secret: stress is not the only feeling that triggers the release of norepinephrine. In truth, this hormone is released any time someone undergoes a sudden and/or powerful emotional shift.

If you swing from happy to sad, angry to scared, or surprised to disgusted this will release norepinephrine and boost memory. Similarly, if you swing from sort-of happy to ecstatic, somewhat sad to depressed, or mildly angry to irate, the same thing will occur.

So when it comes to leveraging emotions to increase influence, we must determine what emotions others might already be experiencing and consider ways to either heighten, lessen or shift these. In a sea of sadness, joy stands out; but in a sea of joy, sadness wins the day.

Furthermore, keeping anyone happy, scared or sad for too long will wear away any potential memory boost. It's therefore important to consider what emotional *journey* you wish to take others on. If you attempt to be upbeat, happy and funny during an entire two-hour presentation you will invariably find the audience wavering by the end. The most impactful lessons don't only make us laugh ... they make us laugh, cry, gasp and growl.

BURNING QUESTION 1:

FLASHBULB MEMORIES

'There are some moments in my life that I remember in incredible detail. What's going on here?'

We all have several ridiculously vivid memories from our past. Some are positive (the moment your first child was born, for example) while some are negative (the moment you heard Princess Diana died).

These lucid, detailed recollections are called *flashbulb memories* and for decades researchers thought they were only created following moments that were deeply *meaningful* (events that form an integral aspect of our personal identity) and deeply *emotional* (events that were intensely shocking, surprising or caused a sudden chemical flux within the body).

Here's the rub: everyone has flashbulb memories of events that were neither meaningful nor emotional. For instance, I can vividly remember a time when I was in the backseat of my mum's Jeep Wagoneer, looking out the front windshield at a personalized licence plate on a nearby car that read 'mop'. As far as I can tell, this moment wasn't particularly startling or life changing — yet there it is: rising like Mount Everest above the mists of my childhood memories.

Needless to say, these 'neutral' memories have led researchers to question everything we thought we knew about this phenomenon. Currently, no one can predict *when* flashbulb memories will occur, explain *why* they form or describe *how* they happen (though most theories emphasize the role of the amygdala and ARC-proteins).

This is all to say that, although flashbulb memories are a cool occurrence, there is nothing we can yet do to leverage them to boost memory or learning.

My apologies for this less-than-thrilling news.

2. Mix it up

Low levels of stress can impair memory and learning. This means that if the process you typically use to influence others becomes formulaic, repetitive and predictable, this could drive others into a low-stress state and hinder their ability (or willingness) to remember new information.

Frequent, short bursts of moderate stress, however, can boost memory and lead to sustained learning improvements. This means if you mix and match the structure, format, activities, discussions and stories you employ when influencing others, you will make it difficult for them to form simple predictions and ensure they must actively engage with each new moment. By keeping others on their toes, you can maintain a moderate level of stress and enhance their ability (and willingness) to remember new information.

BURNING QUESTION 2:

BRAIN TRAINING PART 2

'Wait ... is stress the secret to keeping my brain healthy and active?'

In a manner of speaking, yes.

Novelty is one of the primary ingredients for keeping the brain agile and responsive. Each time you undertake a new activity, learn a new skill or dive into a new situation, this leads to *moderate* levels of stress. As we learnt earlier, moderate stress experienced every day can lead to a steady flow of FGF2 and the continual growth of new neurons within the hippocampus. Since these new neurons process new information, they (in essence) are what keep us learning and growing.

So, as we learnt in Chapter 6, don't worry about brain training games (they will only make you better at chunking information within each game). Instead, try new and scary things. Take up an instrument. Learn a new language. Try cooking a new dish. Continually jumping into novel, unpredictable situations will increase your chances of keeping your mind flexible and your memories active.

Just remember not to take any new activity *too* seriously. Once you begin feeling excess anxiety or undue pressure, it's time to move on. When playing with stress, there is a fine line between helping and harming your brain.

ILLUSTRATION 75. NOVELTY IS THE KEY TO AN ACTIVE BRAIN

3. Beware of state-dependency

In Chapter 4 we explored state-dependency: the idea that the chemicals flowing throughout our bodies as we learn form an integral aspect of what we learn (remember the thought experiment of collecting business cards while at an 'alcohol friendly' networking event?).

By now, you're well aware that *emotions are chemicals*. This means that emotional state-dependency is a real possibility. For instance, information always painted in a sad light might be difficult to access when in a happy situation. Similarly, concepts always presented as frightening could be tricky to recall when feeling relaxed.

The best way to address state-dependency is to embrace *variety*. If you want to ensure information is freely available across any situation, it's worth varying the emotions tied to it during the teaching and learning process. Try to find the good and the bad in any topic: the happy and the sad, the infuriating and the reassuring.

Conversely, if information is best understood only in a certain light (such as the consequences and repercussions of war) or skills applicable only during very specific emotional circumstances (such as combat tactics), then embrace the relevant emotion during all learning and practice sessions.

4. Safety first

It's unfortunate, but many people see learning as frightening, intimidating, threatening … in short, highly stressful. If this feeling is never addressed it's possible some people will switch off before you (as a leader, teacher or coach) have even begun. For this reason, it is worthwhile *early on* to create an environment that allows everyone to feel psychologically safe. Here are some tips to help that happen:

» Ask questions and genuinely listen to the answers. This will allow others to feel as though they have a voice and are respected.

» Display vulnerability and highlight your own imperfections (perhaps by sharing a less-than-flattering story from your past).

This will allow others to lower their guard and view you as an ally.

» Offer options and choices. This will allow others to display agency and recognize the role they play in the learning process.
» Collaborate. This will allow others to feel supported and view you as a partner.

The sooner people feel safe to speak up, interact and make mistakes, the sooner they will re-interpret 'stressful' emotions as exciting, fun and intriguing.

5. Employ physical and mental de-stressing techniques

Seeing as emotions are physical, many primary de-stressing techniques directly target the body. The concept is simple: if you can change the chemicals, you can change the emotion.

Arguably the best (and easiest) example of this is *deep breathing*. As you inhale, receptors in your lungs trigger the release of a chemical that slows the release of cortisol and norepinephrine. As you exhale, different chemicals are released that slow heart rate and reduce blood pressure. After a short time, those physical sensations commonly interpreted as 'stress' are gone and a new interpretation (feeling) can emerge.

Another example is called *progressive muscle relaxation*. In a nutshell, this technique is the systematic tensing, holding and releasing of different muscle groups. As each muscle group is tensed, that physical effort burns off excess cortisol within the body. As each muscle group is relaxed, blood pressure drops and heart rate slows. To experience this sensation, simply make a really tight first with your right hand, hold it for five seconds, then release and relax it. Again, after a short time, the physical sensations of stress will disappear and a new interpretation can emerge.

Importantly, as we learnt earlier, feelings can feedback on and influence emotions. As such, there are many secondary de-stressing techniques that directly target the mind. Meditation; mindfulness; exposure therapy. The main goal of these mental de-stressing techniques is not to stop the physical sensations of stress from occurring; it's to re-frame and re-build interpretations. The idea is that if you can re-label stressful emotions as exciting, intriguing or funny (or if you can remove every label full-stop), this will shift the chemical response of your body.

BURNING QUESTION 3:

MIND BLANKS

'Sometimes when I'm in the middle of a presentation, I suddenly blank out. One moment everything is there; the next I can hardly remember my name. What's going on?'

Ah, the dreaded mind blank!

In Chapter 5 we learnt about the mind wipe. As a reminder, whenever the ventral attention network registers a threat, it will automatically erase anything you were just thinking about (presumably so you can focus all your attention on the threat).

During a mind blank, the process is the same: something catches your attention (say, a flash of light in your peripheral vision); this registers as a threat and your mind is suddenly wiped clean. However, what makes mind blanks unique is that they occur during *important moments*: presentations, performances, exams. For this reason, we tend to interpret this sudden memory dump as highly stressful which, in turn, triggers the release of cortisol and starts a stress feedback-loop, making it incredibly difficult to get back on track.

In other words, a mind blank is an innocuous mind wipe laden with stress and pressure.

So is there anything you can do?

The best remedy is to target the body. My favourite technique is the squat. When a mind blank occurs and the stress feedback-loop begins, step away from whatever you're doing, place your back against a wall, dip into a deep squat and hold for 30 to 60 seconds. This is meant to be difficult. As you struggle to maintain the squat, your exhausted muscles will begin burning off excess cortisol and you will start breathing deeply. This will almost certainly lead you to re-interpret your rapid heartbeat and tingling skin as exhaustion instead of stress.

Once you've re-interpreted the bodily sensations, the stress cycle will abate and you can re-engage with the task at hand. However, *do not* return to the exact point you were at when the mind blank occurred. Rather, return to a previous, already completed moment: for instance, quickly repeat a story you've already told, re-answer a question you've already tackled or re-read a paragraph you've already scanned. By returning to an earlier moment, you will have a much easier time accessing information and triggering relevant associations which will help you push past the mind-blank moment.

Now, I'm not an idiot. I realize there will be times when you can't stand up and say 'Gimme a sec, y'all, I'm just gonna pop a squat real quick!' Luckily, if squatting is not an option you can mimic this by sustaining a tight fist, pushing your hands down hard against a table top, or shifting all your weight over one slightly bent leg. Anything that drives a particular muscle or muscle group to exhaustion should have the same impact.

AT A GLANCE

Moderate stress can boost memories and general learning (though high stress and no stress can be detrimental).

- » Emotions are physical sensations within the body. Feelings are mental interpretations of these physical sensations.
- » Stress is a feeling, not an emotion.
- » During moderate stress, ARC-proteins support neurons in the hippocampus (boosting memory) and FGF2 grows new neurons (boosting learning).
- » During high stress, cortisol kills neurons and the hippocampus withers.
- » During no stress, neurons naturally degrade and the hippocampus withers.

APPLICATIONS

1. Leverage emotional *shifts* to boost memory.
2. Mix up activities to maintain moderate stress.
   - » *Novelty* is one of the best tools to maintain brain health and flexibility.
3. Beware of emotional state dependency.
4. Safety first.
5. Employ physical and mental de-stressing techniques.
   - » Mind wipe + stress = mind blank.
   - » Remember to pop a squat!

12.

Distribution

All things live forever, though at times they sleep and are forgotten.

— H. Rider Haggard

Finally, after all that build-up, it's time for the big reveal.

Questions

You've no doubt noticed (and possibly been confused by) the five 'intermissions' interspersed throughout this book.

Intermissions 1, 2, 4 and 5 were identical. Without flipping back, can you recall the date, image and relevant phrase/motto from those?

Date:

___

Image:

___

Phrase/motto:

___

Intermission number 3 was different. Without flipping back, can you recall the date, image and relevant phrase/motto?

Date:

___

Image:

___

Phrase/motto:

___

Now, flip back and check to see how you did …

If you're like most people, you probably remembered very little from intermission number 3 but had no problem recalling some details of the other four.

Your first inkling might be that this is due to repetition: you saw the headless man four times, so of course you remember him better. But look again at intermission 3: the globe and compass were also repeated four times. This means something else must be going on here.

What you've just experienced is the power of *distributed practice*, arguably the most applicable, adaptable and powerful tool in our influence arsenal.

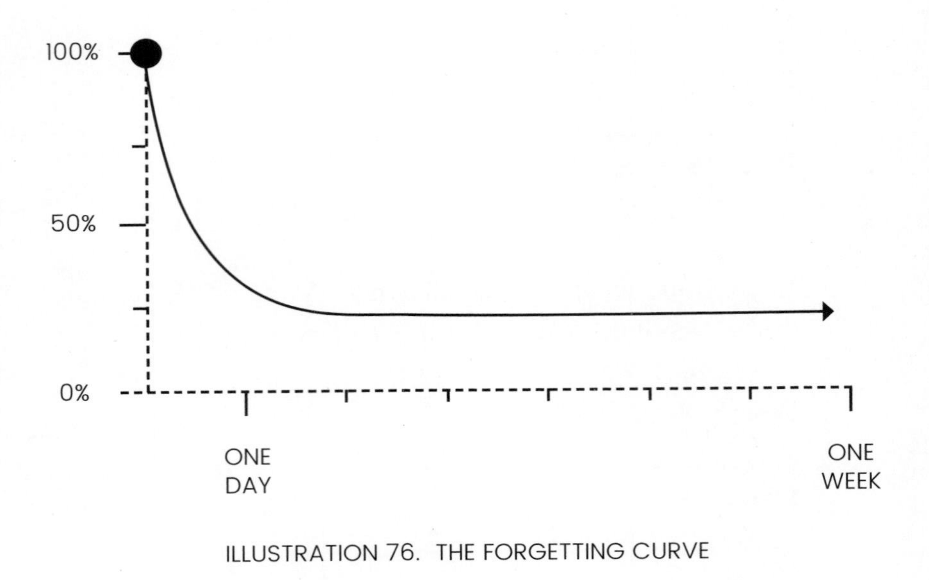

ILLUSTRATION 76. THE FORGETTING CURVE

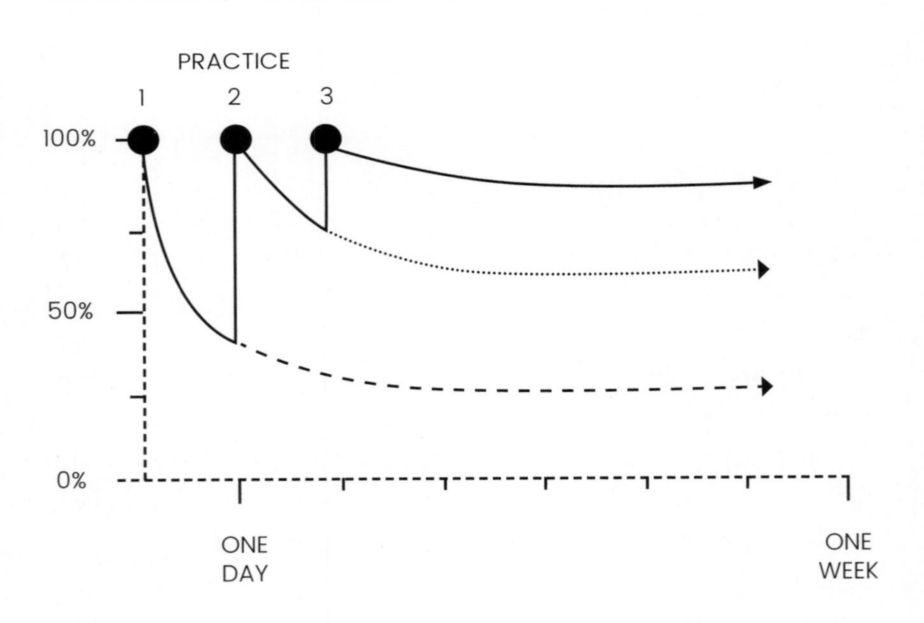

ILLUSTRATION 77. DISTRIBUTED PRACTICE COMBATS THE FORGETTING CURVE

Forgetting

When it comes to forgetting, people often envision memories as clouds: ephemeral objects destined to fade away and disappear with the passage of time.

Unfortunately, this isn't a very accurate metaphor. As we learnt in Chapter 8, memories are like huts within a jungle: as long as we continue to retrieve them (i.e. to forge a path) they will always be accessible. Only when we stop accessing memories do they become overgrown and lost within the jungle … but this does not mean they disappear! Have you ever heard a song from your past and suddenly remembered vivid details from a high school party you've not thought about in decades? No matter how old or lost they become, it only takes *one* association to rediscover and re-forge a pathway to presumably forgotten memories.

This leads to an interesting question: how quickly does the jungle grow? In other words, how often do we need to retrieve memories to keep them active and accessible?

This question was most comprehensively addressed in the late 1800s by Hermann Ebbinghaus. This German researcher would spend hours memorizing lists of completely meaningless syllables (ZOF; YAT; DAX) then he would simply wait. After different periods of time (ranging from hours to months), he would test his memory to see how much he had forgotten from each list. In a display of near super-human patience, Ebbinghaus repeated variations of this experiment for years — simply memorizing and forgetting nonsense syllables day after day.

What he found is represented in the top image on the opposite page.

This image, called the *forgetting curve*, suggests that the jungle grows quite rapidly. In fact, it appears people forget around 70 per cent of what they learn after only 24 hours. Luckily, this decline quickly levels off and plateaus; but it can still be unnerving to realize that a week from today, you will likely remember a paltry 20 per cent of what you read in this chapter.

Fortunately, Ebbinghaus wasn't only interested in tracking how quickly we forget things; he also wanted to determine how best to *remember* things. To explore this, at different intervals he would return to and *re-learn* various word lists and measure how this impacted his forgetting curve.

The first thing Ebbinghaus found was that the more time he devoted to practising a specific list of nonsense syllables, the longer he would remember it. Nothing really surprising there.

The second thing Ebbinghaus found was that the way in which he scheduled his practice had massive impacts on his memory. More specifically, if he crammed practice into a single, long session (say, three hours in one sitting) this would boost his memory for a short period, but the forgetting curve would soon reappear. However, if he spaced practice across several days (say, one hour per day for three days) this would boost his memory and stave off the forgetting curve for a much longer period. Put simply, by spacing out his practice sessions, Ebbinghaus was able to remember *more* information for a far *longer* period of time (represented in the bottom image on p. 264).

Let's return to the jungle metaphor. If you cut a path to a particular memory, you can expect the jungle to overgrow and reclaim around 70 per cent of that path within 24 hours. What Ebbinghaus discovered was that if you continuously re-cut this path for *three hours straight*, not much will change: it will take only 72 hours for the jungle to reclaim 70 per cent of that path. However, if you re-cut this path over *three consecutive days*, this will slow the jungle significantly: in fact, it might take *weeks* for the jungle to reclaim 70 per cent of the path. It's almost as if, with successive cuttings over several days, the jungle *learns* that it's no use growing over the path and starts growing in different directions, leaving the path free and clear.

Researchers call this phenomenon *distributed practice*. Put simply, if practice is broken up and distributed over an extended period, this will lead to longer lasting memories than if the same amount of practice is crammed into a single, long session. Returning to the start of this chapter, this is the reason why you remembered more details from intermissions 1, 2, 4 and 5: even though you saw that image four times and studied it for a total of about 60 seconds (same as intermission 3), these exposures were distributed over a longer timespan, leading to deeper and longer-lasting memories.

Importantly, this phenomenon has been demonstrated in nearly every living creature (monkeys; bumble bees; sea slugs; plants ... read that again: *plants*). In addition, it appears to work with anything you could ever want to remember, from basic information (vocabulary) to highly complex skills (flying an airplane). For this reason, distributed practice is as close to a fundamental law as we've ever found when it comes to memory and learning.

But *why* does it work? It turns out there are three key drivers (two of which we've explored previously).

VARIABILITY

When we cram practice into one long session, chances are this will occur in a single, unchanging context. For instance, if you sit down and devote five straight hours to study, all of this will occur at *one* table, in *one* room, with *one* set of smells, noises and physical sensations. As we learnt in Chapter 4, when practice occurs in a single context, relevant memories become difficult to access and apply outside that context.

However, when we break practice into several shorter sessions distributed over a longer time period (say, one hour per day for five days), there is a much better chance each session will occur in a different and unique context. Even if you practised at the same table each day, there is a good chance one session would occur in the morning and another in the evening; one would occur while you're hungry and another while you're satiated; one would occur on a rainy day and another on a sunny day. All these subtle shifts in context or state will form deeper, more nuanced semantic memories leading to easier access and transfer across novel situations.

RETRIEVAL

When we cram practice into one long session, we need only retrieve memories once. After accessing relevant ideas or skills at the start of the session, we can simply hold them within our prefrontal cortex for the duration of practice, then re-store when we're done. Unfortunately, as we learnt in Chapter 8, the key to forming deep memories is *multiple* retrievals.

Luckily, when we break practice into several shorter sessions distributed over a longer timeframe, we retrieve and re-store memories multiple times. This repeated path-cutting to relevant ideas or skills leads to stronger memories and staves off jungle growth for a much longer period.

CONSOLIDATION

A concept we've not yet explored in this book is memory consolidation. If *encoding* is inserting new information into the brain, and *storage* is finding a home for this information within the brain, then *consolidation* is the act of tying this information securely into place so that it cannot shift from its home. This makes that information much easier to locate in the future.

Although no one is 100 per cent sure of the exact mechanisms, a large portion of consolidation occurs at night during sleep. When asleep, the brain slows down. However, on occasion, short bursts of intense activity will arise. These bursts (called sleep spindles) are thought to represent the brain 'replaying' ideas and information learnt that day. In a very simplified manner, during sleep new memories (encoding) seek out an area of the brain to lay down roots (storage), and this area of the brain will 're-enact' the relevant memory several times to lock it into place (consolidation). It's possible that dreams are snippets of these re-enactments reaching conscious awareness.

Here's the twist: consolidation doesn't happen all at once. In fact, this process typically takes months (if not years) to complete.

Luckily, consolidation can be accelerated through repeated retrieval. In addition, there is a limit to the amount of consolidation that can occur each night. Typically, information encountered that day will be the first to be consolidated that night. This means any memories not accessed during the day might fall into a consolidation backlog and take much longer to become firmly rooted in place.

When we cram practice into one long session, we really only allow for one evening of sleep-based consolidation to occur. This means relevant memories won't be securely tied down, making them susceptible to interference and more difficult to access in the future. However, when we break practice into several shorter sessions distributed over a longer timeframe, we allow for several evenings of sleep-based consolidation to occur, making memories more stable and easier to access.

ILLUSTRATION 78. DON'T WAKE ME — I'M CONSOLIDATING MEMORIES

Less is more

When first learning about the power of distributed practice, a natural question arises: what is the perfect distribution schedule to maintain strong and everlasting memories?

Unfortunately, as you may have already guessed, there is no single answer to this question. The ideal number of practice sessions, duration of each and interval between each will necessarily change depending upon each unique situation. Simple skills might require fewer sessions than complex skills; mastery might require longer practice durations than competence; mental skills might require more frequent sessions than physical skills; etc.

With that said, there is a rule of thumb we often use:

Deadline	***Distribution delay***
1 week	*daily*
1 month	*weekly*
1 year	*monthly*

When preparing for a *specific* purpose (say, an upcoming presentation), then practice can be scheduled according to this deadline. If the presentation is one week away, practise each day (rather than cramming the night before). If the presentation is one month away, practise once a week. If the presentation is one year (or longer) away, practise once a month.

If there is no deadline and you want others to remember information indefinitely, then combine all these schedules. When starting out, run short practice sessions every day. After a week or so, begin to add more and more space between each practice session — perhaps extending to every other day, then every week, then fortnightly, then monthly. With time, it is wholly possible you will need to only run one short practice session *each year* to maintain strong and easily accessible memories.

Caveats

'Distributed practice'. Most people focus on the first word: distributed. However, the second word is equally important: practice. Put simply, all the benefits we've explored above occur when people are practising something that they have *already learnt*. Unfortunately, there is little-to-no direct evidence that distributing new learning has the same impact on memory. As such, if you are exploring a brand new topic it's important to devote adequate time to learning prior to distribution.

Also, for distributed practice to be effective, *people must actually practice*! Studying maths for one minute a day over 30 days will not work as well as studying maths for 30 minutes in one day. Practice must be realistic, focused and relevant to the skill at hand. Importantly, this will change depending upon the skill you are practising. Whereas 30-minute sessions might suffice when studying vocabulary words, practising complex computer coding could require four- or five-hour sessions.

Finally, whereas the short-term benefits of a single, long practice session are immediately apparent, the long-term benefits of distributed practice only become obvious with time. As such, some people are wary of embracing this technique. Perhaps the only way around this is to consider ways in which to measure and compare growth over time (quizzes; surveys; before-and-after photos; free-writing examples; videos; etc.). Once people recognize the personal advantages gained by distributed practice they will be more inclined to adopt it.

Implications for leaders, teachers and coaches

1. Distribute, distribute, distribute

There's not much more to say here: if you have the time and opportunity to distribute practice over several sessions — do it. As long as the practice is realistic and meaningful, it's difficult to think of a scenario where this won't be beneficial.

BURNING QUESTION 1:

CRAMMING

> 'I managed to make it through school by cramming the night before each exam. Where's your distribution now?'

Cramming works. If you spend ten hours studying immediately prior to an exam, chances are you're going to perform quite well.

However, as we saw above, cramming will only stave off the forgetting curve for a short while. In fact, only 72 hours after a cram session you can expect to forget around 70 per cent of what you learnt.

On the other hand, people who spread those ten hours of study over five days will likely perform just as well on any exam *and* retain memories for a much longer period. Indeed, with this distribution schedule, it's possible memories will remain prominent and easily accessible for up to six months after the final study session.

With that said, people love to cram. This means, if you want others to remember information or skills for an extended period, you'll likely need to explicitly address cramming practices and employ techniques (such as those below) to embed distributed practice as much as possible.

BURNING QUESTION 2:

BINGE-WATCHING

'I binge-watched the final season of *Breaking Bad* in one day. Is that the same as cramming?'

Unfortunately, yes.

When people binge-watch television shows they display the same pattern as people who cram: strong memories for about 72 hours followed by a precipitous drop. On the other hand, people who watch nightly or weekly episodes display the same pattern as people who distribute practice: strong memories that sustain for months.

Luckily, people tend to watch television shows for enjoyment. Who cares if you don't remember every detail from *Breaking Bad*? It's a diversion meant only to entertain.

Bad news: it turns out that people who binge-watch television programs also *enjoy* them significantly less than people who watch the same programs in nightly or weekly instalments.

With that said, I don't expect this information will stop anyone from binge-watching: it's too deeply engrained in the way we consume media. However, where all this information becomes extremely important is in the realm of digital education.

ILLUSTRATION 79. JUST ONE MORE EPISODE ...

As more people film presentations, lessons and training sessions, and move into online platforms, a new behaviour has emerged: binge-learning. People are now cramming hours of digital videos and online learning into a single sitting. Unfortunately, as you can predict, this means people will likely forget much of what they've learnt incredibly rapidly.

If you want people to remember digitally-presented material, it is worth considering ways to combat binge-learning — perhaps by restricting access to particular video lessons according to a distribution schedule (e.g. people must wait 48 hours and undertake a digital review session of video lesson 1 before they can access and watch video lesson 2).

BURNING QUESTION 3:

DISTRIBUTED LEARNING

'Wait a second — earlier you said distribution only works with practice. But binge-watching isn't like practice at all. What gives?'

Very shrewd!

Although they build upon each other, each new episode of a television show is wholly unique and original. This means watching a television program is more akin to learning (experiencing new material) than practice (re-hashing already learnt material).

If distribution only works for practice, why would people who watch programs on a nightly or weekly basis remember more than people who binge-watch?

If you look closely above, I did not say distributed learning was *impossible*: simply that there is *little-to-no evidence* for it. It's wholly possible that stretching learning over a longer timespan will prove more effective than cramming it into a short period. In fact, there is some evidence to suggest that distributing training programs over several half-days is more effective than squeezing the same program into a single full day.

Unfortunately, until clear, robust and explicit evidence is established, it's best to let distributed *learning* percolate in the background while focusing your energies on the tried-and-true distributed *practice*.

2. Don't save review sessions for the end

It's quite common to run a single, large 'review session' on the final day of a program or course exploring all the topics covered in previous days, weeks or months. As you might have guessed, this tends to have the same impact as cramming.

A stronger idea is to devote time at the end of each day or week to review concepts. By doing this, you will ensure material learnt early in a course is recalled numerous times (making durable memories) while giving newer information a consolidation boost.

If you only get to work with people for a single session, try to employ distributed practice using digital means. Each week send a video, newsletter or activity to help people retrieve and practise relevant material. If you can inspire others to *recall* information (such as via quizzes, discussion topics or games), even better. With time, you can begin spacing these mini-review sessions more and more until, ideally, a single yearly reminder will suffice to keep ideas sharp and strong.

As an example, where I work everyone has to sit through an eight-hour health and safety seminar every year. As you can guess, nobody ever remembers much and most people view this as a wasted day. Imagine if, after the initial seminar, they instituted a 30-minute refresher each week … then extended this to each month … then every other month. Eventually, a single 30-minute refresher once a year could work better than the full-day session.

3. Don't demand perfection from square one

As we saw above, Ebbinghaus didn't begin distributed practice until he had first *perfectly* memorized each word list.

Lucky for us, this 'perfection' is unnecessary. Distributed practice will still work its magic even if you have not completely mastered a certain skill or topic: simply knowing *enough* to begin practice will suffice. Furthermore, distributing the practice of material you have yet to perfect can actually speed up mastery.

4. Combine distribution with all other strategies

The best thing about distributed practice is that it is an overarching principle. This means it can be applied to any number of more specific techniques. Interleaving, recall, context, stories, priming: these practices boost memory and learning. However, like a steroid, distribution can be used in conjunction with these strategies to boost that impact even further.

There is no technique explored within this book that will not benefit from distribution.

AT A GLANCE

Spacing practice out over several distributed sessions will improve memory and accelerate learning.

- » People forget new information rather quickly.
- » This forgetting can be dramatically slowed and reduced by stretching out practice sessions over multiple days. This is called distributed practice.
- » With continued distributed practice, memories can be maintained while spacing practice sessions further and further apart.

APPLICATIONS

1. Distribute, distribute, distribute.
   - » Cramming for exams does not stave off the forgetting curve for long.
   - » Binge-watching television shows (and online lessons) is the same as cramming.
   - » Employ distribution during *practice*, not during *learning.*
2. Don't save review sessions for the end.
3. Don't demand perfection from square one.
4. Combine distribution with all other strategies.

So Now Then

Afterword

You are a teacher.

Hopefully, through reading this book you've not only gleaned a number of useful techniques to help boost your influence, but have also begun to understand *why* each works. As a quick refresher, here's what we've explored:

1. It's impossible to simultaneously read words while listening to someone speak.
2. Listening to speech while looking at images can improve learning and memory.
3. Predictable spatial layouts free up mental resources and can boost learning and memory.
4. *Where* people practice and *how they feel* during practice form an integral aspect of *what* they learn.
5. Human beings *cannot* multitask. Trying to do so impairs learning and memory.
6. Interleaving skills during practice can boost performance and skill transfer.
7. Embracing errors can lead to improved memory, learning and predictions.
8. Recall (as opposed to review and/or recognition) leads to stronger, deeper and more accessible memories.
9. Pre-activate facts, expectations and strategies to influence others' learning.
10. Use stories to guide understanding, memory formation and thinking.

11. Moderate stress can boost memories and general learning (though high and no stress can be detrimental).
12. Spacing practice out over several distributed sessions will improve memory and accelerate learning.

As noted in the introduction, these are *foundations* of learning supported by a wealth of brain and behavioural research. If you'd like to dig into this scientific literature or dive deeper into any specific topic, please visit the website below for a generous list of references: http://www.lmeglobal.net/references

My hope is that, by drawing upon the deeper knowledge examined throughout this book, you will be able to begin modifying, adapting and personalizing each of these techniques to match your unique situation. With time, you'll soon be innovating and creating effective teaching and learning strategies of your own.

In other words, you are well on your way to becoming a Picasso of teaching.

ILLUSTRATION 81. ... AND WE'RE BACK!

References and Resources

For a complete list of the references and resources that have informed this book, please visit: www.lmeglobal.net/references

Image credits

INTRODUCTION

p. x, *Sketch of a Horse in One Continuous Line* by Pablo Picasso, © Succession Picasso/licenced by Viscopy, 2018; *Sketch of a Pink Unicorn* by Athena Drysdale, used with artist permission, 2018.

p. 2, by Pablo Picasso: *Plaster Male Torso Sketch* (1893) © Succession Picasso/licenced by Viscopy, 2018; *Portrait of the Artist's Mother* (1896) © Succession Picasso/licenced by Viscopy, 2018; *The Old, Blind Guitarist* (1903) © Succession Picasso/licenced by Viscopy, 2018; *Girl with Mandolin* (1910) © Succession Picasso/licenced by Viscopy, 2018; *Olga* (1923) © Succession Picasso/licenced by Viscopy, 2018; *Bather with a Beach Ball* (1932) © Succession Picasso/licenced by Viscopy, 2018.

CHAPTER 1

p. 6, shutterstock_404493943

p. 6, shutterstock_479653255

p. 9, Morgan Freeman by Reamronaldregan available at https://commons.wikimedia.org/wiki/File:Morgan-Freeman.jpg under a Creative Commons Attribution 4.0. Full terms at https://creativecommons.org/licenses/by/4.0.

p. 12, brains listening to speech by Sarah Johnston, 2018.

p. 12, bottleneck illustration by Jared Cooney Horvath, 2018.

p. 15, brains silently reading illustration by Sarah Johnston, 2018.

p. 18, shutterstock_1007858200

p. 22, computerized notes by Jared Cooney Horvath 2018; Handwritten notes by Sacha Chua, available at https://www.flickr.com/photos/65214961@N00/12798461515 under a Creative Commons Attribution 2.0. Full terms at https://creativecommons.org/licenses/by/2.0.

CHAPTER 2

p. 28, Baba/Fafa image by Jared Cooney Horvath, 2018.

p. 30, brain processing visual information diagram by Sarah Johnston, 2018.

p. 30, sensory, integration diagram by Jared Cooney Horvath, 2018.

p. 32, three people playing cards by Jared Cooney Horvath, 2018. Inspired by Anderson, R.C., Reynolds, R.E., Schallert, D.L., & Goetz, E.T. (1977). Frameworks for comprehending discourse. *American Educational Research Journal*, 14(4), 367-381.

p. 34, three people playing instruments by Jared Cooney Horvath, 2018. Inspired by Anderson, R.C., Reynolds, R.E., Schallert, D.L., & Goetz, E.T. (1977). Frameworks for comprehending discourse. *American Educational Research Journal*, 14(4), 367-381.

p. 36, man with guitar and balloons, *Journal of Verbal Learning and Verbal Behavior*, 11(6), John

D. Bradman & Marcia K. Johnson, 'Contextual prerequisites for understanding: Some investigations of comprehension and recall', pp. 717–26, 1972, with permission from Elsevier, 2018.

p. 37, quote from: Shelley, M. Frankenstein, Or, The Modern Prometheus: the 1818 Text. Oxford; New York: Oxford University Press, 1998. Print.

p. 38, Frankenstein's monster by Dr Macro, available at https://commons.m.wikimedia.org/wiki/File:Frankenstein%27s_monster_(Boris_Karloff).jpg under a Public Domain Attribution. Full terms at https://creativecommons.org/publicdomain/zero/1.0.

p. 42, projection screen by Clker-Free-Vector-Images, available at https://pixabay.com/en/screen-projector-projection-tripod-37075 under a Creative Commons Attribution CC0; train by ben299, available at https://pixabay.com/en/engine-train-railroad-track-3080936 under a Creative Commons Attribution CC0; space shuttle by WikiImages, available at https://pixabay.com/en/rocket-launch-rocket-take-off-nasa-67649 under a Creative Commons Attribution CC0; racecar by MikesPhotos, available at https://pixabay.com/en/lamborghini-car-automotive-drive-1334993 under a Creative Commons Attribution CC0; horse and carriage by nastogadka, available at https://pixabay.com/en/cart-chaise-travel-cab-the-horse-2942512 under a Creative Commons Attribution CC0. Full terms at https://creativecommons.org/publicdomain/zero/1.0.

p. 42, projection screen by Clker-Free-Vector-Images, available at https://pixabay.com/en/screen-projector-projection-tripod-37075 under a Creative Commons Attribution CC0; mountain by sakhshar, available at https://pixabay.com/en/nature-panoramic-mountain-travel-3076910 under a Creative Commons Attribution CC0. Full terms at https://creativecommons.org/publicdomain/zero/1.0; graph by Jared Cooney Horvath, 2018.

p. 44, pop-out effect diagram by Jared Cooney Horvath, 2018.

INTERMISSION 1

p. 50, 1952 headless man adult education poster by unknown, available at http://www.publicdomainpictures.net/view-image.php?image=157286&picture=adult-education-vintage-poster under a Public Domain Attribution. Full terms at https://creativecommons.org/publicdomain/zero/1.0.

CHAPTER 3

p. 54, brain erase by Lightspring, used under licence from Shutterstock.com, 2018; HM brain slice by Henry Gray, adapted by Jared Cooney Horvath, available at https://commons.wikimedia.org/wiki/File:Gray748.png under a Public Domain Attribution. Full terms at https://creativecommons.org/publicdomain/zero/1.0.

p. 55, HM brain slice by Henry Gray, adapted by Jared Cooney Horvath, available at https://commons.wikimedia.org/wiki/File:Gray748.png under a Public Domain Attribution; Electrocardiogram by ElisaRiva, adapted by Jared Cooney Horvath, available at https://pixabay.com/en/electrocardiogram-heart-care-1922703/ under a Creative Commons Attribution CC0. Full terms at https://creativecommons.org/publicdomain/zero/1.0; newspaper design by Jared Cooney Horvath, 2018.

p. 56, man with hippocampus by Umberto NURS, adapted by Jared Cooney Horvath, available at https://commons.wikimedia.org/wiki/File:Hippolobes_it.gif under a Public Domain Attribution; hippocampus proper by Professor Laslo Seress, adapted by Jared Cooney Horvath, available at https://commons.wikimedia.org/wiki/File:Hippocampus_and_

seahorse_cropped.JPG under a Creative Commons Attribution 1.0; neurons by Internet Archive Book Images, adapted by Jared Cooney Horvath, available at https://commons.wikimedia.org/wiki/File:A_text-book_of_physiology_for_medical_students_and_physicians_(1911)_(14592099789).jpg under a Public Domain Attribution. Full terms at https://creativecommons.org/publicdomain/zero/1.0.

p. 57, GPS device by Clker-Free-Vector-Images, adapted by Jared Cooney Horvath, available at https://pixabay.com/en/gps-navigation-garmin-device-304842 under a Creative Commons Attribution CC0; head with map by OpenClipart-Vectors, adapted by Jared Cooney Horvath, available at https://pixabay.com/en/brain-chart-diagram-face-fringe-2029363 under a Creative Commons Attribution CC0; maze by Royalty Free HD Wallpapers, adapted by Jared Cooney Horvath, available at http://thewallpaper.co/download-mobile-dark-backgroundspattern-samsung-colourful-maze-display under a Creative Commons Attribution CC0. Full terms at https://creativecommons.org/publicdomain/zero/1.0; man sitting by Jared Cooney Horvath, 2018; comic book design by Jared Cooney Horvath, 2018.

p. 58, 1980s magazine cover model by izusek, used under licence from iStock.com, 2018.

p. 59, Male model by RoyalAnwar available at https://pixabay.com/en/model-businessman-corporate-2911330/ under a Creative Commons Attribution CC0 Full terms at https://creativecommons.org/publicdomain/zero/1.0; magazine design by Jared Cooney Horvath, 2018.

p. 60-61, fossil by Daderot, adapted by Jared Cooney Horvath, available at https://commons.wikimedia.org/wiki/File:Heterodontosaurus_tucki_cast_-_University_of_California_Museum_of_Paleontology_-_Berkeley,_CA_-_DSC04696.JPG under a Public Domain Attribution. Full terms at https://creativecommons.org/publicdomain/zero/1.0.

p. 62-63, L and T grids by Jared Cooney Horvath, 2018.

p. 68, projection screen by Clker-Free-Vector-Images, available at https://pixabay.com/en/screen-projector-projection-tripod-37075 under a Creative Commons Attribution CC0; drawing of pig by OpenClipart-Vectors, available at https://pixabay.com/p-576570/?no_redirect under a Creative Commons Attribution CC0. Full terms at https://creativecommons.org/publicdomain/zero/1.0.

p. 68, projection screen by Clker-Free-Vector-Images, available at https://pixabay.com/en/screen-projector-projection-tripod-37075 under a Creative Commons Attribution CC0; drawing of pig by OpenClipart-Vectors, available at https://pixabay.com/p-576570/?no_redirect under a Creative Commons Attribution CC0; drawing of duck by Clker-Free-Vector-Images, available at https://commons.wikimedia.org/wiki/File:Yellow_duckling.png under a Creative Commons Attribution CC0; drawing of rabbit by PDP, available at http://www.publicdomainpictures.net/view-image.php?image=154464&picture=rabbit-cute-clipart under a Public Domain Attribution. Full terms at https://creativecommons.org/publicdomain/zero/1.0; scared cat by Sparkle Motion, available at https://www.flickr.com/photos/54125007@N08/15634745431 under a Creative Commons Attribution 2.0. Full terms at https://creativecommons.org/licenses/by/2.0/.

p. 72, 180-degree rule by Grm wnr, adapted by Jared Cooney Horvath, available at https://commons.wikimedia.org/wiki/File:180_degree_rule.svg under a Creative Commons Attribution 3.0. Full terms at https://creativecommons.org/licenses/by/3.0.

CHAPTER 4

p. 78, man with hippocampus by Umberto NURS, adapted by Jared Cooney Horvath, available at https://commons.wikimedia.org/wiki/File:Hippolobes_it.gif under a Public Domain

Attribution. Full terms at https://creativecommons.org/publicdomain/zero/1.0.
p. 78, shutterstock_288982655
p. 80, scuba diver illustrations by Sarah Johnston, 2018.
p. 82, drunk man illustrations by Sarah Johnston, 2018.
p. 86, episodic/semantic memories: part I by Jared Cooney Horvath, 2018.
p. 86, chalkboard episodic/semantic memories: part II by Jared Cooney Horvath, 2018.
p. 94, Statue of Liberty image by Ronile, adapted by Jared Cooney Horvath, available at https://pixabay.com/en/statue-of-liberty-new-york-ny-nyc-267948/ under a Creative Commons Attribution CC0. Full terms at https://creativecommons.org/publicdomain/zero/1.0.

INTERMISSION 2

p. 100, 1952 headless man adult education poster by unknown, available at http://www.publicdomainpictures.net/view-image.php?image=157286&picture=adult-education-vintage-poster under a Public Domain Attribution. Full terms at https://creativecommons.org/publicdomain/zero/1.0.

CHAPTER 5

p. 106, Lat PFC brain illustration by Sarah Johnston, 2018.
p. 106, Nintendo game cartridge by Evan-Amos, adapted by Jared Cooney Horvath, available at https://commons.wikimedia.org/wiki/File:NES-Cartridge.jpg under a Creative Commons Attribution CC0; robot by thehorriblejoke, available at https://pixabay.com/en/video-game-8-bit-old-school-retro-175621 under a Creative Commons Attribution CC0; Nintendo game console by Evan-Amos available at https://commons.wikimedia.org/wiki/File:NES-Console-Set.jpg under a Creative Commons Attribution CC0; television clipart by Clker-Free-Vector-Images, adapted by Jared Cooney Horvath, available at https://pixabay.com/p-308962/?no_redirecthttps://pixabay.com/p-308962/?no_redirect under a Creative Commons Attribution CC0. Full terms at https://creativecommons.org/publicdomain/zero/1.0.
p. 108, brain illustrations by Sarah Johnston, 2018; shutterstock_126644501
p. 108, man with hippocampus and striatum by Umberto NURS, adapted by Jared Cooney Horvath, available at https://commons.wikimedia.org/wiki/File:Hippolobes_it.gif under a Public Domain Attribution. Full terms at https://creativecommons.org/publicdomain/zero/1.0.
p. 120, teacher sitting on desk by Duettographics, adapted by Jared Cooney Horvath, used under licence from Shutterstock.com, 2018.

CHAPTER 6

p. 123, brain illustration by Sarah Johnston, 2018; bartender by RetroClipArt, used under licence from Shutterstock.com, 2018; serving tray with drinks by RetroClipArt, used under licence from Shutterstock.com, 2018; waitress by Clker-Free-Vector-Images available at https://pixabay.com/en/server-servant-table-lady-293966/ under a Creative Commons Attribution CC0. Full terms at https://creativecommons.org/publicdomain/zero/1.0.
p. 126, chunking letters image by Jared Cooney Horvath, 2018.
p. 128, waiter's hand with serving tray by Jared Cooney Horvath, 2018; beer glass by Own work, adapted by Jared Cooney Horvath, available at https://commons.wikimedia.org/wiki/File:Pint_Glass_(Mixing).svg under a Creative Commons Attribution CC0; beer pitcher

by Own work, available at https://commons.wikimedia.org/wiki/File:Pitcher_(Beer).svg under a Creative Commons Attribution CC0. Full terms at https://creativecommons.org/publicdomain/zero/1.0.

p. 128, shoelace tying chunk diagram by Jared Cooney Horvath, 2018.

p. 131, interleaving diagram by Jared Cooney Horvath, 2018.

p. 140, shutterstock_721226998

INTERMISSION 3

p. 144, 1959 headless man adult education poster by unknown, available at http://www.publicdomainpictures.net/view-image.php?image=157289&picture=adult-education-vintage-poster under a Public Domain Attribution. Full terms at https://creativecommons.org/publicdomain/zero/1.0.

CHAPTER 7

p. 148, Paris in the spring triangle by Jared Cooney Horvath, 2018.

p. 150, anterior cingulate cortex diagram by Sarah Johnston, 2018; error alarm illustration by Jared Cooney Horvath, 2018.

p. 150, error alarm illustration by Jared Cooney Horvath, 2018; theta brain wave by Hugo Gamboa available at https://commons.wikimedia.org/wiki/File:Eeg_theta.svg under a Creative Commons Attribution 3.0; beta brain wave by Hugo Gamboa available at https://commons.wikimedia.org/wiki/File:Eeg_beta.svg under a Creative Commons Attribution 3.0. Full terms at https://creativecommons.org/licenses/by/3.0; silhouette head by PDP, adapted by Jared Cooney Horvath, available at http://www.publicdomainpictures.net/view-image.php?image=74363 under a Public Domain Attribution. Full terms at https://creativecommons.org/publicdomain/zero/1.0.

p. 155, black blobs by werner22brigitte, adapted by Jared Cooney Horvath, available at https://pixabay.com/en/frog-jungle-amphibian-animal-266885/ under a Creative Commons Attribution CC0. Full terms at https://creativecommons.org/publicdomain/zero/1.0.

p. 157, frog on a log by werner22brigitte available at https://pixabay.com/en/frog-jungle-amphibian-animal-266885/ under a Creative Commons Attribution CC0. Full terms at https://creativecommons.org/publicdomain/zero/1.0.

p. 163-164, speed limit signs by Jared Cooney Horvath, 2018.

p. 166, woman with wine by Adam Blasberg from the Stockbyte Collection, used under licence from Getty Images, 2018.

CHAPTER 8

p. 172, silhouette man's head by PDP, adapted by Jared Cooney Horvath, available at http://www.publicdomainpictures.net/view-image.php?image=74363 under a Public Domain Attribution; globe clipart by GDJ, available at https://pixabay.com/en/world-earth-planet-globe-map-1301744/ under a Creative Commons Attribution CC0. Full terms at https://creativecommons.org/publicdomain/zero/1.0.

p. 175, sketch of a duck by Clker-Free-Vector-Images, available at https://commons.wikimedia.org/wiki/File:Yellow_duckling.png under a Creative Commons Attribution CC0. Full terms at https://creativecommons.org/publicdomain/zero/1.0.

p. 176, brain by Sarah Johnston, 2018; conductor by HikingArtist.com, available at http://

www.publicdomainpictures.net/view-image.php?image=2698& under a Public Domain Attribution. Full terms at https://creativecommons.org/publicdomain/zero/1.0.

p. 178, brain by Sarah Johnston, 2018; conductor by HikingArtist.com, available at http://www.publicdomainpictures.net/view-image.php?image=2698& under a Public Domain Attribution. Full terms at https://creativecommons.org/publicdomain/zero/1.0.

p. 178, four women by SensorSpot, used under licence from iStock.com, 2018.

p. 181, association network diagram by Jared Cooney Horvath, 2018

p. 188, notecards by Jared Cooney Horvath, 2018.

p. 192, doorway by qimono, adapted by Jared Cooney Horvath, available at https://pixabay.com/en/door-bad-luck-13-thirteen-unlucky-1587023/ under a Creative Commons Attribution CC0. Full terms at https://creativecommons.org/publicdomain/zero/1.0; man in front of doorway by Jared Cooney Horvath, 2018.

INTERMISSION 4

p. 194, 1952 headless man adult education poster by unknown, available at http://www.publicdomainpictures.net/view-image.php?image=157286&picture=adult-education-vintage-poster under a Public Domain Attribution. Full terms at https://creativecommons.org/publicdomain/zero/1.0.

CHAPTER 9

p. 197, towel by Program Executive Office Soldier, adapted by Jared Cooney Horvath, available at https://www.flickr.com/photos/peosoldier/4997103062 under a Creative Commons Attribution 2.0. Full terms at https://creativecommons.org/licenses/by/2.0; shampoo bottle by bijutoha, available at https://pixabay.com/en/shampoo-shampoo-bottle-1860642/ under a Creative Commons Attribution CC0; blueberries by Clker-Free-Vector-Images, available at https://pixabay.com/en/blueberries-leave-ripe-forest-306718/ under a Creative Commons Attribution CC0; apple by Clker-Free-Vector-Images, available at https://pixabay.com/en/green-apple-fruit-tree-smith-304673/ under a Creative Commons Attribution CC0; strawberry by GDJ, available at https://www.goodfreephotos.com/vector-images/shiny-strawberry-vector-graphic.png.php under a Public Domain Attribution; showerhead by kboyd, available at https://pixabay.com/p-653671/?no_redirect under a Creative Commons Attribution CC0. Full terms at https://creativecommons.org/publicdomain/zero/1.0; all images adapted by Jared Cooney Horvath.

p. 201, newspaper headlines by Jared Cooney Horvath, 2018.

p. 202, shutterstock_320661278

p. 210, male and female brains by Jared Cooney Horvath, 2018.

CHAPTER 10

p. 218, golfer with shovel by OpenClipart-Vectors, adapted by Jared Cooney Horvath, available at https://pixabay.com/p-2028116/?no_redirect under a Creative Commons Attribution CC0. Full terms at https://creativecommons.org/publicdomain/zero/1.0; association network diagram by Jared Cooney Horvath, 2018.

p. 223, kid with aviator cap by Sunny studio, used under licence from Shutterstock.com, 2018.

p. 225, storyteller and audience synchrony by Christophe Vorlet, used under licence from the artist, 2018.

p. 230, physical thrust diagram by Jared Cooney Horvath, 2018.
p. 230, psychological thrust diagram by Jared Cooney Horvath, 2018.
p. 235, puzzle pieces by HomeStudio, used under licence from Shutterstock.com, 2018.

INTERMISSION 5

p. 238, 1952 headless man adult education poster by unknown, available at http://www.publicdomainpictures.net/view-image.php?image=157286&picture=adult-education-vintage-poster under a Public Domain Attribution. Full terms at https://creativecommons.org/publicdomain/zero/1.0.

CHAPTER 11

p. 241, inverted-U diagram by Jared Cooney Horvath, 2018.
p. 242, happy baby by vborodinova, available at https://pixabay.com/en/babe-smile-newborn-small-child-2972222/ under a Creative Commons Attribution CC0; scared baby by Mcimage, used under licence from Shutterstock.com, 2018; angry baby by Sarah Noda, used under licence from Shutterstock.com, 2018; surprised baby by freestocks-photos, available at https://pixabay.com/en/people-baby-blanket-boy-child-2942977/ under a Creative Commons Attribution CC0; sad baby by TaniaVdB, available at https://pixabay.com/en/baby-tears-small-child-sad-cry-443390/ under a Creative Commons Attribution CC0. Full terms at https://creativecommons.org/publicdomain/zero/1.0; disgusted baby by 2xSamara.com, used under licence from Shutterstock.com, 2018.
p. 244, cast of characters by Jared Cooney Horvath, 2018.
p. 247, act I by Jared Cooney Horvath, 2018.
p. 249, act II by Jared Cooney Horvath, 2018.
p. 251, act III by Jared Cooney Horvath, 2018.
p. 256, skydivers by Woody Hibbard available at https://www.flickr.com/photos/65214961@N00/12798461515 under a Creative Commons Attribution 2.0. Full terms at https://creativecommons.org/licenses/by/2.0.

CHAPTER 12

p. 264, forgetting curve diagram by Jared Cooney Horvath, 2018.
p. 264, distributed practice diagram by Jared Cooney Horvath, 2018.
p. 269, shutterstock_142164154
p. 274, shutterstock_167358809
p. 279, So Now Then title card by Jared Cooney Horvath (inspired by *Magnolia* by Paul Thomas Anderson, 1999: one of the top-10 films ever made … honestly, if you've not seen it, now is the perfect time!).

AFTERWORD

p. 281, *Sketch of a Horse in One Continuous Line* by Pablo Picasso, © Succession Picasso/licenced by Viscopy, 2018; *Sketch of a Pink Unicorn* by Athena Drysdale, used with artist permission, 2018.

Index